W9-AEP-894

WITHDRAWN

DICK ENBERG

Oh My!

DICK ENBERG

with

JIM PERRY

www.SportsPublishingLLC.com

ISBN: 1-58261-824-0

Publishers: Peter L. Bannon and Joseph J. Bannon Sr.
Senior managing editor: Susan M. Moyer
Acquisitions editors: John Humenik, Scott Rauguth, Dean Reinke
Developmental editor: Elisa Bock Laird
Art director: K. Jeffrey Higgerson
Dust jacket design: Christine Mohrbacher and Joseph Brumleve
Project manager: Alicia Wentworth and Kathryn R. Holleman
Imaging: Kenneth J. O'Brien and Christine Mohrbacher
Photo editor: Erin Linden-Levy
Vice president of sales and marketing: Kevin King
Media and promotions managers: Scott Rauguth (regional),
        Randy Fouts (national), Maurey Williamson (print)

Printed in the United States of America

Sports Publishing L.L.C.
804 North Neil Street
Champaign, IL 61820

Phone: 1-877-424-2665
Fax: 217-363-2073
Web site: www.SportsPublishingLLC.com

To Arnie and Belle, for giving me the genetic gumption to succeed.

CONTENTS

FOREWORD

Dick Enberg is old enough to be my father!

So what? Is there something wrong with that?

Early in my career, when he first started covering tennis, Dick started sounding like my father. I could almost hear him cringing in the booth trying to explain one of my on-court outbursts. Where do you think "Oh My!" came from? (Just kidding.)

So it was with a little uncertainty (for both of us) that I stepped into the NBC booth for the first time in 1992 to cover a match between Michael Chang and Nicklas Kulti in the third round of the French Open. Forget that the match had already taken place and we were only announcing one of the five sets that had been taped that day. I was working with the legendary Dick Enberg, whom I had first seen hosting *Sports Challenge* as a kid and later heard in football, baseball, and basketball stadiums throughout the country. Anyway, Jimmy Connors had preceded me as color commentator for NBC, so I figured Dick had at least dealt with someone with whom he had disagreed—shall we say—"philosophically!"

What he said to me that day I'll always appreciate. It was so simple: "Just be yourself and stay the hell out of my way." (Just kidding!) Actually, he told me, "People want to hear what you have to say, so just work hard and you'll be fine." It was nice that he was willing to accept me for who I was—in fact, insist upon me being me—give me a chance to prove myself, and willingly help me along the way. I wanted him to be happy with the results.

Over the last 12 years, I have had the good fortune of learning from a true pro. What I have come to realize over time is how much he cares. He's "old school," a consummate professional. He earns your trust, whether you are the player, the viewer, or his partner. You know you can count on Dick Enberg.

I know this is hard to believe, but Dick and I are quite similar. I know what you are thinking, "You cannot be serious!" But it's true; we're both perfectionists. Okay, maybe we do show it in different ways, but we have that attitude just the same. We're never satisfied, we're always striving to prove ourselves, and our demanding nature makes it frustrating not only for the people around us, but also for the two of us. Love us or hate us, we just can't change.

Dick used to complain that the tennis players weren't accessible enough. He would say sport is a form of entertainment, after all. Initially, I just thought he was blowing off steam. Only now, after a dozen years of calling this great sport, do I realize, sadly, how right he was. What I respect is that he didn't have to say that. He could have just dialed it in. He just… cares.

Above all, Dick is prepared. Never once during a tournament would I arrive before Dick and rarely would I leave after him. He was tinkering with the next day's opening or putting a finishing touch on one of his "memories" pieces at Wimbledon. NBC covers only the last 10 days of the tournament. I would arrive Monday morning to work the early days for the BBC. Who would I see first? Dick Enberg. At the U.S. Open? The same thing, just a different location. I'd wonder, "What the hell is Enberg doing here already? He's just the play-by-play guy, he doesn't need to watch the matches. He could do this in his sleep." But he doesn't. He cares.

This is not to say we haven't had fun. We've called matches with streakers in them, endured rain delays that became comical, matches where we wished we could have streaked out of the booth, and classics that gave us goose bumps. Through it all, Dick maintained his professionalism, his *joie de vivre* (translation: love of life, and knowing Dick, and his large collection of wine, it could also be *joie de vin*, a love of wine!), and an effort level that any athlete or commentator would respect.

Only once did Dick really piss me off, and even then it was for the right reason. At the endless Sports Emmys Awards show one year, I was sitting at Dick's table when my category, Sportscaster of the Year, finally came up. At the podium, Keyshawn Johnson announced, "And the winner is John Ma—" Dick quickly reached over and congratulated me as I heard John Madden's name being announced. I thought to myself, "Should I give him one of my infamous McEnroe tantrums?" Forget it. He's old enough to be my father.

Dick, congratulations on a great career and a great book!

—John McEnroe
New York City

ACKNOWLEDGMENTS

Like all books, this one was accomplished with the support and assistance of many, many people, including my family. My special thanks go to Team Enberg, including my wife, Barbara, for her encouragement, enthusiasm, and suggestions; my brother, Dennis, and sister, Sharyl; and my children, Jennifer, Andrew, Alexander, Nicole, Emily, and Ted.

—Dick Enberg

≪ઇ

As Dick and I reach the end of this long editorial journey, a warm thank you to my wife, Catherine, for her eagle-eyed help with the manuscript; my children, Lisa and Jon, for their inspiration and good humor; and my mother, Dorothy, for her unwavering support. I'd also like to offer an affectionate toast to my late father, Frank.

Dick and I also thank the following for their invaluable assistance: Jack Bailey, Van Barbieri, Jim Bell, Pat Bennett, Rich Bertolucci, John Bianco, Steve Bisheff, Ronnie Bradford, Jerry Caraccioli, Vince Casey, Stan Chambers, Don Chargin, Stan Charnofsky, Bud Collins, P.J. Combs, Gary Cunningham, Dean Davenport, Dick Ebersol, Eddie Einhorn, Jeff Evans, Jim Gigliotti, Paul Goldberg, John Gonzalez, Pat Haden, Tom Hammond, Ed Hookstratten, Chris Hughes, Katie Hyde, Tunch Ilkin, Gary K. Johnson, Phil Jones, Laurie Joseph, Bill Keenist, Kit Klingelhoffer, D.C. Koehl, Dave Lockett, Bill Madrid, Paul Maguire, Nancy Mazmanian, Don McGuire, Pat McGuire, Tim Mead, Dr. Michael Mellman, Chennelle Miller, Dave Niehaus, Merlin Olsen, Billy Packer, Joe Quasarano, Rich Rice, Ross Schneiderman, Tom Seeberg, Dan Smith, Bob Speck, Stan Spero, Bob Steiner, Larry Stewart, Jack Teele, Artis Twyman, Bob Uecker, Leslie Visser, Bill Walton, Michael Weisman, John Wooden, and Richard Yoakam.

In addition, we would like to thank our intrepid agent, Mike Hamilburg, along with Scott Raguth, John Humenik, and Dean

Reinke of Sports Publishing L.L.C., for making this project happen. We offer our appreciation, too, to John McEnroe for writing the foreword and to editor Elisa Bock Laird for her enthusiastic support and sound advice.

—Jim Perry

INTRODUCTION

A few years ago, a passenger stopped me in the Indianapolis Airport, and, pointing his finger at me, declared, "I know you! You're someone famous!" Then he paused. "Who are you, anyway?"

When I answered politely that I was Dick Enberg, he shook his head and said, "No... that's not it."

This is one of the amusing aspects about being a public figure. People on the street try to guess who you are but often mistake you for someone else. During the 1996 presidential campaign, a bellman shook my hand in a Detroit hotel lobby and said with great enthusiasm, "You've got my vote, Mr. Dole."

Recently, my wife, Barbara, and I were walking down the main street in La Jolla, California, a few blocks from our house. As we walked by a restaurant, a woman spotted me and started walking quickly after us.

"Wait a minute, wait a minute!" she cried. "I know you. I've seen you on television. Doggone, who are you?"

When I said, "Dick Enberg," she smiled and said, "Good for you."

Well, I guess it is good for me. I'd rather be me than anyone else I know, and not just because I'm happily married and have six great children. I enjoy my life, because I delight in what I do for a living. My career has been too good to be true. As a play-by-play sportscaster for CBS, I have a job that is coveted by millions of people. It provides me with a game-day seat on the 50-yard line or at midcourt—the very best seat in the house, in fact—and then my bosses assign a Hall of Fame analyst to sit next to me in the booth, someone I can chat with in depth during the course of the game.

However, my work is not without some stress. It would be interesting to monitor the blood pressure of an announcer as he calls a game. I'll bet it shoots up dramatically. To be able to speak for three hours off the top of your head, using a full range of emotions, is very demanding. All the while, the producer is giving instructions in your ear, adding to the challenge. And, like a defensive back in football, whose mistakes are right out in the open, I'm fully exposed. Everyone hears the verbal fumbles. There are no erasers on the microphone. There are no proofreaders.

Occasionally, it upsets me when a newspaper columnist takes shots at me for an error I make on the air. We all make them. But that critic who is zinging me has had the luxury of proofreading his column and having an editor read it again before it ever gets into print. I don't have that luxury. When I say something, it's out there. As much as I might wish to, there's no way to call it back.

And there's a lot of information swirling through my brain. One of my job requirements is memorizing the names and numbers of the players before every game—nearly 100 players each week during the NFL season. Of course, as soon as the game is over, I have to wash my mental chalkboard clean. To learn new numbers, I have to immediately forget the old ones.

Socially, this trait is a disaster. My wife will invite new friends or neighbors to our house, and as soon as they leave, I forget their names. It's a terrible habit that drives my wife crazy.

"Sometimes, you can't even remember our neighbors' names," she said one day. "It's embarrassing."

"You know what we ought to do?" I suggested. "Why don't we get jerseys with numbers on them for the neighbors? The Blackmores, for example, will be No. 1, the Baileys No. 2, and the Bradleys No. 3. When they come in the door, put the jerseys on them. Then, I'll be able to remember. It will be more like my usual routine."

She didn't take me up on my brilliant suggestion.

When we're not entertaining, often I can be found watching a TV game at home. As a big fan, I openly cheer in my den. Thus, friends often ask, "When you're calling a game for the network, do you secretly root for one team to win?"

Absolutely not. On the air, it's as if somebody draws a heavy drape to block any bias. I don't even feel it inside. It's the same curtain that keeps you from swearing. I've known broadcasters who can't get one sentence out in normal conversation without being profane, and yet, they can go on the air and talk for three hours and never slip once. I marvel at that. The magic curtain says, "Don't use profanity, don't say something stupid, and don't show any rooting interest." We have a fabulous defense mechanism.

I will admit that network announcers do have one bias. We want the team that's getting drubbed to catch up. If it sounds like I'm getting overly excited for one team, it's because that team, after falling behind 21-0, has scored a touchdown, and I'm still hoping we'll have a close game. A tight game will keep the audience and please our superiors. It will even please the critics, who tend to think the announcer is doing a better job when the game is exciting. The ideal sports event is one where the broadcast comes down to the final two minutes with the score tied. If it's won on a last-second shot, last-second field goal, or 15-foot putt on the final green, the network is the winner.

⤶

I began my half-century of sportscasting on radio, and early in my career, most of my play-by-play work was done in that medium. On radio, the demands are so much more intense. From day one, I was warned about "dead air." If you go three, four, five seconds without saying anything, the audience starts wondering, "Uh, oh, has the station shut down?" The worst sin of all is to have dead air.

Although radio is more challenging, it allows for more creativity. The announcer is not only describing the action, he's verbally painting a total picture for the audience.

On television, of course, the picture is already painted for you. In many ways, television gives you the punch line to the joke before you tell it. We often work backward. The play takes place, and then we describe it, analyze it, and put it in perspective.

In contrast to radio, not talking is a good thing on television. A timely pause, when accompanied by the sound of the crowd complementing dramatic pictures, is a wonderful device. If there's a great moment in a game, the producer quickly orders, "Don't talk. Let it play." The celebration of the winning team, the despair of the losing team, the expressions on the faces of the winning and losing coaches, the fans hugging in the stands—Ernest Hemingway couldn't write prose any better than the pictures themselves. So, it's foolhardy for the announcer to try.

However, in touching moments, the pictures often call for a few well-timed words from the announcer. I'm still frustrated for a comment I didn't make in the 1988 Olympics in Seoul.

Among my assignments that year was the women's basketball final. I did the game as the U.S. team, coached by Kay Yow of North Carolina State, won the gold medal. Yow, who is still the head coach at North Carolina State, had undergone surgery for breast cancer before the Olympics, and in my research before Seoul, I came across a quote from her that was so beautifully inspiring, that I put it in my notes for possible use: "When life gives you a kick," she said, "make sure it kicks you forward."

After Yow's team won the gold medal, the camera lingered on the members of the U.S. team, hugging, crying, laughing, and cheering. We panned from the victory podium to the bench, and there was the coach, on one knee, watching them with great satisfaction and affection. Her face reflected the pride that a mother would have for her successful children. The scene cried out for a comment from me. It was a chance to say, "This is the woman who battled breast cancer and said, 'When life gives you a kick, make sure it kicks you forward.' Not only has she gone bravely forward, she's pushed a terrific team all the way to a gold medal."

But I didn't say it. To this day, I'm not sure why. I still wish I could go back, call the game over, and use her quote.

I still agonize over every broadcast, and I agonized over this book, too. It was a daunting, but pleasurable, task for me to condense 50 years of memories into these pages. I hope you'll enjoy my recollections as much as I enjoyed reminiscing.

As I look back, I remember New York, in 1982, when I was nominated as one of the five finalists for the 1981 Emmy as National

Sportscaster of the Year. It was the first time my name was included with all of the giants of our profession, and when they announced my name as the winner, I almost ran across the tabletops to the stage to receive the award. After stumbling and stammering through my acceptance speech, I wandered off stage. Soon I found myself near the kitchen of the hotel, and my emotions began to boil to the surface. This was the culmination of so many things in my life. It meant that I had reached a pinnacle of my profession. My thoughts drifted to memories of my mom and dad and my childhood dreams. I started to cry—a proud, happy cry.

Suddenly, I felt this big strong arm squeeze my shoulder. It was Hall of Fame catcher Johnny Bench, one of the presenters that evening.

"Enberg," he said, "now you know what it's like to win a World Series."

That was all he said, before walking away. He had taken what was a high moment in my life and boosted it to an even higher level. I'll never forget that emotional Emmy evening and what Johnny Bench's sensitivity added to it.

How do I express my thanks to Bench and all the others who shared this last half-century of experiences with me? Hopefully, my sincere gratitude will emerge within these covers. And so I share my lifelong love for sports and 50 years of experiences broadcasting them. I sincerely hope that through my life story the reader will find a more thorough appreciation of the exclamation, "Oh My!"

DICK
ENBERG
Oh My!

1

A TIME TO DREAM

"Son, the day you think you're so good that you can't improve, you can go only one way—down."

—Arnie Enberg

In 1942, when I was in the second grade, I was playing in front of my house in Glendale, California, when a Helms Bakery truck came slowly down the street, stopping at various homes to deliver bread, pastries, and other baked goods. I wanted to catch the eye of a little girl who lived nearby, so impulsively I decided to grab the truck's rear bumper before it departed from her house. I planned to run behind it and dazzle her with my speed.

As I seized the bumper, it didn't occur to me that her house was the last stop on the block. When the driver took off, he started accelerating around the corner to go to the next street. I held on, but he was going faster and faster, and my little legs were whirling like a pinwheel. Finally, I had no choice but to let go, sliding like Pete Rose on my face, hands, and arms on the pavement.

There was blood all over me, but I was more scared than hurt. As my mother recalled years later, she could hear me screaming from several houses away, "Oh, don't let my dad spank me. Don't let my dad spank me." I just knew that if my dad learned of the stupidity of my act, he was going to punish me. In those days it wasn't child abuse. Physical punishment was expected when you didn't behave properly.

I frightened the hell out of my mom when I walked in the door, bloody abrasions all over my face, hands, and arms. When Dad got home, my mother, as she often did with her children, took my side and pointed out that my punishment was already self-inflicted. It worked. I looked so terrible that Dad took pity on me and left me alone. It was an early lesson on how tough it was to impress the ladies.

∽

Although I risked pain and suffering to win the heart of a girl, my driving ambition early in life was to be a great athlete. For most of my early years, I dreamed about playing right field for the Detroit

Tigers, although as I tell everybody, Al Kaline (inducted into the Hall of Fame in 1980) beat me to it. He was born three weeks before I was.

As the first child of Arnie and Belle Enberg, I barely made it into the world on January 9, 1935, in Mount Clemens, Michigan, just north of Detroit. At the end of a long, difficult labor, there was fear that my mother and I might not survive. Doctors were particularly worried about me, because I was blue from lack of oxygen, but, fortunately, both of us recovered quickly.

My dad's parents were immigrants from Finland, whose original family name was Katajavuori, which means juniper mountain. Kataja wood, or juniper wood, is used for cooking in Finland. Before arriving in America, the family name had been changed to the Swedish word Enberg, which means roughly the same thing, but had they elected to use the English derivation, I would be Dick Juniper Mountain.

We moved to Bridgeport, Connecticut, when I was two, and then the four of us—my brother, Dennis, was born in 1939—took a transcontinental train to Southern California in 1940. We lived in several homes in the Los Angeles area, landing in Canoga Park in the San Fernando Valley in 1943 when I was eight. The Valley was very rural in the early 1940s—dirt roads intersected with orange and walnut groves, with plenty of room for young boys to run and play. We went barefoot all summer long.

There were no major league sports in Southern California in those days, but baseball fans followed the exploits of the Hollywood Stars and Los Angeles Angels in the Pacific Coast League. Sunday was doubleheader day in the Coast League, and when I emerged from Sunday School, Dad would be waiting to take me out to old Gilmore Field or Wrigley Field. To a young baseball fan, that was heaven.

When we returned from the games, my dad would often say, "Let's get out the gloves and play some catch." I would start out as the pitcher and he was the catcher, and he would urge me to throw strikes. Then it was his turn to pitch. My dad had big hands and could throw a forkball. For many years of my youth, it was such a clever pitch that I couldn't catch it. He would chuckle and say, "One day, you'll be big enough to handle me."

I was lucky to have my father around. His two brothers, Norman and Toivo, fought in World War II, Norman in Italy and Toivo in the Pacific, but Dad was exempt from the draft because he had a heart murmur. It never caused him any problems, but with the less sophisticated tests they had then, the doctors didn't like the sound of his heartbeats and classified him 4-F. He worked in a defense plant.

While I rooted for the Angels and Stars in person and listened to Fred Haney call their home games on the radio, I created my own games between the two teams on a half-acre lot next to our house. A self-taught switch hitter, I would take a bat and tennis ball and imagine myself as each of the players in their lineups. If the player was left handed, I would hit the ball left handed. If he was right handed, I would bat right handed. Starting in the center of the field, I'd hit the ball in one direction for the Stars, and in the other for the Angels, retrieving the ball myself. Whenever the ball carried over the fence at one end of the lot, or the hedge at the other, that team scored.

As I played, I announced the various hitters and described the action. In reality, these were my first broadcasts, although I never thought this was something I would actually do for a living. I wanted to be, and believed that someday I would be, a big league player, not an announcer.

When I came into the house one night, dinner was on the table, and as I sat down, my mother, intrigued by my imaginary games, asked me who won that day.

"The Stars won 8 to 5," I said, as I started wolfing down my food.

"Sounds like a good game," Mom said, "but why are you hurrying now? Slow down. You don't have to gobble your food."

"Yes I do, Mom," I said. "I'm trying to get in a doubleheader."

Boy, I must have been something in those days. I truly did eat and sleep baseball.

Life went blissfully along for me in this way, until it changed suddenly and dramatically in 1946 when I was 11. By this time, there were five Enbergs. My sister, Sharyl, was born in 1945.

My mother and father had not seen their parents since we moved west in 1940, so in the summer of 1946 we drove to Michigan to visit her folks and to Minnesota to visit his. In Michigan, my dad bumped into one of his old friends who was a real estate agent, and he showed my father a 40-acre fruit farm just outside the little town of Armada (pronounced r-MADE-ah). Dad, who had grown up on a farm, fell in love with it and bought it, just like that.

After we returned to California, Mom and Dad put our house in Canoga Park up for sale, which was disappointing. I was happy in the Valley and didn't want to leave my friends and move across the country but had no choice.

Moving from a house in the San Fernando Valley to a farm in Michigan was the equivalent of moving to a different planet. In California, we had indoor plumbing, which I had always taken for granted. I mean, what other kind is there? In Armada, 40 miles north of Detroit, we lived in a drafty, two-story wooden farmhouse that was built around the time of the Civil War. There was no insulation in the walls. There was no running water. There was no central heating. Worse yet, there were no bathrooms.

There *was* a well that went dry almost every year by the middle of summer and stayed dry until November or December. There *was* a two-hole outhouse. And, a quarter of a mile away, sitting on a dirt road, there *was* a one-room schoolhouse, where I attended the seventh and eighth grades. There were only two other kids in my class in Barringer School. The basic one-two education, I always called it. The one-room school and the two-hole toilet.

The winters were just brutal. The temperature often dropped to zero or below, and when the wind blew, it sliced right through the house. My brother, Dennis, and I slept in the same bed, wearing sweatshirts and sweatpants, while the dog slept on our feet at the bottom of the bed for extra warmth. I left a glass of water out in the bedroom one night, and when I found it in the morning, it was half frozen.

There was a kerosene furnace in the kitchen downstairs, so we opened the upstairs bedroom doors at night, hoping some warm air would rise. Of course, the lower part of the house felt like the inside of a refrigerator the next morning. Meanwhile, we kept a big tub filled with water on the furnace at all times, so we'd have hot water for bathing or washing our hands or doing the dishes.

When the well went dry, we hauled water from another farm, picking it up in old Coca-Cola one-gallon syrup jugs that Dad bought for a nickel from the pharmacy. We would bring 10 cases of those bottles, four bottles to a case, to carry the water home.

When I was 16, we finally got running water, but the piped-in water came from the same well that always went dry, so we still had to haul water for several months almost every summer and fall. We never owned a hot-water heater.

The move to Armada was not only difficult for the kids, it was often challenging for my mother. Unlike my father, she had not grown up on a farm, and she missed the "luxury" of indoor plumbing. One afternoon, she went out to the outhouse, and the door, which didn't fit right, had frozen shut. First, she had to kick it open, then she had to brush snow off the seat. When she came back inside, she snapped, "I wish that thing would burn down."

My brother, Dennis, who was a bona fide hellion as a kid, overheard her. He was about eight or nine at the time.

"I decided to get rid of the outhouse for her," he said years later. "I didn't like it either. So I dropped lighted matches down the hole to set the toilet paper below on fire. But it was wet and all it did was give off a lot of smelly, black smoke.

"But the smoke scared me and I ran into the house, yelling that the outhouse was on fire. My mother had to pour a couple of buckets of rainwater down the hole. Thank God that Dad wasn't home."

If Dennis had succeeded in setting the outhouse on fire, we probably would have been homeless. The outhouse was next to another small building, which had a storage shed on one side and a sauna on the other. Next to that was our house. Everything was wood, so the fire would have jumped quickly from building to building before Armada's volunteer fire department could have responded. Even if they had arrived, where would they have found enough water?

The sauna that was next to the outhouse was an important part of our lives, too. It had been built by my dad, and every Saturday night we all took our steam bath, which was a Finnish ritual. Dad had grown up in a small town in Northern Minnesota, and his parents, like all of their Finnish neighbors, had a sauna on their farm. According to Finnish custom, everyone, family and friends, went in the sauna naked. It was no big deal to us.

Obviously, in winter no one loafed on the way to the sauna, particularly when it was snowing. Going back was easier. Your body was so super-heated that you didn't feel the cold at all. In fact, cooling off in a hurry is part of an old tradition for Finns, whether it's jumping into an icy lake or walking back through the snow. It's a wonder every Finn hasn't died of pneumonia.

The Enberg spread was a real working farm. We grew 20 varieties of apples, and we also raised pears, plums, cherries, sweet corn, and popcorn, made apple cider, and collected honey. In the early fall, we operated our own little fruit stand on one edge of our property, next to North Avenue, the two-lane paved highway that led north from Mount Clemens to Armada. On weekends, I would serve as the sole proprietor, which was a relaxing job. Based on the other farm labor, I was taking a weekend holiday.

Often a car wouldn't stop for hours, so there was considerable time to kill, and I could listen to my trusty radio that brought me Detroit Tigers baseball, Detroit Lions football, Michigan and Michigan State football, and, in October, the World Series. Van Patrick was the silky voice of the Tigers and Lions and my direct connection to my Detroit athletic heroes.

During one weekend in the middle of apple harvesting season, business was unusually brisk, and I was able to sell just over $100 worth of produce, which was a record for us. I felt rich, because Dad promised me five cents on the dollar for my work. Five percent this time was five bucks, five big ones! I was always good at math.

Well, money was always scarce on the farm, and Dad wouldn't give me the five dollars. He only gave me three. I can remember my mother fighting on my behalf.

"Come on, Arnie," she said. "You know five percent was the deal."

"Five dollars is too much money for a little bit of work on a weekend," he argued. "Three bucks is plenty."

And it was a lot of money in those days. You could go down to Simpson's Pharmacy in Armada and get a big bag of peanuts and a cherry root beer for five cents each. So I got three dollars instead of five.

I can also remember fighting with my dad over getting a haircut, because it cost a whole quarter. It was a pretty simple haircut because I wore a crew cut until I was 30 years old. But I can hear Dad complaining now.

"What do you mean you need a haircut?" he would say. "You just got one."

"Dad, that was over a month ago," I'd say.

"Well, you look fine."

Although I adapted to life in Armada, there came a specific day that definitely altered my life's path. My female pig had delivered a large litter, and one day Bob Bower, the high school agriculture teacher and director of the local FFA (Future Farmers of America), told my father that it was time to castrate the young male pigs. Because I was 13, he said this was a good opportunity to teach me how to do it.

The local vet, Orv Krause, was my instructor. He must have been deaf, because the incredible, high-pitched squeals of his first patient didn't deter him even slightly. I faintly recall his unemotional directions.

"It's easy," he said. "Hold him down, make the incision, and it's just like popping a grape."

Mr. Bower went next. Then Dad took a turn. No one could find me.

I was only in the ninth grade, but I now knew that farming would not be part of my future.

◈

My father, Arnie Enberg, was the first person in his family to finish high school, but he had to work extraordinarily hard for every dime he earned—and he didn't earn many. Before he died, he told me that the most income he ever made in a year was $8,000.

He was a typical Finn—stubborn, tough to know, and not free with his feelings. He rarely gave compliments to anyone; I can remember my mom begging him to say something sweet about her. He was emphatic that you can only improve if you work hard, and he insisted that you should never get too high on yourself, because you're only setting yourself up for a fall. He didn't want to show any weakness, and he didn't want us to show any weakness. He was a tough disciplinarian. If we misbehaved, he would grab us by the hair, pull on it, and lead us off for a spanking. He never said too much, but when he talked, we listened. He wasn't an outwardly affectionate person until his later years, but we knew he loved us.

Belle Enberg, my mother, was a very caring person who made us feel important. If we were sad, she would comfort us, usually with hugs. If we needed a boost, she encouraged us; she wouldn't let us get down on ourselves. She was sensitive, compassionate, always thinking of others before herself, and a good listener, and she had a lively sense of humor. We always knew, no matter how bad we were as kids, that she loved us.

My mother was not Finnish, and her parents were not immigrants. Her father was German, and her mother, who died shortly after her birth, was a mixture of nationalities, including English, French, and American Indian. Mom, whose maiden name was Weiss, was raised by a stepmother. She grew up in Mount Clemens, where her baseball-loving father, my grandpa Rudy, owned a small neighborhood grocery store.

So, I was raised with the charge from my dad to move on with your life and keep improving, while, on the other hand, Mom was there to give heavy doses of love, laughter, and encouragement. Because they matured during the Depression, both of them pushed me hard to succeed. You could never quite do enough for Dad, while even Mom insisted on all As in school. This was their way of trying to prepare me for the future. As parents, they really complemented each other very well. But the obvious differences in their personalities added up to a marriage under strain.

As was typical of the times, my father expected my mother to raise the kids and cook the meals and do the washing and ironing, and from his point of view, there was no obligation to thank her for doing it. That was her job, just as it was his job to work his tail off all day in a Detroit auto factory or on the farm, so there would be food on the table. The farm was a terrible size—too big for one man to work, but too small to make a comfortable living. When the weather didn't cooperate and we had a poor year, Dad was forced to get a part-time job in a factory in Detroit—40 miles away—to make ends meet. So he often worked two jobs and was seldom around. When he was home, he was exhausted. Looking back, I don't think there was much time, nor energy, for affection.

I remember one night when Mom had cooked a very nice meal, Dad was silent as we ate. Finally, she said, "Well, Arnie, what do you think of supper?" Obviously, she was fishing for a compliment.

And his idea of a compliment was, "I'm eating it, aren't I?"

My mother, as I said, cared about everyone. She was an extremely empathetic person. A married couple lived just down the road from our farm, and the wife was terminally ill with cancer. My mother helped take care of her and tried to offer comfort to her and her husband. After a long illness, the woman died.

A few months later, when I was 14, our neighbor came over to visit, and, as he entered the house, he briefly touched my mom's back, and I noticed this. At dinner that night, I mentioned this to her in front of my father.

"I didn't understand why Mr. Dixon [a pseudonym] put his hand on your back like that," I said.

It was the beginning of the end. Over the next few days, as Dad questioned her, Mom admitted she was involved in an affair. Dad insisted that the marriage was over, and he also insisted that he was not leaving the farm or giving up the kids. Because she had committed the wrong, he demanded that she leave. And weighed down with guilt, she agreed.

Although Dennis and Sharyl were definitely staying with Dad, he gave me a choice, because I was much older than my brother and sister. I wasn't about to leave my home, my family, and my friends in high school, and I elected to stay. If Dad had moved out, I still would have stayed on the farm. So Mom really got short-changed. She left her family and moved north to the central part of the state, working first as a waitress at a hotel in Clare and then as a secretary at Central Michigan College in Mount Pleasant.

I'm convinced the two of them never stopped loving each other. Two years later, Mom tried very hard to put the marriage back together, but my dad just wouldn't do it. I really believe he still loved her, but he couldn't forgive her. It was a tragedy because she really was a good person. It probably was the only bad thing she had done in her life, and she got caught.

After Mom moved away, she regularly came south to visit us. One day she arrived earlier than Dad expected. He was upstairs when she walked in the door, and to avoid meeting her face to face, he climbed out of his bedroom window onto the roof over the kitchen and jumped to the ground. He sprinted to his car and drove away. You don't do that if you don't love somebody. I believe it hurt him too much to see her.

A few years later, Mom married another man, whom she met at Central Michigan, and had two more children. Some 20 years after the divorce, Dad also got remarried when he moved back to California, but it only lasted a couple of years.

I regret that I was never as close as I should have been to my mother, first, because she moved away, and, second, because it was awkward to visit her after she married again. However, I'm eternally thankful to my sister, Sharyl, who lived nearby, for her loving care of Mom until Mom's peaceful death in 1994.

As time went on, I buried myself in my schoolwork and athletics and was convinced that the divorce was for the best because they had argued for years, beginning in California. Now there would be no more fighting. But down deep, it left an indelible scar, which I didn't realize until my own divorce 25 years later.

In the divorce settlement, Dad legally won the right to keep Dennis, Sharyl, and me, because his sister, Beatrice, agreed to move into the house to help raise us. She joined us with her husband, Uncle John, who worked in a factory in Detroit, and their son and daughter, David and Jeannie. Aunt Beatrice was a second mother to the Enbergs. Somehow she balanced her love between her own son and daughter and the three of us. She was a 1950s version of Wonder Woman.

By the time my parents were divorced, I was attending Armada Rural Agricultural High School, playing football, baseball, and basketball for the Armada Fighting Tigers and still dreaming of becoming a star athlete. I was small and matured late, however, and in my first two years I played either on the JV teams or as a varsity reserve, mostly sitting on the bench. As a freshman, I weighed 95 pounds and stood barely five feet tall.

Meanwhile, I continued to play one-man baseball games as I had in California. The area around the fruit stand provided an endless supply of cherry-sized rocks that served as perfect batting practice ammunition. Using an old Louisville Slugger (Hank Greenberg model), I'd target the telephone lines across the road. Line drives under the wires were doubles and triples, high drives over the wires were home runs. When I wasn't batting my way through a team's lineup, I imagined myself as Ted Williams, swinging left handed and hitting majestic high drives over the wires.

During the football season, I'd refine my punting and placekicking skills, propelling a football instead of a rock over the wires. As I kicked the ball, I pretended to be my football idol, Doak Walker.

It was a time to dream, a time to envision myself as the great athlete, the guy Van Patrick would describe circling the bases in

Detroit's Briggs Stadium or spiraling a long punt out of bounds at the Packers' two-yard line. I wanted that very much. In fact, as a teenager, that's *all* I wanted.

There were only 150 kids in the high school, so freshmen could take a date to the prom, and I did, which is memorable, because she had to be the only girl who's ever been driven to the big dance while sitting on an apple crate. My dad had an old Chevrolet panel truck, which had only one seat, and he sat on it as he drove us to the dance. He had ripped out the others to leave room for crates of fruit that we took to market.

To pick up my date, we stuck an apple crate where the passenger seat should have been and covered it with a blanket. She sat on that in her prom dress and corsage, while I crouched behind them. It wasn't exactly the best way to impress your date at the big dance.

The panel truck did serve an important sports function. On Saturday nights, my only contact with the NHL was to hear Foster Hewitt's call of *Hockey Night in Canada* through the Chevrolet's radio. With the antenna up, I could get a station in Sarnia, Ontario. You didn't need to start the truck for the radio to work, so I'd sneak out of the house, slump down in the driver's seat out of sight, and listen to the second period. I didn't dare stay for the entire game for fear of killing the battery. I'd hold my breath every Sunday morning when Dad started the engine.

Dad also used the panel truck to take our fruit to Eastern Market in Detroit for sale. Later, around 1950, he bought a Chevrolet Suburban, his first purchase of a new vehicle. After Mom moved out, he worked full time as a farmer, and on demand, I spent a lot of time helping him. On high school Friday nights, I was allowed to stay out late, after playing in a game and attending the postgame dance, but I understood that whenever I got home, even if it was after midnight, I would have to get right to work, helping him load our truck or Suburban for the drive to market.

We needed to reach the maze of open-air stalls in Detroit by dawn in order to rent one, so I might get a couple of hours of sleep in my own bed and maybe another hour wedged in the corner of the Suburban as Dad drove to the city. When we arrived, we sold as many crates of apples wholesale as we could to markets in Detroit, but, invariably, there were a lot of apples left. We would display them in various sized baskets for sale to the public, along with honey (clover and buckwheat), cider, popcorn, and in the summer, pears, plums, cherries, and sweet corn. We peddled apples all year.

Selling fruit in the Eastern Market was a great educational experience. Dad would stay in the truck, loading our fruit baskets—from half-pecks to bushels—and I would deal with the public. It helped give a young farm boy social confidence. You had to think on your feet as you quickly made change and answered questions; you had to be pleasant, no matter how tired or cold you were; and, obviously, you had to be a good salesman. It *was* cold, though. In the winter we were lucky if the temperature wasn't below freezing, and we were out in the open air all morning.

If we had a really good day, there was a great reward. Right across the street was a restaurant, which made the best hamburgers I've ever eaten, although maybe that's because I thought about the meal all day and was hungry enough to eat the wrapping. But the hamburger was oversized and juicy, and the meat, tomato, and lettuce were so fresh that it all crunched when you bit into it. If we'd really done well that day, Dad would also buy me a chocolate malt. That was the ultimate prize.

We'd thaw out on the drive back to the farm, and it was the one time Dad seemed really happy. He always said, "Money can't buy happiness, but it's way ahead of whatever's in second place." The trip home was a bonding experience, too, because he seemed to relax and allowed me to be close to him. Now we were a team and we'd earned enough money to get us through the next week.

Dad was always looking for new ways to make money. One winter, he decided to make maple syrup, because one whole side of the farm was lined with stately maple trees. So we tapped all of the trees, collected buckets and buckets of sap, and boiled it. It turned into an immense project that seemed to take forever. When we got through, I think we had about a pint and a half of maple syrup.

"That's all right, Dad," we teased. "We'll just make smaller pancakes."

We didn't wait for his reaction. We ran like hell.

&

All of us kids in the outlying area bused to the high school in our small village. After practice, whether it was football, basketball, or baseball, I walked or hitchhiked home. It was about two miles to the farm.

I didn't grow much until the end of my sophomore year, and then I grew five inches in five months. By the time I was a senior, I was five foot 11 and had "bulked up" to 140 pounds. I still thought I was going to be a professional athlete because I did have some skill and I had become a big frog in a little pond at Armada High. In my senior year, I was the quarterback on the football team, the pitcher on the baseball team (we only played one game a week), and the center and captain on the basketball team. As a center, I fouled out of every game. My profile today suggests I might have done some boxing. Actually, it was the direct result of my nose being the perfect height for the elbows of guys four to six inches taller whom I tried to guard.

I should have had an inkling that my future might lie in a different direction after a memorable football game at Memphis, another high school in a small farm town. Trailing by six points late in the fourth quarter, we drove to our opponent's two-yard line, where it was first and goal. On fourth down, the ball was just inches from the goal line. One last play would spell victory or defeat.

Unlike today, when coaches signal plays in to their quarterbacks, I called my own. Because I rarely carried the ball, I figured that Memphis would look for one of our backs to run the ball inside and wouldn't expect me to keep it. So I took the snap, faked the handoff to our halfback, and took my first step toward circling right end for the winning touchdown. But I tripped over the right guard's foot and was smothered short of the goal line. Memphis ran out the clock.

If California were closer, I would have walked there that night. So I did the next best thing. When the final gun sounded, I started off through the cornfields and woods, determined to walk the entire 12 miles back to Armada. I had lost the game and felt I didn't deserve to ride back to school on the team bus. Of course, I was still wearing my orange and black uniform, and in the late sun of autumn, I must have looked like a caricature of Halloween.

As I was about to disappear into the woods, my dad, my Uncle Norman who was visiting from Minnesota, and my coach chased after me and brought me back to the bus. The ride home with my teammates and the cheerleaders was even more painful than the embarrassment of losing the game. My capture and the forced bus ride were humiliating, and my eyes never left the floor of the bus until we arrived back at school to shower and dress.

With Dad focusing full time on farming after Mom left, he had the flexibility to go to all of my games, including road games, and he rarely missed one. He never cheered or clapped, but it was still important to know that he was there. He was in our gym one night during my senior year when we hosted Capac High School, another equally inept team of farmers' sons, in a basketball game. Although I was often overmatched at center, I had a career game that night, scoring 23 points and leading Armada to a rare victory.

After the game, when I climbed our rickety stairs at home and headed for my bedroom, I noticed that Dad was still awake. I invited myself into his bedroom, thinking I would finally hear a positive reaction to my starring effort that night. I sat on the edge of his bed and asked for his evaluation of our big victory.

"Great to win for a change," he muttered.

I threw out several other comments, all designed to give him a chance to praise my performance. Nothing.

Finally, in frustration, I said, "I scored 23 points."

He looked at me. "How about your man?" he said. "I had him for 26."

Suddenly, I started to cry and blurted out, "It's really going to hurt you to ever say something nice about me, isn't it?"

"Son," he answered, "the day you think you're so good that you can't improve, just remember you can go only one way—down."

I stomped away to my room, still in tears. I didn't want wisdom; I wanted praise. Here was the best game I'd ever played, and my team won, and to get that reaction—you're not as good as you think you are; you could be a lot better—was painful. It's true, of course. We can all be better, but it's not what I needed to hear at the time.

But there was no way to know the profound impact those words would have on the rest of my life. It explains, in part, my competitiveness today. Even after 50 years as a broadcaster, I'm rarely satisfied with my work. I'm driven by that early philosophy that regardless of any acclaim, you must strive to improve. And you can.

By this time, Mom was in Mount Pleasant, working on the campus of Central Michigan University, known as Central Michigan College of Education in the early 1950s. She took several classes at the college and also met her second husband there. When I hitchhiked up to see her as a high school junior, it was my first exposure to the campus.

As my high school years came to a close, however, Dad wasn't offering me any encouragement to continue my education, and I probably wouldn't have gone to college. But fate, fabulous fate, stepped into my life, as it would several times in the next few years.

On graduation day in June 1952, our little class of 33 seniors was flattered and impressed that Dr. Charles Anspach, the president of Central Michigan, had come down to give the commencement address. Anspach was one of the finest speakers of that era, an academic celebrity whose services were in constant demand throughout the state and upper Midwest. Everyone was puzzled as to why a man of such stature had chosen to speak at our little school. I found out years later that he believed that Central Michigan's strength was based on attracting students from small towns throughout Michigan, towns such as Armada. With his graying hair and spectacles, he reminded me of President Franklin D. Roosevelt, impressive and eloquent.

After Dr. Anspach finished the commencement speech, captivating us with his inspiring comments and well-timed sense of humor, I mustered up my courage and approached him.

"Do you happen to know my mother, Belle Enberg?" I asked. "She works at your college and also takes classes there."

"I do," he said. "She works in Warriner Hall, the administration building where my office is located." Then he looked at me kindly. "And what kind of a student are you? Do you have any college plans?"

I told him that I had earned mostly As and ranked third in my class (third of 33, I thought, big deal). I also said I had no plans to go to college. For one thing, my dad couldn't afford it.

"Ask your principal to send your grades up to me," he responded. "I'll take a look at them."

I did it the very next day. Three weeks later, a letter arrived from Central Michigan.

"Congratulations," it said, "you've been accepted," and I was offered a $100 academic scholarship.

"Are you kidding me?" I thought with excitement. "You're going to pay me $100 to go to college?"

So off I went. When I began school at Central Michigan in 1952, war was still raging in Korea, so I enlisted in the naval reserve's two-and-six program. It included two years on active duty and six in the reserves, which would allow me to complete my college education before going on active duty. I majored in physical education, planning to be a high school coach.

During the summer before I went to college, I played first base and outfield for Armada's town baseball team, the Athletics. We had a game every Sunday. I was a good hitter, and playing with older men kept my dream of being a professional athlete alive. I was 17.

However, my athletic dreams soon died at Central Michigan. In baseball, I spent two years on the JV team as an outfielder, never making the varsity. In football, I was the sixth or seventh quarterback on the freshman team. I just tried to stay out of the way and not get hurt. I didn't even attempt to play basketball.

Because I had failed as an athlete, I eagerly accepted a chance to join the debate team as a sophomore. Here was something that had competition, and, what the heck, I always talked a better game than I played. It turned out to be the most valuable educational experience of my undergraduate life. It forced me to be able to see beyond my own beliefs and realize that there's always someone who may have a better argument than you do, and you should listen to it and respect it.

The national topic in debate that year was free trade. One week I would argue for it, and the next, our coach, Emil Pfister, would force me to argue against it, as he did with all of my teammates. It was a fantastic lesson. I realized I could make just as strong an argument on the other side of an issue. It's easy for each of us to get trapped when we believe something so passionately that we don't want to listen to what might change our minds. It's great to have strong beliefs, but be able to support them and at the same time be ready to accept opposing views.

With the help of on-campus work, plus money from home and summer employment, I had managed to pay for my first two years of college. But in 1954, the summer after my sophomore year, employment opportunities were slim, and I made less than $300 pruning trees for the village of Armada. I realized there was no chance of returning to college for the fall semester.

Because I was two years into my naval reserve commitment, I decided I might as well get my active duty in the Navy out of the way. But the Korean War had ended the year before, and the Navy wasn't looking for personnel. Remember the old posters, "Uncle Sam Wants You"? Well, Uncle Sam didn't want me.

However, I still needed to make money for school. With the help of my dad who joined me on the job, I went to work on the assembly line at the Dodge plant in Hamtramck, near Detroit. I'm so non-mechanical that I can barely get out of my own locked bathroom, but I was hired to help attach bumpers on 1955 Dodges. I used to wonder how far the cars would get out of the factory before the bumpers fell off.

I was part of a three-man bumper crew on the assembly line. After the other two men unloaded the bumper from an overhead track and slid it onto the frame, my job was to slide bolts in holes on either side of the bumper to secure it, then fit washers on the bolts, and fasten nuts to the bolts with an air-pressure gun. As you do this, you're lying on your back on a sled under the car and pushing yourself with your feet to follow the bumper. It's a lot to do in a short amount of time. If records were kept, there's no doubt that in my first week I fumbled more bolts, nuts, and washers than anyone in Dodge history. Meanwhile, the line kept moving. The more nervous I got, the more bolts, nuts, and washers I dropped and the farther behind everyone else got.

Working in the next area were my dad and a crusty, wrinkled woman adorned in an ever-present hair net. They were installing carburetors. As I delayed them, forcing them to play catch-up, I quickly tried the woman's patience.

On my third day on the job, she charged over to me.

"You little f-----!" she screamed. "If you don't speed up your little ass, I'm going to kick it right outta here!"

She meant it, too. Not only was it the first time I heard a woman swear, but I got f-bombed.

A month later, Dad and I were able to laugh over the episode, because I did improve, and I quickly learned how fortunate I was to be a college student. I couldn't wait to get back to Central Michigan. Now, I fully realized how incredibly important education was, and I returned to campus in January 1955, with a new attitude and sense of appreciation.

Working in the Dodge plant had fattened my bank account, but, as I returned to school, I needed to continue earning money. One of my teammates on the debate team was the PA announcer for

Central Michigan's football and basketball teams, a lucrative position that paid three dollars a game. Because he was graduating, I asked him to help me follow in his footsteps, which he did. I announced the school's games in the fall and winter of 1955 to 1956. It was the first time that I ever worked behind a microphone, but I had no desire to do any real broadcasting work.

In the spring of 1956, as I neared the end of my junior year, I discovered that Chuck Miller, one of my fraternity brothers who was graduating, was relinquishing his job as janitor at Mount Pleasant's only radio station, WCEN. This position paid the princely sum of one dollar an hour, and I decided to pursue it. Chuck suggested that I contact the station's general manager, Russ Holcomb. I did, and he invited me in for an interview.

When I, now 21 years old, walked in the door at WCEN, it was the first time I had ever been in a radio station. Holcomb told me that he would hire me as the custodian, if I wanted, but he added that the station had a more important position that needed to be filled—weekend disc jockey.

"Enberg, you have a nice voice," he said. "Why don't you step into this little studio and read for me?"

I agreed to do it, but my palms were sweating and my mouth was unusually dry, so I asked if I could read the material before auditioning.

"Oh, no," he said with a chuckle. "We don't often get a chance to rehearse around here. Most of the time the announcer has to read the material *cold* on the air."

Nervously, I did my best. The reel of audiotape on the far wall turned slowly, recording my efforts to sound like a real announcer. I read a five-minute newscast and two 60-second commercials. When I was finished, Holcomb told me he would call me in a few days. Departing the station, I prayed that my nervousness in the booth wouldn't cost me the dollar-an-hour custodial job.

A couple of weeks later, Holcomb informed me that I had been hired by WCEN, "The Pleasant Voice of Central Michigan," as the station's new weekend disc jockey. It was a more glamorous position than janitor, but it also paid a dollar an hour, apparently a true measure of my novice value. Totally by accident, my broadcasting career had begun! As my critics have wryly suggested, somewhere in the great beyond the key to the broom closet is waiting for me.

Timing is everything. Shortly after I was hired, WCEN's sports director became embroiled in a dispute with management and left. Knowing of my intense interest in sports, the station offered me the position. Soon I was writing my own nightly 15-minute sports show, doing play-by-play for Central Michigan and two local high schools when there wasn't a scheduling conflict (calling as many as three football or basketball games in a weekend), and continuing my studies toward a teaching degree in physical and health education. It was a heady, busy time.

On holidays, such as Thanksgiving and Christmas, I worked 16-hour days at WCEN. Because no one else wanted to be there for those shifts, I volunteered to work all day and much of the night. There was no overtime, but I was thrilled to be earning $16 a day.

They taught me how to throw the switches to turn the station on and off, and, inept as I am mechanically, I learned to do it and also run the record turntables. I brought the station on the air before 7:00 a.m. and signed it off at 11:00 p.m. While records were playing, I would run into our little newsroom and rip the five-minute news summary off the UPI ticker. I read the news, gave the weather forecast, read the commercials, and played and announced the records. Except for clanging cymbals between my knees, I was a one-man WCEN band.

As I sat there playing carols on Christmas Day, people in Mount Pleasant noticed that they had heard the same voice all day long and started to feel sorry for me. Several compassionate souls came by with plates of turkey and pumpkin pie, hand-delivering holiday spirit. That wouldn't have happened in a big city.

I worked at WCEN for a year, until the spring semester of my senior year, in 1957, when WSAM Radio in Saginaw, known informally as "Big SAM," offered me two dollars an hour to work weekends. At the time, I was making $1.25 an hour at WCEN but would have stayed for less than two dollars, because the drive to Saginaw took more than an hour. But, when I asked for a raise, WCEN wouldn't budge. It was $1.25 or nothing. I left for the big money, signing on with Big SAM as its weekend disc jockey.

There was no sports show at WSAM, which was disappointing, but I did everything else. Besides working weekends that spring, I was there the next three summers, subbing for each announcer when he went on vacation. I was the morning disc jockey, the afternoon disc jockey, the evening disc jockey, the newsman—whatever they needed me to do. Our music was middle of the road—Frank Sinatra, Bing Crosby, Johnny Mathis, big band, show tunes, and other instrumentals.

We also carried the Lions' and Tigers' games, which was a bonus. For some of my shifts, all I had to do was break in every half hour for the mandatory station identification and then spend the rest of the time listening to Van Patrick call the game—and get paid for it.

My senior year was eventful in other ways. I had been chief justice of the campus supreme court as a junior, and someone suggested I run for student body president. Unlike today, this position had very few responsibilities and was more of an honor than anything else, so I agreed to do it. My work as a radio broadcaster had provided me with some notoriety. Perhaps that helped me to be elected.

After I won, the campus newspaper did a feature on me, casually mentioning a nickname I had been given three years earlier. Tom Dezelsky, one of my teammates on the JV baseball team who had a mischievous sense of humor and rhyme, had called me the "Armada Tomata." My dad got a clipping of the article, "Enberg Is Student Body President," and sent it to his parents in Virginia, Minnesota, a small city on the Mesabi iron ore range in the northern part of the state. My grandparents, in turn, brought it to the local newspaper, which reprinted the whole article, word for word, except for my nickname. Instead of the "Armada Tomata," I became the "Armada Tornado." I prefer that. It also taught me to appreciate good editing.

⚬⚬

As graduation loomed, my new goal was to be an educator, perhaps at the university level. I had been fascinated by education since I was in the eighth grade in the one-room schoolhouse back in Armada. Our burdened teacher often asked me to work with the first and second graders while she taught other children. I helped them with their reading and spelling, and to see them "get it" was a big thrill.

I was encouraged by my professors to apply for a graduate assistantship to further my education at a master's degree level, and I wrote to Columbia, North Carolina, Michigan, UCLA, USC, and

Indiana—all universities with well-regarded health science programs—for application forms. The shortest, least complicated form
was Indiana's, and I sent that one back first. I was quickly accepted by
Indiana and offered a stipend of $1,000 a year, and, without further
hesitation, I decided that this was my new school. This education
thing was starting to become a big-money deal.

A month later, on a warm May evening on campus, President
Anspach delivered a farewell speech to the Central Michigan graduating class of 1957. His theme was "Will You Dare to be Great?" As
I applauded his final remarks, I silently thanked him for changing the
course of my life five years earlier. As I headed for Indiana, would I
dare to be great?

TIMEOUT

The Luckiest Day of My Life

IN THE SUMMER after my freshman year at Central
Michigan, I went home to Armada and was hired by Flynn
Construction Company on a crew that was paving roads. It
was hot, hard, physical labor, but I made $2.35 an hour,
working 10 or 12 hours a day and socked away enough
money for my next year in college.

The work comprised either tamping hot asphalt in new
parking lots or resurfacing paved roads with hot tar and
gravel. A 10-ton roller would crush the gravel into the tar,
smoothing out the rebuilt road surface.

Near the end of the summer, the guy who drove the
roller quit, and they asked me if I could operate it. Because
this assignment gave me a chance to work sitting down, I said
sure. You simply sat on top of the roller and drove it back and
forth over the tar.

But it almost cost me my life.

I had only been piloting the roller for a week when I
was told to drive it onto the back of a flatbed truck because

we were moving to a new construction site. It was a tricky operation because the roller had to be backed up a pair of planks onto the truck. When I started up, I got going sideways, and it started sliding. Unfortunately, I didn't have enough experience to know how to correct it. While I furiously worked the controls, it kept sliding, sliding, sliding, and as it was about to plunge off the boards, I quickly decided I didn't want to ride it down. In a panic, I jumped off and landed in a roadside ditch.

Big mistake.

As I landed on my back, I looked up and the roller—all 10 tons of it—was coming right after me! But it hit first on the soft road, and because it was so heavy, it dug in, and, at a 45-degree angle, stopped. If it had flipped into the ditch, I would have been history.

My boss was furious.

"You could have been killed!" he screamed, stating the obvious. "The one thing you never do is jump to the side where it's falling! You should have jumped the other way!"

Fifty years later, I can only shake my head at how lucky I was. Dick Enberg, the announcer, was nearly crushed gravel.

2

COMING TO A CROSSROADS

*"Did you ever consider that with that short hair
you look like a shaved prostitute?"*

—Dr. Arthur Daniels

On a warm September day in 1957, I climbed into my bulky seven-year-old Chrysler Imperial and drove south to Bloomington, Indiana, home of Indiana University. I was proud of that old tank and had given it the nickname "Oyster." If you think that's an odd name, I agree with you. I don't recall how I came up with it. Maybe I hoped to discover an occasional pearl.

When "Oyster" and I showed up in Bloomington, I was 22 years old and planning on a future in education, while encouraged by my modest broadcasting success. For that, I couldn't have come to Indiana at a better time.

My arrival coincided with the hiring of 33-year-old Richard Yoakam as a professor of broadcast journalism. The pipe-smoking Yoakam was a remarkable person. Because he had suffered from polio as a child, he wore leg braces and used crutches, but he maneuvered faster than any of us on two healthy legs and played a solid game of golf. As a professor, he was dynamic—a fascinating lecturer, a wonderful story-teller, and someone who related to students very well.

Yoakam, who had once done play-by-play of Iowa football and basketball, had come to Indiana from KCRG Radio and TV in Cedar Rapids, where he was the news director. With football season about to begin, his immediate goal was to establish a new radio network for Indiana football and basketball that would feature student broadcasters. WFIU, the campus FM radio station, would be the flagship. At the time, a Bloomington station was doing Indiana games.

"Their broadcasts were hokey and corny, and I felt the university was not well represented," Yoakam told me when I visited his home many years later. "I suggested to the university that we could do better ourselves. I personally didn't want to call the games, however, because I was more interested in teaching broadcast journalism than going on the air again. I had two goals: produce better broadcasts and give our students an opportunity to develop skills in sports broadcasting. If I couldn't find the quality I was looking for, I would have done the games myself."

To recruit students for the broadcasts, Yoakam placed an ad in the campus newspaper shortly after he arrived, asking for those who were interested in sports announcing to come to tryouts. If he could find someone skilled enough, that person would be Indiana's new play-by-play announcer. What an opportunity!

Within a week of my arrival on campus, I joined perhaps 15 other students in the press box of Indiana's old Memorial Stadium as the football team gathered on the field below for a scrimmage. We made our own simple little spotting boards, and each of us would be given a chance to announce part of the scrimmage. Yoakam asked who wanted to go first, and most of the guys looked down at the floor. Because I had already announced Central Michigan games, I felt comfortable and volunteered to begin the audition. When I finished, several of the students, none of whom had any experience, had walked out.

When we finished in the stadium, Yoakam took the rest of us back to WFIU and asked us to create a game in our own minds and ad-lib its call. Again, advantage Enberg. All of the names from Central Michigan were still fresh in my memory, so I used my old school's lineup, made up a scoring drive and took the Chippewas right down the field. It was easy.

Shortly after, Yoakam informed me that I had won the audition and would be joined by Phil Jones, a junior at Indiana, as color commentator. Jones, who worked with me for two years, retired in 2001 after spending 32 years on television with CBS News. During his long career with the network, he was a war correspondent in Vietnam, a White House correspondent, chief Congressional correspondent, and a correspondent for the news program, *48 Hours*. It was not a bad partnership for the IU Sports Network's initial voyage.

"We were young, we were ambitious, we were creative, and we felt like nothing could stop us," Jones always said of his years at Indiana. "And Dick Yoakam inspired us. He was loaded with enthusiasm. Anyone who got within 10 feet of him was infected by it."

Under Yoakam's leadership, students continued to call Indiana games for nearly 20 years, with many others serving as engineers and producers. Among the graduates, Pat Williams and John Gordon also advanced to big league radio-TV sportscasting careers.

WFIU was an FM station at a time when AM radio was dominant, but FM technology allowed Yoakam to rapidly build his network. He credited Elmer Sulzer, Indiana's director of broadcasting in 1957, for inventing an FM relay system that helped it expand. FM stations throughout Indiana were offered the broadcasts for free. Each station would tune in an FM radio receiver, pick up the game, and simultaneously re-broadcast it as far as its signal would carry to the next station. In the first year we had eight or nine stations, and then after four years, it expanded to 40, with several AM stations joining the network. Eventually, Yoakam told me it grew to more than 50 stations.

I had grown up a Michigan fan, and to be announcing Big Ten games at the age of 22 was heady stuff. In my first game in historic Michigan Stadium, the Wolverines' broadcaster in the booth next door was the great Tom Harmon, "Ole 98." It was hard to believe. I was not only making $35 a game, but I was in such big-league company.

They were largely lean years for the Hoosiers' football team—IU's record was 11-23-2 from 1957 to 1960—but there were several bright moments in 1958 when Indiana won four games in a row late in the season, including rare back-to-back victories over Michigan State and Michigan.

But basketball was IU's big sport. Indiana, under the great Branch McCracken, who won two national championships during his 24 years at the university, sold out every game. His "Hurryin' Hoosiers" won the 1958 Big Ten title and finished second in 1960. The 1960 team went 20-4 and provided the sports highlight of my Indiana years by handing soon-to-be national champion Ohio State its only Big Ten loss—99-83 behind All-America center Walt Bellamy's 24 points. That was the Ohio State team that featured future NBA stars Jerry Lucas, John Havlicek, and Larry Siegfried, with future Indiana coach Bobby Knight coming off the bench.

McCracken loved the fast break but hated dribbling. He wanted his players to rebound, pass, pass, pass, and shoot. His offensive philosophy was simple. The faster you get the ball down court, the more shots you can take, and the more shots you take, the better your chance to score and win. The Hoosiers wore their crimson jerseys on the road, and as they flashed full speed down court, my call became, "And here come the red shirts."

My excited descriptions of the Indiana fast break were often punctuated with "Oh My!", which was first used during one of those basketball games. One night, when the Hoosiers were on an up-tempo roll, it just came out of my mouth in one loud burst—"OOOOOHHHHH MY!!!" I felt like it capped an exciting moment. The next day, some of my friends on campus greeted me with "Hi, Dick... Oh My!" They liked it!

Those two words have become my great friends as a broadcaster, describing the total range of athletic emotions—from deep despair to triumphant exultation. At the very least, they serve to call back the television spectator who may have wandered off to the refrigerator. I've always tried to use it as an exclamation point, a signal that the play was unique or spectacular enough to warrant the viewer's return to the TV set.

The only negatives to announcing Indiana basketball were the nerve-wracking moments when our little DC-3 airplanes flew through sleet and snow on some of those ominous winter nights to land on tiny airstrips. Flying into Manhattan, Kansas, home of Kansas State, the wind was so strong that the plane literally landed on one wheel with its opposite wing pointed straight up. Oh My!

❧

While I was announcing the Indiana games, I continued to root for my favorite teams, among them the Detroit Lions. In the fall of 1957, the Lions finished the regular season tied for first place in the Western Conference with the San Francisco 49ers, and three days before Christmas, the two teams met in a playoff at Kezar Stadium in San Francisco.

I watched the game from Bloomington, and Jack Bailey, a close college pal of mine, watched from Mount Pleasant, where he was a senior at Central Michigan. As Jack and I cheered in front of our TV sets, the Lions pulled off a remarkable second-half comeback to defeat the 49ers and earn a berth in the NFL Championship Game. Trailing 24-7 going into the second half, Detroit rallied to win 31-27 behind Tobin Rote, the replacement for injured quarterback Bobby Layne.

As soon as the game ended, Jack and I made contact on the phone to celebrate the big victory. The longer we talked, the more excited we got about the Lions, and we decided to meet in Detroit the next weekend for the title game against Cleveland. Our audacious game plan was to pose as a couple of announcers from an imaginary radio station— WCEN, Chillicothe, Ohio—and try to talk our way through the press gate at Briggs Stadium. I still had my ID card from WCEN, Mount Pleasant, so I had that handy if the usher at the gate demanded some proof.

Dressed in our suits, ties, and fedoras, we arrived at the stadium at 11:00 a.m., an hour before the gates were to open. Approaching the press entrance, I identified myself, asking if we could go in early to prepare for our radio reports.

The press usher stopped us.

"You've got to have the press credential, the pink one, to get in," he said.

"No one said it would be a problem," I appealed.

"Without the pink credential, it's a problem," he said, as he sent us on our way.

The game was a sellout, so our only hope now was to find someone with a couple of tickets to sell. At 11:45 we met a teenager on the opposite side of the stadium who was trying to sell two standing room passes for $10 each. That was about all we could afford. Time was running short for him, so he succumbed to our pressure and agreed to sell both for $15.

Tickets in hand we streaked back to the press entrance. Flashing them at the usher, I said the Lions had run out of the pink press passes, and all they had left were a couple of lousy standing-room tickets. With a knowing look, he waved us in. It was 11:55, and we were the first fans in the stadium. We found a choice standing-room spot on the 50-yard line in the lower deck. Not bad for $7.50 each.

It was a wonderful day. We cheered the Lions to an overwhelming 59-14 victory over the Browns as Rote threw four touchdown passes. With less than a minute to go, we decided to wander down to the first row of the box seats behind the Lions' dugout. No one was minding a small gate, so we jumped onto the field. As the players headed for the locker room, we took a chance and followed them down the steps of the dugout. The same usher who allowed us in at the press entrance was now guarding the tunnel that led back to the locker room door. He recognized us and waved us through. What luck!

However, when we arrived at the crowded entrance to the locker room, we encountered another usher who was checking for the pink credentials. As Jack and I tried to figure out how to slip by him, two photographers came out of the locker room.

"We lost our press passes," I said. "If you've finished your work, could we have yours?"

"Sure," they said, handing them over.

The next thing we knew we were standing in the middle of the cramped dressing quarters in direct contact with our football heroes, as they celebrated their NFL championship.

We knew our friends and family wouldn't believe our story. In fact, they had laughed at our plan, suggesting it would be much safer to stay home and watch the game on television. So I edged over to halfback Gene Gedman's locker and asked if I might have a souvenir, and he kindly gave me his chinstrap. Jack got center Charlie Ane's chinstrap. Now, we had evidence.

I've been fortunate to do play-by-play for eight Super Bowls, but none of them can quite match the pleasure of that late-December day in Detroit when Jack and I came to the stadium with no tickets and wound up in the victorious Lions' locker room. Did we have a delicious answer for all those inevitable questions upon returning home? Did we get in? Did we ever!

᠊᠊᠊᠊᠊᠊᠊᠊᠊᠊᠊ ᚛ ᠊᠊᠊᠊᠊᠊᠊᠊᠊᠊᠊

I earned a master's degree in my first year at Indiana, but now I was prepared to take a long break before plunging into work for my doctorate. I had completed six years in the naval reserve but still owed the Navy two years of active duty, so I reported to the local naval officer and said I was ready to go.

"Why do you want to go on active duty?" he asked.

That was a strange question.

"I have to fulfill my obligation," I said.

"I just saw a memo come through here recently," he said, "which says you can do that by staying in the reserves for two more years, with no active duty required."

I was in total disbelief. I didn't even want to celebrate. This was too good to be true.

"Please check that," I said. "I won't believe it until you make sure. I'll come back tomorrow."

So I came back the next day, and he said, "Yep, I was right. Two more years in the reserves and you've done your good deed for Uncle Sam."

That changed my whole life. Instead of leaving for two years, I continued to broadcast football and basketball as our network grew from eight stations to 40, and my popularity grew on campus, as well as throughout the state. It also allowed me to stay on track for my doctorate. Because of the network's success, I got another break when the university waived a requirement that obligated doctoral candidates to leave campus for two years to teach somewhere else before finishing their dissertation. I was able to get credit for my two years by teaching on campus, while still attending classes. So I saved all that time, too.

Because I wasn't sailing around the world with the Navy in the summer of 1958, I went back to Saginaw, Michigan, to continue working at WSAM as a vacation replacement. One day, Bruce Malle, the program director, called me into his office.

"Dick, I've got some advice for you," he said. "I think you're really going to be successful in this business if you decide to stay with it. But you should change your last name."

I asked why, and he said, "Well, I'm Jewish, and I changed my name. Enberg sounds Jewish, and I think you'd be better off if you used another name."

As I look back, there's real sadness in that insecurity, but I was very young and did pause to give it some thought. After all, movie stars change their names. What would my radio name be? My middle name is Alan, so I thought how about Dick Allen? But Mel Allen was a sports-casting legend, and it sounded as if I was trying to copy him. Eventually, I came up with Dick Breen, which had a fresh, sporty sound to it. I even bounced it off some of my buddies, but, obviously, I never did it. In retrospect, it would have been tragic if I'd taken his advice. It would have killed my dad, who was fiercely proud of his Finnish heritage and the relatively uncommon Enberg name. Any pride the Enberg family has had in my success would have been diluted by the fact I had changed my name. But I might have been Dick Breen.

∾

WFIU, the student radio station, was located in an old Quonset hut in the middle of campus. It was not a place one would expect to find romance, but when I dropped by the station, I would often run into a broadcast student who worked there. Her name was Jeri Suer. She was bright, and she looked like actress Audrey Hepburn, who had captivated me and millions of others a few years before in the movie *Roman Holiday*. Jeri and I soon began dating, and because I had grown close to Yoakam, he often joined us at the Olde English Hut next to campus for beer and pizza on Friday afternoons. He liked Jeri, too, and used to kid us, "I want to see you two get married to see what kind of kids you'd produce."

Yoakam got his wish. In the late summer of 1959, we were married in what turned out to be a memorable ceremony. In fact, it was comical. First, Jeri and I asked a minister from our church in Bloomington to marry us, and he agreed. Then, Jeri's mother, who lived in Bloomington, selected and signed us up for Beck Chapel on campus for the ceremony, asking 90-year-old Reverend Beck to marry us. Because the chapel was named after Beck, she felt obligated to ask him to perform the ceremony. On our wedding day, we wound up with two ministers who continuously collided in the cramped chapel quarters. Is this a wedding or roller derby?

Before we were pronounced man and wife, Reverend Beck, whose false teeth rattled every time he spoke, chattered to me, "Repeat after me: I, Richard, take thee, Nancy, to be my lawfully wedded wife."

There was a long pause, before I said, "I, Richard, take thee, *Jeri*, to be my lawfully wedded wife."

I guess Nancy was the bride in the last wedding. In addition to the dueling ministers, Jeri and I spent much of the time trying to keep our two sets of divorced parents apart. It was an exhausting day.

As we settled into married life, living in on-campus housing, I continued to work toward my doctorate while broadcasting Indiana's games. Before my final year, I steeled my courage and asked athletic director Frank Miller for a raise. Shaking as I walked into his office, but feigning confidence, I succeeded. He gave me a boost to $50 a game. It was my only raise in four years.

Shortly after Indiana's basketball season ended in the spring of 1961, a Columbus television station asked about my availability to do play-by-play of Ohio State's NCAA regional final game, which would be played in Louisville. I agreed in a heartbeat. It's hard to believe, but there was no national telecast of the NCAA Tournament then, not even the championship game. The top-ranked Buckeyes, defending national champions, were unbeaten and favored to win the title again. They defeated Kentucky in the regional final at Freedom Hall to move on to the Final Four.

Ohio State then routed St. Joseph's in the national semifinal to take a 32-game winning streak into the national championship game against second-ranked Cincinnati, and the Columbus station, apparently pleased with my work, asked me to call that game. I flew to Kansas City, the site of the Final Four in those days, knowing that my broadcast to Columbus, and now, Cincinnati, was the only telecast of the title game in the entire United States. There wasn't even a nationwide radio broadcast. March Madness was obviously a long way away.

Our telecast was scheduled on air at 9:00 p.m., and as I meticulously went over my notes at courtside, Utah and St. Joseph's tipped off in the consolation game, still part of the Final Four in 1961. I didn't pay any attention to the game, except to glance up occasionally when the crowd cheered.

As our broadcast time neared, Utah and St. Joe's played into overtime. At 9:00 p.m., they were still on the court, slugging it out in a second overtime. I had to drop my notes for the championship game, greet the audience, and pick up the call without any preparation. It was like diving into a cold swimming pool—there was no time to ease into it. Of course, I didn't know any of the players for Utah and St. Joe's, so I quickly grabbed a program and grabbed names on the fly. To everyone's disbelief, the game extended into a third overtime. It was easier for me now, because I could at least identify the players without looking at the program. The marathon ended as St. Joseph's won 127-120 in *four* overtimes.

Now I had a new problem. Instead of a planned five-minute lead-in to the championship game, I had 30 minutes, while Ohio State and Cincinnati warmed up, to fill before tipoff, and I was working without a color man. Dashing around the arena during commercials, I started grabbing people for interviews. I interviewed everybody but the guy sweeping the floor, and I considered asking him about his favorite broom.

Cincinnati won the national championship in an upset 70-65, snapping Ohio State's long winning streak. That game also went into overtime.

❧

As summer approached, I had finished my doctoral work and was working on my dissertation, a document of more than 400 pages. It was entitled *An Analysis and Synthesis of Research and Professional Thought on the Health and Welfare of the Athlete with Emphasis on Prevention of Athletic Injury*. The academic intent was to collect all of the available pertinent information that would be helpful in preventing injuries to athletes. The university library was my home for six months.

At this point, Central Michigan, South Carolina, and Temple had offered me teaching positions, but I knew exactly what I wanted to do the next fall, and it seemed like a fait accompli. My goal was to continue doing the Indiana broadcasts, while serving as one of the assistant professors in the school of health, physical education, and recreation. I knew the athletic department, elated by the success of the IU Sports Network, was campaigning for me to continue in a full-time position. In addition, I had already taught several classes on campus, including one of the toughest in the university—a high-level graduate statistics class, replacing a professor who was seriously ill. I figured the university was busy organizing its hiring proposal for the about-to-become Dr. Enberg.

In May, I got a call from Dean Arthur Daniels, whom I assumed would be my new boss. I was 26, although I looked 21, thanks to my chubby cheeks and military-style short hair.

As I walked in, Daniels said, "Sit down, Enberg. I understand you're interviewing for faculty positions."

"Yes, sir," I said, and proudly threw out the names of the schools that were recruiting me, while waiting for his invitation to join the IU faculty.

"Well," he said, "since you're interviewing, I just thought I'd call you in to give you a little piece of advice."

"What's that, sir?"

"It's about your hair," he said. "Did you ever consider that with that short hair you look like a shaved prostitute?"

And then he dismissed me. I walked in expecting a job offer and walked out with my head down and my shoulders slumped, my future sent into sudden turmoil. He had made up his mind that he didn't want to hire me, perhaps because I looked so young. I'll never know. But it was a pivotal moment. What was I going to do now?

I've always felt that in analyzing anyone's life, you can look at several crossroads over which he or she has no control. We all come to a critical moment in our lives and someone or something else dictates which path we take. For example, I often have wondered how my life would have unfolded if I hadn't gone to Central Michigan, a door that opened when President Anspach asked me if I had any college plans. Without Central Michigan, how would I have gotten into broadcasting? What if the general manager at WCEN Radio had hired me as a janitor, the position I sought? And I probably wouldn't have walked into the radio station in the first place if I had gone on active duty in the Navy in the summer of 1954, but they wouldn't take me. It happened again in the summer of 1958, when the Navy allowed me to finish my military obligation in the reserves, instead of leaving the university for two years. Then Dean Daniels decided that I looked like a shaved prostitute!

If Daniels had offered me the job I expected, I'm absolutely convinced that I'd still be doing Indiana's games. There's no doubt in my mind. I would be on campus broadcasting and teaching, sucking on a pipe like Yoakam—but without tobacco—and probably writing my academic memoirs.

Shortly after my visit with Daniels, Dr. Delmar Oviatt, a recruiter from San Fernando Valley State in California, paid a visit to Indiana. When I lived in the San Fernando Valley during World War II, our home was near the new campus, so, out of curiosity, I signed up for an interview. Oviatt offered me a teaching position in health education, and when he added that they needed an assistant baseball coach as well, I was sold. The right decision was to move to the Left Coast.

As Jeri and I drove west late in the summer of 1961, I was determined to be a college professor for the rest of my life, but in the back of my mind was the lingering thought, I'm pretty good at broadcasting, too. I had done Big Ten football and basketball. I had worked the national championship basketball game. Feedback was positive.

I thought, "I should be able to keep it going in Los Angeles, maybe on weekends or in the summer to supplement my income."

At first, however, my total focus was on the full-time role of teaching and coaching.

Beginning in 1961, I taught four years at San Fernando Valley State, which is now Cal State Northridge, coaching baseball for three of them. I had the freshmen team and was the assistant on the varsity team under former Yankee minor league infielder Stan Charnofsky, who had played college ball for the great Rod Dedeaux at USC. Stan was a fabulous head coach. I thought I knew the game, but I learned more baseball from him in my first season than I had in my previous 26 years.

As an assistant professor, I taught health education and safety, including a class at night for master's candidates in education. I was perpetually nervous. I had diarrhea every morning. Even though I had taught at Indiana, the pressure was much more intense now, because these were *my* classes and I had four or five of them a semester. In health sciences, there are so many things you have to know. One week you're teaching psychology, the next week you're teaching sex education, the next week you're teaching communicable diseases, and the next week you're into anatomy or physiology.

In a class of 40 or 50 students, I was cognizant that somebody in the room knew more about a specific subject than I did, particularly in the night classes. The students at night were older than I was, and most had been teaching in area high schools for many years. They had real-life experiences I didn't have. I often felt like a batter in a baseball game. When they asked questions, I got three strikes. I was allowed two, but if I said, "I don't know" three times, I had struck out miserably that day. So I admitted right up front that I didn't know everything.

I told them, "This is the framework of the class. I'll help you as much as I can to get the most out of it, but you can contribute, too. You can be a resource for me."

Despite my anxiety, I enjoyed teaching. I wanted to be the best in my department. I wanted the word on campus to be, "He may be the most demanding teacher and toughest grader, but if you want the best teacher, it's Enberg." I tried to be entertaining, and it always bothered me if even one student didn't look interested. I went right at him or her with a question or worked even harder to liven up my presentation.

When I think back to those four years as a professor, it was such rich training for what I'm doing now. As a broadcaster, you have to be entertaining, you have to be well informed, you have to be excited about what you know, and you have to have a sense of your audience—just like in the classroom. In fact, when I look into a camera, I'm looking into my classroom. When I'm calling a game, I can envision hands shooting up all over the country with questions. Whoops, I'll think, perhaps we need to explain a concept or strategy a little better. I believe it's an advantage I have over other sportscasters who have never taught.

As my first year at Valley State continued, I went back to Indiana in January for my oral exam and officially earned my doctorate. It was also a chance to thank Dr. Donald Ludwig, my adviser all four years there and one of the university's wisest and kindest faculty members. He was an inspiration to me. And now I was a proud colleague.

෴

During Easter vacation that spring, I tried to line up a summer job in broadcasting. I took my tapes from Indiana and contacted virtually every radio and TV station in Los Angeles to let them know that Dick Enberg was here. Sports was my strength, but I'd been a disc jockey, I'd been a substitute newsman, and I was willing to work any time of day or night. There was silence at the other end of the phone. I couldn't get by the secretaries. No one would even talk to me.

Finally, I decided to introduce myself as Dr. Enberg, and that worked. Secretaries at three radio stations—KNX, KFI, and KGIL— thought I was a medical doctor and made an appointment for me with their program directors. Even better, KGIL in the San Fernando Valley hired me for summer vacation relief as a disc jockey.

It gave us an economic boost as well. With my teaching salary of less than $5,000 a year, we were facing additional pressure with the growth of our family. Jennifer, the first of our three children, would be born that August.

An indication of how thin I was in the wallet came shortly after Jennifer was born. After watching the miracle of childbirth, I decided to celebrate with a hamburger and milkshake at a coffee shop across the street from the hospital. Like any new father, I excitedly shared all the details with other customers seated next to me at the counter and accepted a wave of congratulations. However, when I tried to pay the bill of $1.35, despite digging through all of my pockets, I could find only $1.25. Fortunately, a gentleman on the next stool loaned (gave) me a dime to pay the tab.

(Many years later, I recounted the incident on a local radio broadcast. It's amazing how many letters I received from people who claimed they were the generous soul who stepped forward in time of need. Based on the response, I was in debt for at least a couple of dollars.)

At the end of the summer, the general manager at KGIL, who liked my work, offered me a full-time job as the station's new morning disc jockey. He came up with a salary of $9,500, double what I was making as a college professor. It was flattering, and the money certainly would have been helpful, but I couldn't accept it. I had taught and coached just one year at Valley State and was enjoying it. To leave so soon would have betrayed all the people who had helped me academically and financially through my college years. In addition, I didn't see myself as a disc jockey for the rest of my life. I returned to Valley State for the fall semester.

A year later, in 1963, I got another part-time radio job, this time doing weekend sports at the CBS radio station KNX. That's where I met Chuck Benedict, who would be instrumental in helping me get an opportunity to work on the Rams' broadcasts a few years later. Pat McGuirk was the sports director at KNX, and he pushed for the station to hire me full time. In fact, he thought it was about to happen. He took me in to the program director one day, and I went in expecting a serious offer. The discussion was brief.

The program director looked at me and said, "Enberg, I understand you're an assistant professor out at San Fernando Valley State."

And I said, "Yes, sir."

"If I were you," he said, "I'd hang on to that job."

It was just like the shaved prostitute story. He didn't see my potential either.

During this period of time, I also did weekend sports reports at KLAC Radio, thanks to a recommendation from Benedict, and I began making a name for myself in Los Angeles radio. Then I received a call from Bill Welsh, sports director at KTTV-TV (Channel 11). It was a week before a USC-UCLA water polo match that the station was scheduled to broadcast, and he must have been desperate. He asked me if I could do it.

"Absolutely," I said.

"Ever do one?"

"Sure. It's no problem."

I had never even gone to a water polo match, but I dashed off to watch two in the next week, asked dozens of questions of our coach at Valley State, and pulled it off. I'm as proud of that as anything I've ever done, because when I was hired, I didn't know one thing about the sport. A week later I was on Channel 11, with Olympic swimmer Roy Saari as the analyst, calling the match. As I told some of my friends, "Before this, water polo was a mystery to me. I used to wonder how the hell they got the horses in the pool."

Before the 1964 football season, Channel 11 signed a contract to televise four games for L.A. State (now Cal State L.A.), which was considered one of the nation's top small college football teams that fall. By this time, Benedict was doing weekend sports for Channel 11, and he suggested I audition for the play-by-play job, even though he had applied for it, too. That's an unbelievably good friend. I did the audition and won the right to do the games. I'm not sure how well watched they were, but for me, this was L.A., and I felt like I was given a high-profile chance to show my stuff. Coached by Homer Beatty with future NFL players Walter Johnson and George Youngblood, L.A. State went 9-0 and ended the season as the nation's top-ranked small college football team.

This same year, 1964, turned out to be pivotal in Los Angeles sports television history. Gene Autry, who owned the Angels' baseball team and KMPC Radio, bought KTLA-TV (Channel 5). Autry hired 29-year-old Bob Speck, a bright, creative former sportswriter, as his sports director. He told Speck that he wanted KTLA to become like KMPC, which was loaded with sports programming, including the Angels, the Rams, and UCLA football and basketball.

Late in the year, as one of his first major tasks, Speck was looking for a new sports announcer to replace 10 popular local athletes who had been taking turns doing the sports segment on the nightly news. Although some of these stars had a knack for broadcasting, most didn't, so KTLA was ending the experiment. Among these athletes were two who went on to great success in broadcasting, including many years as my partners—Merlin Olsen of the Rams and Don Drysdale of the Dodgers. Some of the others included Jerry West and Rudy LaRusso of the Lakers, Roman Gabriel and Roosevelt Grier of the Rams, and Jim Fregosi and Jimmy Piersall of the Angels.

As Speck was beginning to consider new candidates to replace the 10 athletes, Bill Welsh from Channel 11 called him.

"Welsh told me that the station had a young guy who had done a lot of fill-in work there and some radio weekend work, and he was pretty good," Speck said, in recalling the phone call. "Welsh asked me to give him an audition as a favor to him, so I did."

The "young guy" was me. I found out about Welsh's phone call 40 years later while writing this book. I wish I had known earlier. It saddens me that I never had a chance to say thank you to Welsh, one of the living legends in L.A. television. He opened the door for me at KTLA, even though it was his station's primary independent competitor.

When Speck contacted me, he said they would ask me to read some sports copy and do an interview for my audition. I brought in a ringer for the interview—Dean Davenport, an assistant basketball coach at Valley State. He was a legitimate guest, but he also had been one of my best friends since our college years at Central Michigan. In fact, I recommended him for his job at Valley State. The subject of our interview was, "Should the Lakers draft UCLA star Gail Goodrich?" Goodrich had led the Bruins to two national titles, but, at slightly over six feet, some analysts thought he was too small for the NBA. Laker star Elgin Baylor would later tag him with the nickname "Stumpy." The Lakers did draft Goodrich that year, and Stumpy played in the NBA for 14 years, averaging 18.6 points a game.

The interview seemed to go well, but when I watched the tape, I thought Davenport was better than I was. Another obvious concern: KTLA had brought in announcers from all over the country for the audition. It turned out, however, that I had a big advantage. The station knew they could get me more cheaply. A short time later, in early 1965, Speck offered me the job, although it hinged on my success during a 13-week tryout. I quickly accepted, but asked if I could start in the summer in order to complete the spring semester at Valley State. It would also allow me to return to the classroom if the summer tryout didn't work out. Speck agreed. Forty years later, Davenport claims that I owe my entire career to him and his terrific answers in the interview.

Imagine, a guy who couldn't even win a varsity letter at Central Michigan replacing a 10-man team of some of the greatest athletes in Southern California history.

Understandably, there was considerable guilt for me in leaving Valley State, but the school graciously made it easy.

President Ralph Prator said, "We'll give you a year's leave of absence. If this isn't the right thing for you, you can come back here and continue as an assistant professor. We'll hold the position for you."

I also have Glenn Arnett, the dean of my department, to thank. He had to give his permission first.

My starting salary at KTLA was $18,000, which tripled my income, but they could have offered me half that amount, and I would have gone for it. I was so naïve at the time that I barely remember the 13-week tryout period. I was just happy to be on Los Angeles television. I started at KTLA in June 1965. Within a year and a half, I was doing the nightly sports news, weekly boxing from the Olympic Auditorium, UCLA basketball, and Angels pre- and postgame shows—all on TV— and the Rams on radio. All in a year and a half. Oh My!

TIMEOUT

Giving Lip Service to My Class

WHEN I TAUGHT FIRST AID at Valley State, mouth-to-mouth resuscitation had just become the accepted method of trying to save the lives of drowning victims. Although I gave a written exam in the course, I decided that everyone who took the class should be able to prove that he or she knew the new technique of administering artificial respiration—clearing the air passage, tilting the head back, pinching the nose, jutting out the jaw (with your thumb in the victim's mouth), and making a seal with your lips over the victim's lips as you began to blow air into his lungs.

While another teacher monitored the written exam, I asked the students, one by one, to come into the next room and demonstrate on me that they knew how to do it—except for putting their lips on mine. Show me the proper technique, explain what you're doing, and you'll pass this part of the test.

Well, you can imagine all of the different-tasting thumbs that went into my mouth. I didn't ask them to wear gloves or anything. I mean, what was I thinking?

There were 30 students in the class, and, after half of them had come through the room, another one of the girls walked in. As usual, I was lying there with my eyes closed, trying to get the taste of those thumbs out of my mouth. She clears my air passage, tilts my head, pinches my nose, tugs on my jaw, and the next thing I know, her lips are right on mine and she starts blowing into my mouth! I was so surprised my body lurched as if jolted by a defibrillator, literally throwing her in the air.

"Very good, Miss Jones," I said, grabbing some oxygen of my own. "Ve-r-r-r-y good."

3

IT'S LIKE WATCHING
AN ACCIDENT

*"Turn on that tape recorder. Your grandchildren
are really going to enjoy this."*

—Muhammad Ali

My first full-time play-by-play assignment in Los Angeles was in boxing, a sport that I had followed as a young fan. One of the fondest sports memories of my boyhood was listening to Joe Louis's fights on the radio. Louis was not only a great, great champion, but I don't think he has ever received full credit for the contribution he made to improved racial relations in this country.

In 1946, when I was 11 years old, Louis fought the clever Billy Conn, who had nearly upset him back in 1941. We were sitting in my uncle's home in Mount Clemens, Michigan, in a crowd around the radio that included my uncle and aunt, their son, our family, and some neighbors. The natural instinct of our family was to root for the underdog, in this case, Conn, but Joe Louis was the man we all wanted to win. Here was an entire household of white folks, in 1946, cheering for the African-American guy. And we celebrated as Louis won by a knockout in the eighth round.

Jackie Robinson broke into Major League Baseball the next year, and his impact on racial equality was momentous, but let's not forget that Louis had already blazed the trail. In June 1938, he represented the United States when he knocked out the German Max Schmeling in their historic rematch in New York. Schmeling, the Nazis' symbol of Aryan superiority, had knocked Louis out in their first bout in 1936 (a year before Louis became heavyweight champion)—the only loss for the Brown Bomber in his first 62 fights. In their 1938 bout, a year before the start of World War II, America needed a hero, and Louis beating Schmeling then was *enormous*. That fight is credited with inspiring sportswriter Jimmy Cannon's famous line: "He's a credit to his race—the human race."

Louis was such a modest sort that the impact he had during his long career was very subtle, and I don't think the American public even realized the enormity of his contribution. When I voted for the most significant American athletes of the last century, I felt there were only two who could be one and two—Babe Ruth and Joe Louis. They delivered at a time when our nation hungered most for a hero.

✑

Although I had listened to fights on the radio while growing up, I knew very little about boxing, a sport I felt had declined in the 1960s. I had been working at KTLA for just a few months in 1965 when sports director Bob Speck lined up a weekly package of Thursday night fights that would originate from the Olympic Auditorium in Los Angeles. When he told me, my first thought was, "There goes my career."

In May of that year, Muhammad Ali had defeated Sonny Liston in the first round of their second heavyweight title bout in Lewiston, Maine, with what many thought was a "phantom punch," and boxing's image was at an all-time low.

"Oh, my God," I thought, "on the heels of the Ali-Liston fight I'm going to make my TV debut with boxing. I'm the one who's going to get kayoed."

Much to my surprise boxing became a popular sport to watch on Thursday nights.

"We were hoping to do a 3 rating," Speck told me later, "and we did it right away. Soon, we were drawing 10s and 11s."

However, even before our first telecast, I was also concerned about my lack of boxing knowledge. So when I first met Aileen Eaton, who ran the Olympic Auditorium, I told her, "I don't know a lot about boxing, but I'll learn."

She told Speck she liked my sincerity and assigned matchmaker Mickey Davies to work with me as the TV commentator. I knew I needed more firsthand information to improve my blow-by-blow descriptions, so Davies arranged for me to meet with a friendly trainer at the Main Street Gym in downtown Los Angeles, where most of the fighters worked out. I didn't want to get in the ring, but I had a couple of sessions where I put on the gloves and the trainer had me hit the bag, teaching me some basic combinations—jab, jab, hook to the body, cross with the right. It gave me an appreciation of how difficult and exhausting it is to box for just one three-minute round, even without defending against someone else's bombs.

However, after the third Thursday night, I was ready to quit. People called Aileen "The Dragon Lady," and I soon found out why. She was tough, very tough, and everyone was afraid of her. She was more than a match for any man. And even though I was the new face in the arena, I wasn't going to be treated with kid gloves. There was no mercy. I had to put on the big-boy gloves and be ready to fight, or she would nail me for every mistake.

Considering that she was a woman in an all-male world, her success was remarkable. She not only promoted fights at the Olympic for more than 40 years, she also staged major matches in the Los Angeles Coliseum and Sports Arena. Boxers who fought for her before her retirement in 1981 included Ali and Liston, Archie Moore, Floyd Patterson, Ken Norton, Jerry Quarry, Eddie Machen, Mando Ramos, Ernie ("Indian Red") Lopez, Danny ("Little Red") Lopez, Bobby Chacon, Hedgemon Lewis, Joey Orbillo, and George ("Scrap Iron") Johnson.

Aileen was a relentless promoter. When she met the young Cassius Clay, before he became Muhammad Ali, she thought he was too quiet. She asked wrestler Gorgeous George to tutor him in self-promotion.

"You've got to sell yourself and sell tickets," she said to Clay, thereby helping to create one of the more loquacious sports figures of all time.

But it was very difficult to work with Aileen. During the live call of a bout, she would walk up to me at ringside, lift up one of my headphones, and yell in my ear, "Plug roller derby and wrestling!"

That was certainly a new experience. People don't come up to you in the middle of a football broadcast, lift one of your headphones, and start yelling at you to promote next week's game. The first thing I had to do was cover the microphone so her words wouldn't scream out on the air. I was desperate to do well, and it's difficult to succeed when someone is interrupting you. But she was the boss, and I was the 30-year-old rookie.

I admit that she broke me down. It seemed like there was nothing that I could do to please her, plus in the first few weeks, there were very few people at the fights, and I felt like I was going down with a sinking ship. After the third broadcast, when she had yelled at me again and told me I didn't do enough of this and enough of that, she had me practically in tears.

"I'm going to quit," I told Davies as we sat at ringside. "I'm going to tell KTLA to get somebody else. I can't handle it."

One of the crusty old cameramen from KTLA overheard me.

"Forget about her, Enberg," he said. "She eats her young."

Despite my frustration, I couldn't help smiling. That cameraman had been around a long time, and at least his comment had lightened the mood.

But it was Davies, an amateur boxer in his Pittsburgh days, who fought for me. As one of Aileen's two matchmakers (with Don Chargin), I think he realized that this marriage between KTLA and the Olympic could be very good for everybody. Even though crowds were small at first, people were watching on television and becoming hooked. Mickey became more than my color man—in effect, he held my hand. He encouraged me and softened the blows from Aileen by becoming a buffer. She stopped bothering me so much, because he told her, "Tell me what you want us to promote. Don't tell him when he's on the air, because it messes with his train of thought. I can handle it just as well."

So I stuck it out, as boxing became the No. 1 regularly scheduled program on KTLA. Everywhere in the city people were talking about it, and it gave my career a terrific early boost. I called the weekly fights for more than three years until I became the Angels' broadcaster in early 1969. Meanwhile, those boxing telecasts from the Olympic Auditorium lasted more than a decade on KTLA, before moving to another L.A. station.

In a sport that is often so cruel and filled with so many vulgar people, Davies was unique. He was charming and gentle and had the demeanor of a professor. He even smoked a pipe and looked like he should have leather patches on the elbows of his sport coat. He was a good matchmaker because he was sensitive to lining up two fighters in a bout that was fair instead of putting together a setup where the lesser talent could get hurt. He had the best interests of the sport and the fighters at heart, and they trusted him.

Mickey was a good color man as well, because he knew the backgrounds of all the fighters and was not afraid of tough questions. If we had a disappointing fight, I could turn to him and say, "Mickey, you put these two guys together. Why is it so lopsided?" And he'd have a good answer.

He might say something like, "I wanted to match one guy who was a good boxer—who would jab and move—and another guy who usually looks for the knockout. I didn't know that my knockout fighter was going to decide he wanted to be a boxer, so now we've got two men dancing around the ring and there's no action. I made the fight thinking I'd get a toe-to-toe result. Instead, we've got a waltz."

Because Mickey convinced the fighters, managers, and trainers that it was okay, we were the first television station to put microphones in the corners so the audience could hear what went on between rounds. One of the more interesting comments involved Jerry Quarry, who matured as a fighter on those Thursday night fights and became one of the top heavyweights of the era.

Quarry's dad, Jack, was his co-manager, and during one bout his dad told him, "I don't want you to get hit now. Go out there, but don't let him hit you."

And I thought, "That's a strange statement to make. Of course, you don't want your son to get hit, but how is he ever going to be successful as a professional boxer if he's worried about getting hit?"

As I watched Quarry throughout his career, I always felt his dad's message, "Don't let him hit you" was part of his boxing personality, and that mentality took his aggression away. Sadly, great boxing champions don't have that luxury.

Ironically, Quarry did take too many punches in a career that went on too long. He died at 53, suffering from dementia pugilistica—severe brain damage caused by repeated blows to the head.

∾

If you've only watched boxing on television, it's a staggering experience to go to a fight and sit in the first two or three rows. Up close, it's like watching an accident. From a distance, you don't realize how ferocious the punches are, but I was often no more than three feet away. From there, you not only hear the punches, you hear the reaction to them and you see the spray that flies off the fighters.

After one of my early telecasts, I couldn't determine what had caused the spots on my sport coat until I realized that it was perspiration, spit, and blood. I've even had a mouthpiece land in my lap. Wearing a raincoat at ringside might look silly, but I wouldn't advise wearing a white sport coat, either.

Of course, many athletic events are different when you're close to the action. On a non-working weekend a few years ago, I was given a field pass for an NFL Monday night game in Dallas. When you're that close, the collisions are stunning. I played high school football, but these players are so much bigger and faster, and artificial turf makes them even faster. You marvel at the way the human body can absorb those blows and bounce up for more.

Even in basketball, the game is much different up close. You get a real feel for how big the players are, how strong they are, how quick they are, and how powerful they are as shot blockers and rebounders. They're incredibly better than they appear on television.

As I called the action at ringside, I lived in constant fear. What if a fighter died in the ring on one of my Thursday nights? I quickly realized that the referee, with his power to stop the fight, has enormous responsibility. If a fighter can't defend himself, do we need to see him be totally pummeled, knocked down, and knocked out before we're satisfied? I say let's stop it, and let him have another day. Meanwhile, the guy in the 20th row wants the fight to continue. The farther you are from the scene, the less real it seems. It's like watching a video game.

During one of my early bouts, a fighter was pinned against the ropes and was taking a tremendous beating from his opponent. When the referee stepped between the two boxers and stopped the fight, the fans booed. On television, I defended the referee's decision, and I was emphatic about it.

"Obviously, the fight was over," I said on the air, "and we don't need to see a man driven to the canvas and be counted out. The ropes were holding him up. The referee only has two choices—whether to stop a fight too soon or too late. He picked the better option. No one wants this fight to end with a tragedy."

There wasn't much feedback on my comments. A couple of months later, I was calling another bout in which one fighter was outclassing the other, not as badly as in the first fight, but the referee stopped this one, too. In my own mind, I actually thought he stepped in too quickly. But few people booed.

And I thought, "Wow, that's surprising." I'm not saying the crowd's more compassionate reaction was solely because of my comments, but I did feel my commentary helped. It taught me a meaningful lesson about the responsibility that comes with being a reporter and the power of the microphone. There are moments in a sports event when you have a chance to use the microphone as a force for good, and you should do it.

❦

My career as a boxing announcer ended in 1969, but it had a brief revival with NBC in 1976. I did about a dozen fights, including one in Munich, Germany, where I called one of Muhammad Ali's many heavyweight title bouts, this one against Richard Dunn, a Welshman. Today, almost every decent fight is on pay-per-view, but the Ali-Dunn bout was shown free, airing live at 9:00 p.m. in New York. It was difficult to sell all the tickets in Munich, however, because the fight in the Olympiastade began at 2:00 a.m.

It was an interesting week. Munich was graced by glamorous actress Candace Bergen, who was on the scene for NBC to do a photo essay on the fight. I was between marriages, so I asked her to join me at a Mozart concert in a romantic castle setting, just a couple of nights before the fight. She said yes, which immediately rated as one of the more exciting things that has ever happened to me. But she had second thoughts and backed out. I should have figured that might happen, because she could never get my last name right. When she autographed one of her action photos of Ali for me, she misspelled my name, even though the syllables are just the reverse of hers—ENberg, as opposed to BERG-en.

On fight night, when she appeared, dressed like she was going to the Academy Awards, every man in the NBC crew sighed in unison.

The weigh-in was also quite a scene. There were so many people standing on a makeshift platform, constructed for the event, that it collapsed. It looked like a trap door had opened as Ali fell five feet through the floor. He could have broken both of his legs, but he pulled himself out of the rubble, smiled, and shrugged it off. I don't think he ever stopped talking.

To properly prepare for the match, I needed to talk to Ali myself, and a few days before the fight, I was allowed to join him and his entourage in a limousine as he went out in the scenic Bavarian countryside to do his final roadwork. We drove down a little one-lane country road, and after a while, Ali left the car and started jogging in front of the limo. Word had spread that the champ was running in the area, and out of nowhere a crowd materialized, filling both sides of the road to cheer his every stride. As the limo followed Ali, we were surrounded, too, and I will never forget the sight of all those adoring faces as we passed by.

When Ali finished his run, he climbed back in the car and agreed to do an interview on the drive back to Munich.

"Turn on that tape recorder," he said. "Your grandchildren are really going to enjoy this."

Unfortunately, I lost the tape. He answered everything in full-spirited detail and couldn't have been more gracious or more entertaining. A few days later, he defended his title with a fifth-round knockout.

Twenty years later, Bob Costas and I were announcing the opening ceremonies at the 1996 Olympics in Atlanta when Ali lit the flame to officially open the games. His selection for that role was as much a surprise to us at NBC as it was to the viewing audience.

As usual, there was a lengthy buildup to the torch-lighting ceremony, but when the champ arrived via a small, hidden elevator and was revealed to the world, his hand holding the torch was shaking so badly because of Parkinson's disease that it was painful to watch. It was live television, and, as we watched, we were seriously worried that, with one of his involuntary spasms, he might set himself on fire.

I had just seconds to react. I explained that Ali suffered from Parkinson's disease, a neurological disorder that had left his hands weak but quickly added that his spirit was still strong. As we watched, holding our breath, he was able to steady himself, light the caldron, and dramatically open the games. It's one of the moments I'll never forget.

Ali's Parkinson's disease was first diagnosed in the mid-1980s, but there has to be brain damage from boxing, too. People say he wasn't hit that often because he was such a great defensive boxer, but we know Joe Frazier got him, we know Ken Norton nailed him, and there were many others, particularly late in his career. What everyone also overlooks are the many hours in the gym—all the sparring sessions required before every bout. Even with a protective helmet, you're still taking blows, and every one of those punches has some impact. Fighting too long, that's what gets them all. Tragically, for the bigger names, in particular, the money is so good that it's difficult to say goodbye.

❦

Of all the sporting events that I've witnessed, including the Super Bowl and the World Series, there's nothing more powerful than the moment when, with the houselights dimmed, the two fighters in a heavyweight match walk down the aisle, climb through the ropes, and enter the ring. It's unbelievably electric. Nothing like it.

The boxers themselves, no matter the weight class, are probably the most beautiful characters in all of sports. It seems like a contradiction, but they're really sweet guys. They can fight 10 rounds and hammer the hell out of each other and then, when the final bell sounds, embrace their adversary. It's a matter of mutual respect. In my experiences with them, they couldn't be nicer, although the people around them—promoters, publicists, even some of the fans—are often the worst. And that hasn't changed.

But, in a civilized society, boxing is a puzzling sport for me. Injuries are indigenous to all sports, but professional boxing is still the only one where the ultimate goal is a serious injury—rendering an opponent unconscious. It takes us back to barbaric times. The scene at a big fight is an interesting sociological phenomenon. I've seen a sophisticated woman come down the aisle, wearing her best clothes and looking charming and beautiful. Later, in the middle of the fight, I've looked over and she's standing, screaming for one guy to kill the other, venom literally dripping from her fangs.

Although I fully appreciate the difficult art of self-defense, I've thought many times that with the sport the way it is now, in all political correctness it should be called "knockout," and not boxing. That's what satisfies its audience. If we had a ballot measure on whether this professional sport should continue as it is, my conscience says I don't think it's right. I would vote against it.

TIMEOUT

Knock a Coconut

BESIDES BOXING, AILEEN EATON'S Olympic Auditorium empire included roller derby and wrestling. Announcer Dick Lane, a KTLA institution, whose signature phrase was "Whoa, Nellie!" called both of those "sports" for the station.

One night, Lane's regular floor manager for roller derby at the Olympic couldn't be there, and the station sent my assistant, Eddie Toler, to the event. Eddie, who was a dedicated lifetime sports fan who knew all the statistics and facts, was sitting next to Lane during the broadcast and handing him commercial drop-ins, when, with about 20 minutes to go before the 10:00 p.m. news, Lane leaned over and whispered, "Knock a coconut, kid."

Toler looked at him blankly.

"I thought I knew everything about every sport there is, and I've never heard that expression before," he said to a nearby cameraman. "Dick Lane wants me to knock a coconut. What's that?"

"Take a minute off the clock," the cameraman answered. "Knock a coconut means take a minute off the clock so we can finish on time."

A switch that controlled the game clock was in the TV booth, so the floor manager would wait for an exciting moment, and while the skaters were pushing and shoving each other in a jam with, say, 6:48 to go, he'd set the clock ahead to 5:48. In the next jam, he might take another minute off.

Roller derby had to be off the air by 10:00 p.m. when the nightly news began, and if the game was running long, they simply knocked enough coconuts to make their 10:00 p.m. deadline. It was a very efficient system.

Not only did they control the clock, but they also controlled the hardest-hitting action on the track, choreographing the major player collisions and flips over the rail right in front of the track's one and only camera.

Do you think roller derby's fans ever wondered why the games always managed to conclude right at 10:00 p.m., or if they were curious why the most dramatic crashes always occurred in the same spot on the track? Whoa, Nellie!

4

WHO DOES THIS GUY THINK HE IS?

"Money doesn't mean a damn thing."

—George Allen

I am not an aggressive person, but being assertive—heck, being pushy—started me down the road to becoming the Rams' play-by-play announcer in 1966.

At the time, broadcast pioneer Bob Kelley had been calling the team's games for nearly 30 years, joining the Rams at the tender age of 20 when the franchise was founded in Cleveland in 1937. Kelley, who came to Los Angeles when the Rams moved in 1946, was a standout play-by-play announcer. He was quick, he was smart, he had a theatrical style, and he taught the new Los Angeles fans the game of pro football. But, although he was still young, his health was deteriorating in the mid-1960s, and it was affecting his work. He wasn't the same announcer who excited pro football fans earlier in his career.

I had started working at KTLA in 1965 and missed calling football games. Inspired by my four years as Indiana University's announcer, plus the four games I had called for L.A. State in 1964, I sent a letter to Dan Reeves, the owner of the Rams.

The letter was out of character for me, because it had all the subtlety of a note from a collection agency. In effect, I told Reeves I was this tremendous young talent who used to do Big Ten football and basketball, I was as good as Bob Kelley, and, furthermore, they should seriously consider me as their announcer.

Reeves handed the letter to Jack Teele, the team's publicity director, and huffed, "Who does this guy think he is?"

The whole matter should have died there, but, fortunately, Chuck Benedict, who had worked with me at KNX Radio and KTTV-TV, was one of the team's assistant publicity directors. Chuck was a wonderful ally and supporter of mine over the years, and he was patient with me despite my infamous letter.

First of all, however, he scolded me for its tone.

"That was an awfully strong letter you wrote," he said. "You could have promoted yourself a little more diplomatically."

"I was trying to get their attention," I said.

"Well, you did," he said, arching his eyebrows.

Although I didn't have much experience, I believed in my talent and decided that I needed to prove my case by doing an audition tape of a Rams game so they could compare me directly with Kelley and see if I had the goods.

I asked Chuck, "How can I make a tape of a Rams game?"

"Leave it to me," he said. "I can help you out."

Chuck went to Teele and told him that he had worked with me before and knew I had talent, and that I really wasn't a wise guy. He also told Teele that I wanted to submit a tape for a possible job with the club but needed a location in the press box to do the live-to-tape call. Teele, who distributed all the credentials, said he would find a place for me—and he did, putting four folding chairs and a portable table on top of the Coliseum press box roof.

"You were probably the first broadcaster to ever call a game from the roof," Teele told me later.

He gave me four passes for the Rams' last game of the 1965 season against the Baltimore Colts.

I wanted to do my audition in a professional manner, so I hired a friendly engineer at a bargain rate of $50 to set up the equipment and brought a couple of gratis friends with me, one to work as a spotter and one to serve as a statistician. Of course, it was not only cold and windy on top of the press box in December, it was also a long way from the field, kind of like watching the Tour de France from atop the Eiffel Tower. For that matter, if not for the Hollywood Hills in the near distance, you could have seen the curvature of the earth. And no one was listening to my broadcast but a flock of seagulls, who were ready to harvest fans' leftovers. But I was appreciative and excited to have the opportunity.

Fate was on my side. It turned out to be a momentous game. Don Shula's Colts defeated the Rams 20-17 to force a tie for the NFL's Western Conference title between Baltimore and the Green Bay Packers. Remarkably, the Colts won even though they took the field without both injured quarterbacks, starter Johnny Unitas and backup Gary Cuozzo. Shula's emergency quarterback was halfback Tom Matte, who wore a list of plays taped to his left wrist. Today, many pro quarterbacks wear a wristband during the game, but in my NFL experience it all began with Matte.

A few days after the game, Teele listened to the tape and played it for Reeves. They both liked what they heard, so they recommended me to KMPC, the Rams' flagship radio station. KMPC radio and KTLA television were both part of Gene Autry's Golden West broadcasting empire, which was also fortuitous for me. I wasn't offered a job yet, but I was in the right place at the right time, and now I was on everybody's radar screen for the Rams.

Meanwhile, I continued to seek other opportunities in football. Before the 1966 season, I applied to CBS-TV for a chance to work on the network's regional postgame scoreboard shows that originated in the NFL's three western cities—Los Angeles, San Francisco, and Dallas. A CBS announcer was sent to each of the games in those three cities to do the show at the stadium site, and I thought, "I can do that." My confidence was based on my ad-lib scoreboard shows after Angels telecasts on KTLA, as well as my work on the evening news. I sent CBS some of those tapes after KTLA gave me permission to bid for the CBS job.

Imagine the thrill the day I received the call from CBS in New York that they would hire me to do eight scoreboard shows a year. This farm boy from Armada was going to be on network television for the first time!

However, when word circulated that CBS had employed me, things changed again. Loyd Sigmon, the general manager of KMPC and president of Golden West Broadcasters, decided the time was right to hire me as the Rams' No. 2 announcer as a replacement for longtime Kelley sidekick Bill Brundige. Realizing that Kelley's health was not good, KMPC and the Rams were receptive to developing a young announcer for the future. They offered me the job, and I accepted faster than a quick kick.

My KTLA broadcast assistant, Steve Skinner, later to become executive producer of *ABC World News Tonight*, questioned my sanity.

"Are you crazy?" he said. "Here's your chance with the CBS network, and you're going to call New York and turn it down?"

Actually, choosing between the Rams and CBS wasn't a difficult decision. I would now be working a full NFL schedule with the possibility of someday sitting in the play-by-play seat. However, it was embarrassing calling CBS to turn down the scoreboard show. Here I was telling the network, which had given me a big break, "Thanks a lot for offering me this job that I begged you for, but now I don't want it."

Unlike today, the second announcer on those Rams broadcasts wasn't an analyst. His work was limited to reading commercials, giving scores, and doing halftime interviews. But, as the Rams began the 1966 season, I was delighted to be working next to the legendary Kelley.

However, neither of us was prepared for what happened in the club's third preseason game at Minnesota. In the second half we were hit with a torrential summer rainstorm, complete with thunder, lightning, and high wind. The driving rain pelted against the windows of the radio booth. It was as if somebody had turned a fire hose on the glass.

It was painful to sit there helplessly and watch Kelley squinting through a virtual waterfall. The field was a total blur. It was like trying to call a game with 20–500 vision. He did the best he could until the deluge finally stopped, but it had to be a very stressful experience.

A few days later, Kelley, who had a history of heart trouble, was told by the team physician that he should not broadcast any more games the rest of the season because of his health problems. On August 30—10 days after the Minnesota game—he was rushed to the hospital unconscious after a serious heart attack, his condition complicated by intestinal bleeding. The Rams' announcer never regained consciousness, dying on September 9, two days before the team's first regular-season game. It was a tremendous shock. He was only 49.

Although I had called the last two preseason games, there was a meeting at KMPC to determine who the team's new play-by-play announcer would be. The decision was made by Bob Reynolds, president of the Angels, former KMPC general manager, and an All-America football player at Stanford in the mid-1930s; Sigmon, who succeeded him as general manager; and Stan Spero, the general sales manager who would later succeed Sigmon. With the blessing of Dan Reeves, they agreed that I should move over one chair to replace Kelley on a full-time basis. Dave Niehaus took my place as the second announcer. (Niehaus later became an icon in Seattle as the voice of the Mariners.)

I could only shake my head in disbelief. What if I had chosen the CBS job? What if I had not done the audition tape for the Rams? What if I had not written the pushy letter in the first place? What if Chuck Benedict had not been there to open doors for me? Like so many other times in my life, it was a remarkable intersection of events.

There was a small catch. KMPC told me that I should consider the 1966 season only as a one-year audition for the permanent job of play-by-play announcer. No problem. I was ready for the challenge, and, in fact, I would go on to call Rams football for the next 12 seasons.

∽

Although I had enjoyed broadcasting Big Ten action at Indiana, it was an intoxicating experience being the Rams' announcer. Now I was in the National Football League and calling games from the world-famous Los Angeles Coliseum. I couldn't get to the games soon enough. I'd arrive at the press box early and have a grilled hot dog with mustard and onions and a cup of coffee before most of the media had arrived. It became part of my pregame ritual. To this day, I kick start before kickoff with a hot dog and coffee.

After that, I would walk down to the field, where I might pick up some interesting information and meet with the TV announcers and some of the opposing coaches. Then I would walk through the Coliseum tunnel into the locker room to soak up more of the atmosphere. Coming back into that stadium as the fans started filling the seats remains one of the most powerful experiences I've ever had as an announcer. Like the players, I was hit with an adrenaline rush as I turned the blind corner in the tunnel and saw the massive stadium spread out in full view, ready for the three-hour drama to come.

After the game, I was never in a hurry to leave, especially if the Rams won. I wanted to go back to the locker room to hear the interviews and absorb more of the experience. The expression, "This is as good as it gets," is so overused that it has become a cliché, but Sundays with the Rams were just that for me.

Even the drive home was entertaining, because KMPC played highlights of our game broadcast and I could listen on the car radio and anxiously critique myself. Throughout the years, I've never forgotten what former Hall of Fame Brooklyn Dodger announcer Red Barber told me about this high-wire act of doing play-by-play.

"Richard," he said, with that soothing Southern drawl, "what the audience doesn't realize is, we turn on the microphone for a sports event, and we'll ad-lib for some three hours. Then the game is over and we get in the car and we don't know one word we've said!"

He was absolutely right. It's kind of frightening, because you really get lost in the game as a play-by-play announcer and most of the time you don't know what you've said. There's an exception, of course. In a one-sided game you tend to remember some of the broadcast, because you'll wander from the action and use more of the notes and stories you've prepared, trying to keep the audience interested. But when you're calling a close game, you do get lost in the action, the game carries you, and there's no register of what you're describing.

Think of it. Three hours of basic ad-libbing and there are no erasers on the microphone. No editors to correct mistakes. Once you've said it, it's out there. No wonder after 50 years, I've yet to have that perfect broadcast.

As I motored back to my home in the San Fernando Valley, a KMPC announcer would say, "Let's go back to the fourth quarter of today's exciting victory by the Rams. Time was running out when Roman Gabriel hit Tommy Mason for the winning touchdown. Here's Dick Enberg's call… "

When the highlights came on, I would worry to myself, "Oh, I hope I was good." Sometimes I would think, "Boy, that was pretty ordinary." Other times, I was pleasantly surprised: "I said that? That was really good. That line came out of my mouth, and my brain didn't even know I was saying it!"

It was Vin Scully of the Dodgers who made Los Angeles a transistor city a few years before I arrived. People not only listened to his broadcasts at home and in their cars, but also brought their radios to the games, and, in quiet moments, you could hear Scully's voice reverberating around the stadium. Soon, football fans started bringing radios to the Coliseum. During a timeout on the field, I might say, "Here's a score from San Francisco. Atlanta leads the 49ers 14-0." And a roar would go up in the stadium. "Oh My!" I'd think. "They're listening to *me!*"

On December 9, 1967, the Rams and Packers played a game at the Coliseum that sharply illustrated the power of that microphone. The NFL had only 16 teams and four divisions at the time, and George Allen's Rams needed to defeat the Packers and then the Baltimore Colts the following week to capture the Coastal Division title and earn the right to play Green Bay again in the playoffs. The Packers had already clinched the Central Division crown.

The Rams had lost only one game all season, but they trailed Vince Lombardi's defending Super Bowl champions 24-20 with 1:10 left after coming up short on fourth down at the Green Bay 44-yard line. As the Packers took possession of the ball, depressed fans starting filing out of the stadium. The Rams' playoff hopes were ticking away with the seconds on the clock.

However, three Packers running plays and three timeouts consumed only 16 seconds, so with 54 seconds left, Green Bay's Donny Anderson dropped back to his own 27-yard line to punt. While those who stayed watched in joyful disbelief, L.A.'s Tony Guillory, a reserve linebacker, burst through the middle untouched and blocked Anderson's punt, and defensive back Claude Crabb scooped up the ball and headed for the end zone. With the crowd on its feet, Anderson denied the score with a tackle at the Green Bay five-yard line.

The Rams needed a touchdown to win, and, with 44 seconds left, they had no timeouts. On first down, quarterback Roman Gabriel threw the ball out of bounds to stop the clock.

On second down, with 34 seconds to play, Gabriel struck for the winning touchdown, faking a handoff to Tommy Mason and lobbing a five-yard pass to wide receiver Bernie Casey. Inside the Coliseum, fans celebrated the remarkable 27-24 victory. As I found out later, so did thousands more who were gathered outside the stadium.

In typical Los Angeles fashion, people hurrying to beat the traffic had poured out of the Coliseum and were headed for their cars when the punt was blocked. Those who carried transistor radios were like magnets. They quickly attracted crowds of listeners throughout the parking lot. It was quite a scene, groups of human satellites huddling around my call and then cheering wildly as the game ended.

It was an important early lesson. You never know how many people are listening. Although it's flattering to think of so many hanging on to your every word, it's sobering as well. With the power of the microphone comes journalistic responsibility. The audience expects, demands, an accurate account. Be emotional if the game warrants it. But above all, be right.

Like all play-by-play announcers who quickly become involved with their teams, I went home happy that day. I wanted to be the announcer for a successful team. That meant larger, more enthusiastic crowds, more people talking about the team, and larger radio audiences. If you're working for a losing team, it can be empty and agonizing, as I was to find out later when I became the broadcaster for the Angels.

However, I always felt that although you wanted your team to win, you had to swallow that feeling. You could root on the inside, but not on the outside. You needed to pay equal tribute to the opposing team, know how their coaches thought, be well versed in their anecdotes and strategies, as well as your own team's.

In the Midwest, where I grew up, broadcasters were much more provincial than they are in Southern California. When the late Harry Caray called a baseball game (he worked for the Cardinals, A's, White Sox, and Cubs in a 53-year career), there was never any doubt which team he wanted to win. It wasn't a balanced broadcast. He was kind to the opposition, but he openly rooted for his team.

I remember a night in the late 1950s when Caray told his audience, "All right, the Cardinals are coming up in the bottom of the ninth, and we're down 8-1 to the Phils. But, hey, a walk, a couple of base hits, maybe another walk or two, they drop a fly ball, a couple more hits, maybe an error, and we're right back in it! Holy Cow!"

Although I grew up in that environment, I felt differently. Besides my urge to be fair, it also was obvious to me that in this mobile society of ours, with so many people moving to the West Coast, that many of the fans listening to my calls were cheering for the other team. As a kid, I rooted for the Detroit Lions and Detroit Tigers. When I first came to the West Coast in 1961, I continued to pull for them even when they faced L.A. teams. It took a while before I embraced the local teams. The lesson learned was you couldn't ignore the audience of people rooting for the other team. It was crucial to connect with them as well.

⚬

The team had suffered through seven losing seasons in a row when George Allen took over as coach in 1966, my first year as the announcer. He immediately went 8-6 and, overall, in his five years with the team, was 49-19-4.

Allen was one of the most detail-oriented people I've ever known. Early in our relationship, he told me, "Dick, I can tell you're really serious about your business."

I thought maybe he noticed that I asked a lot of good questions and took copious notes. But I was curious and wondered what gave him that impression.

"Because every time you come into my office your shoes are shined," he said. "That tells me you care about how you appear. It indicates that you're taking your job seriously."

I guess it does make a statement about who you are. I wish Allen had been around for some of the arguments I had with my kids when they claimed that it doesn't matter if your hair is combed or how you're dressed when you're meeting people for the first time. Of course it makes a difference. You do have only one chance to make that first impression.

Allen was fastidious himself, always neat. He did have one odd quirk. Whether on the football field or not, he would constantly lick his fingers when he talked, much like a quarterback just leaving the huddle. It usually meant he was deep in thought and was getting a grip on an idea before delivering.

Although he respected me, Allen could be frustrating, particularly on Wednesdays. We had the usual 15-minute coach's show on KMPC, and every Wednesday I drove to the team's practice facility in Long Beach to tape the show, which we agreed would take place at 11:00 a.m. So I would arrive at 11:00 a.m. and sit in his outer office with my tape recorder, and wait and wait and wait, and at 11:30 he would ask me in.

It became a consistent pattern. Every week he made me wait a half hour. My interpretation was that he was showing me how busy he was. So I attempted an end run. I started coming at 11:30—and then he made me wait until noon.

I finally had to confront him.

"Coach," I said, "we're playing a game here. Please tell me the time that you're really going to be available, because that half hour is important to me, too. I'm driving all the way from Hollywood to Long Beach [a one-hour round trip] to do this show."

So we split the difference. He only made me wait 15 minutes.

One week, when I was finally in his office, Allen starting giving me one of his lectures about the importance of winning in sports.

"There are some rewards that come with it, like money, but money doesn't mean a damn thing," he preached, as he pounded his desk. "Money isn't important. It's success. It's winning."

Right in the middle of his speech, the phone rang and Allen answered.

After the caller said a few words, the coach responded, "For what? For $20,000? No. Are you kidding me? Only $20,000? I can't... no... no... I've got to get at least twice that. I'm sorry. That's it."

He hung up and turned his attention back to me, without even breaking stride.

"Money doesn't mean a damn thing," he said again, as if the phone conversation had never happened.

Despite his sermon, Allen was not averse to using money as a tool. One year, at the end of the season, Rams owner Dan Reeves wasn't pleased when his accountants informed him of an expense that ran well into five figures—for payments to players for Saturday naptime. Apparently, the coach felt that on road trips a Saturday siesta would not only keep the team in the hotel, but save energy for the next day's game. Thus, an assistant coach would do a room check, and if the player was tucked under the blankets, he got a $50 cash bonus. Of course, the players happily took the money while lying under the blankets fully clothed.

Reeves, however, didn't appreciate how much this strange budgetary item added up over the course of the season.

Reflecting on incidents like this, Rams star Merlin Olsen once remarked: "Why is it that coaches treat you like children on Saturday and expect you to play like men on Sunday?"

✥

As an assistant coach, Allen trained in Chicago under the venerable Bears coach, George Halas. It wasn't beyond the crusty Halas to try to spy on an opposing team's practice. Although a good student, Allen was caught once when a couple of Rams scouts were spotted with binoculars outside a Dallas Cowboys' practice.

Allen, in turn, was paranoid about someone spying on him, even hiring a full-time house detective to make certain no one was sneaking around the Rams' practice site, Blair Field in Long Beach. The players called Ed Boynton, the team's counterspy, "007" and would have him rushing, binoculars in hand, from one sideline to the other as they claimed they saw movement in the trees beyond the field.

"007, look beyond the goalposts, in that eucalyptus tree," a player would cry. "I thought I saw a guy in camouflage dress and the sun reflecting off a camera lens." Boynton would run dutifully to investigate, while the players would hide a good laugh. Allen never thought it was funny. He really believed every leaf that rustled might be hiding the enemy.

Despite his odd habits, Allen was a deep thinker. Give him credit for recognizing the importance of special teams play. He was the first to hire a full-time NFL assistant to do nothing but coach special teams. His choice in 1969 was Dick Vermeil, later to become a highly successful head coach with UCLA, the Eagles, the Rams, and the Chiefs.

In his 12-year NFL career as a head coach with the Rams and Washington Redskins, Allen was also a shrewd judge of talent. I've never forgotten one of his most profound comments about players. It was very simple.

"Every team in every sport has players just good enough to make you lose," he said. "They're fast, they're strong, they look good in the uniform, they say all the right things, but they don't deliver. It's the guy who misses his block on fourth-and-one, it's the back who fumbles, it's the baseball player who takes strike three in the ninth inning with the game on the line. They're great in practice, but in the game they're just good enough to make you lose.

"No one gets rid of all of them. Every coach, every team, has a player good enough to make you lose. But the real good teams have only a few. The bad teams have a bunch of them. The key to coaching, then, is to limit the number of those guys on your team."

I've thought about that theory many times in the last 35 years, and I've concluded Allen had brilliant insight.

◈

Most of my 12 years with the Rams (1966-1977) were highly successful seasons for the franchise. Allen (five years), Tommy Prothro (two), and Chuck Knox (five) were the coaches, and the Rams went to the playoffs seven times, twice under Allen and five years in a row under Knox.

The team's defensive line, the Fearsome Foursome, led by end Deacon Jones and tackle Merlin Olsen, both Pro Football Hall of Famers, was a legendary group that tormented offenses for years. When they started retiring, more All-Pros, such as ends Jack Youngblood (another Hall of Fame selection) and Fred Dryer and tackle Larry Brooks, took their place.

Dryer, who went on to become an actor, was not only a star player, but also a delightful free spirit who was a master at mimicking Prothro's Southern drawl and Knox's penchant for clichés. Whenever the team needed a laugh, he would string all of Knox's clichés together in one long, humorous pep talk. Every season he'd promise to set his hair on fire and dance the hucklebuck if he ever scored a touchdown, so we all held our breath in 1975 when he actually did prance into the end zone with an interception. Fortunately for his future acting career, he didn't burst into flames, nor could he dance.

Although the defense was powerful, the Rams' offense had its share of great players, too. Tom Mack was a Hall of Fame guard who never missed a game in his 13-year Los Angeles career, and Hall of Fame tackle Jackie Slater, the only player in NFL history to play 20 years with the same franchise, began his long career in 1976. The inspirational quarterback, Roman Gabriel, is still the second-leading passer in the team's history, and running back Lawrence McCutcheon had four 1,000-yard seasons. Jack Snow and Harold Jackson were dangerous wide receivers. In all, the team had 85 Pro Bowl selections on offense and defense from 1966 through 1977. Hey, let's face it. Good players and good teams make good announcers.

But it was a frustrating time, too. The Rams had a 3-7 record in playoffs during my years behind the mike, including three successive losses in the NFC Championship Game (1974-1976), denying them ascension to the Super Bowl. Five of those seven playoff losses were on the road, including three in a row in Bloomington, Minnesota, to Bud Grant's Minnesota Vikings. The Rams never beat the Vikings in the playoffs during the Enberg era, going a demoralizing 0-4.

The games in 1974 and 1976, when the two clubs played for the right to go to the Super Bowl, were particularly galling. The Rams were in the middle of their streak of five successive division titles under Knox, but they fell short of the Super Bowl each time.

In 1974, the club lost at Minnesota 14-10 largely because of one critical penalty in the third quarter. Trailing 7-3, the Rams had driven 98 yards to the Vikings' one-yard line, but, on second down, Mack was called for illegal motion and the ball was moved back to the six. Mack swears to this day that even his nose hairs didn't flinch. On third down, quarterback James Harris had to pass, and his throw was intercepted in the end zone. The Vikings took over on their 20-yard line and drove 80 yards for the touchdown that gave them a decisive 14-3 lead.

In 1976, even though the wind-chill factor in Bloomington was 12 degrees below zero, the team from balmy Los Angeles should have won. The Rams rolled up more yards, more plays, and more first downs as they drove inside the Minnesota 40-yard line four times without scoring and lost 24-13. The final score was totally misleading. In the first half, Minnesota had 89 yards of total offense and five first downs and led 10-0 thanks to a blocked field goal and a blocked punt.

The blocked field goal in the first quarter was a huge psychological blow. At the time, the game was scoreless, but the Rams mounted an impressive drive to the Minnesota four-yard line. On second and goal from there, flanker Ron Jessie ran a reverse that fooled the Vikings. Jessie thought he scored before he was shoved out of bounds, but the ball was spotted inches from the goal line.

"I was in," he insisted later.

On third down, quarterback Pat Haden tried a sneak. The Rams argued that he, too, had crossed the goal line, but again the ball was spotted inches away.

"I made it," Haden said. "I know I made it in the end zone on my second surge."

Now it was fourth down and inches. Knox, haunted by the team's previous failures in Minnesota, called for a field goal to put some points on the board. On defense, the Vikings weren't worried about a fake kick, because Knox was a conservative, straightforward guy. He would never have called for a fake field goal. In fact, many felt the Rams didn't have one in their playbook.

Tom Dempsey lined up for a kick that was shorter than an extra point, but cornerback Nate Allen blocked it. The ball bounced as if ordained into the hands of safety Bobby Bryant, and he raced 90 yards to a touchdown.

Up in the press box, I knew the game was over. In 12 years of calling the Rams, it was the single most disheartening play.

The next year, when the Rams finally got to play Minnesota in Los Angeles, the skies opened up and we had an unlikely midwestern downpour in the Coliseum. Vikings weather. Chuck Foreman sloshed through the mud for 101 yards, and Minnesota won again 14-7. It was my last game as a Rams announcer.

TIMEOUT

My Heart Got in the Way

FOR SEVERAL REASONS, my favorite Rams player was defensive tackle Merlin Olsen, later to work as my partner for more than a decade at NBC. Not only was he a Hall of Famer as a player, but he was always the most gracious, most articulate, most insightful of the Rams.

They didn't lose very often in my 12 years with the team, but in those rare defeats, we knew we could always go to Olsen for the obligatory postgame interview. Not only would he be willing to do it, but he'd say something that was perceptive and pertinent. Of course, he was fully aware that he was bailing us out. He knew that very few of his teammates were as capable or as cooperative.

"Why don't you ever have me on when we win a game?" he grumbled. "I'm always on when we lose."

Well, our standing guarantee was that if and when the Rams won the Super Bowl, he'd be our first postgame guest.

Sadly, Olsen's 15-year career as an All-Pro player and postgame guest came to an end in 1976 with no Super Bowl ring. The team's final three games that year were on the road, including a playoff victory over

Dallas and the heartbreaking 24-13 playoff loss to Minnesota. But on a Saturday in early December, Olsen played his last game at home, and it was a memorable one as the Rams overwhelmed Atlanta 59-0.

Olsen had already announced his retirement and when Chuck Knox took him out of the game with just a few minutes remaining—his final farewell in the Coliseum—he got a rousing, lengthy standing ovation. With time running out, however, the crowd urged Knox to give him one more chance. Tens of thousands of fans rose to their feet and started chanting, "We want Olsen… We want Olsen."

As a coach, Knox could be stubborn, but he was also sentimental, so he sent his star defensive tackle back onto the field, all to the roaring approval of the partisan crowd. The two teams lined up, and, as Atlanta reserve quarterback Kim McQuilken went back to pass, all eyes, including mine, were on Olsen. Calling the action on the Rams Radio Network, I excitedly described how, in his final curtain call, he burst into the Falcons' backfield, aiming for one last sack.

"McQuilken back to pass," I shouted into the microphone, "AND OLSEN HITS HIM!!!" Then I paused. "No, it's not Olsen… My heart got in the way… I wanted it to be Olsen… It was [tackle] Mike Fanning."

"When I went back in, I knew I had no chance for a sack," Olsen said later. "Everybody blocked me, which meant all of our other guys had a shot. In effect, the Falcons were saying, 'Even though our quarterback may get killed, you're not going to get the sack.'"

When he came off the field to another standing ovation, I apologized to the audience.

"It wasn't Olsen," I repeated, "but Merlin Olsen in my heart made that sack."

5

THE BRUIN BALLET

"Never cease trying to be the best you can be."

—John Wooden

As the UCLA team bus crawled through the wheat fields of Eastern Washington, heading for the next night's basketball game in Pullman with Washington State, I sat in the back of the bus and admired the scenery. My schedule had been frantic in the last few days, and it was pleasant to relax for a couple of hours.

My nose was on the window when the team's manager approached.

"Dick, Coach Wooden would like you come up to the front of the bus and sit with him."

If I had catapulted off a trampoline, I couldn't have bounced up any faster. Gone was my reverie. "Fantastic," I thought, "I'm going to sit next to the greatest coach in the game for two hours and get loads of inside information on the team. Tomorrow night's broadcast could be the best we've ever done."

As I sat down next to the coach, his first words were, "Do you like poetry?"

What was I going to say, no?

"Of course, Coach," I said, trying to sound convincing. "I love poetry."

"How about Edna St. Vincent Millay?" he asked.

"Oh, absolutely. She's a joy to read," I feigned.

For the next two hours of that bus ride, he proceeded to quote from the poems of Edna St. Vincent Millay, the famed American poet. There was not one word about the game. In fact, the word *basketball* never came up. He discussed the meaning of many of Millay's poems, explained why he liked them, and talked about the enjoyment he derived from writing his own poetry. I had rushed to the front of the bus to get an insight into the UCLA team; instead I got added insight into the coach.

From the fall of 1966 to the spring of 1975, encompassing the last nine seasons of Wooden's career as UCLA coach, I announced Bruins games for KTLA-TV. We did most of the road games live and showed the home games on tape delay at 11:00 p.m. after the news. UCLA won eight national championships in those nine years (and 10 in 12 years, dating back to 1964), a run of success that will never be approached again.

It was my incredibly good fortune to team up with the Bruins. Because I was their announcer, there was the perception that I was something special, too. I loved doing baseball and football, but it was my connection with UCLA that shot me into the national limelight and triggered my move to NBC-TV in 1975. My entrée to the network was the success of UCLA. I rode the Wooden wave.

It all began in the exhilarating fall of 1966—shortly after I had been named Rams play-by-play announcer. Bob Speck, KTLA's sports director, negotiated a TV package with UCLA that included football, basketball, and spring sports. When he told me I would be calling the basketball games, I was excited. However, when he told me that we were going to delay televising the home games until 11:00 p.m., I thought it was a ridiculous idea.

"That'll never work," was my response. "Who's going to watch a three-hour-old basketball game? You already know who won."

I underestimated the power of UCLA. The delayed televised games developed a cult following in Southern California. On Friday nights, we outrated *The Tonight Show* with Johnny Carson. Even the fans who went to the games and the players who took part in them went home and watched them all over again. Much of the rest of the public avoided learning the scores and tuned in faithfully at 11:00 p.m. On KTLA's newscast, just before the replays, the score was never flashed on the screen, and announcers would warn the audience, "If you don't want to know the score of the UCLA game, don't listen for the next 10 seconds."

One night, newscaster George Putnam, introducing sportscaster Jerry Coleman, said casually, "What a thrilling game that was in Westwood tonight."

And Coleman, without warning the audience, said, "It sure was, with UCLA winning by a point."

KTLA's switchboard was immediately overwhelmed with hundreds of angry phone calls.

My father was living with me during many of those years and refused to answer the phone after 8:00 p.m., afraid he might learn the score.

"Dad, please answer," I would beg before leaving for the game. "It could be an emergency."

But he would never comply.

UCLA center Bill Walton, the Bruins' three-time National Player of the Year from 1972 to 1974, told me many years later that the players couldn't wait to get back to their rooms to watch the replays. The more spectacular the game, the more times I said, "Oh My!" It was how the players gauged their performance.

"Right after the game, we started guessing how many times you'd shout 'Oh My!' that night," Walton said. "We always had a contest to see who would be closest to the actual number. Whenever you belted your signature phrase, one of the guys would mark it down to make sure we got an accurate count."

In Wooden's last 10 years as coach, which were also UCLA's first 10 years in Pauley Pavilion, the team's record at home was 149-2. People often asked me if the predictability of the games, particularly the home games, made my task more difficult. Not only did UCLA win 99 percent of the time in Pauley, but most of the games weren't even close. I told my friends that I tried to look at it differently. I felt I wasn't assigned to call a basketball game, I was assigned to cover the Bruin Ballet. Everyone knew what the outcome was going to be, the only question was how the choreography would be staged that night. How could you tire of it when experiencing the very best? It wasn't the Des Moines Ballet; it was the Royal Ballet. At times, UCLA's play was so efficient and so well constructed, and the players so brilliant that it seemed almost perfect. That made calling the games an absolute delight.

However, as I said earlier, I've always believed in doing a balanced broadcast. If you're a play-by-play announcer for one team, it's important to pay equal tribute to the opposing team and be well versed in their personal anecdotes and strategies. Because I anticipated that most of the games were going to be lopsided, it was doubly important to collect enough information on the other team to try to make the broadcast more interesting.

I would watch the opposing team's practice when the coach allowed me to visit and then talk with him, plus a player or two. Most of them were very cooperative. Teams that played UCLA on Friday night stayed in town to play USC on Saturday night, and they would often watch our replays. I received several letters from coaches who had watched, thanking me for my fairness. As a broadcaster, you develop a reputation, and this helped me continue to gain important access with UCLA's opponents. I never wanted to be known as the UCLA announcer. I was determined to be an announcer who called the UCLA games.

I did the Bruin games solo. No color man. In those days there was no producer. Venerable John Polich was the director, and, in essence, I was the producer. I basically did whatever I wanted, allowing me all the satisfaction borne of creative license.

As UCLA embarked on its run of eight national titles in my nine years, including seven in a row from 1967 to 1973, more Bruin games were televised nationally. The great bulk of the audience tuned in to see if anybody could beat this team. And when they did, it was a big, big deal. Wooden has often kidded me that whenever I talk about the games that I remember most, they're games that UCLA lost, and that's true, because you always expected his team to win. In fact, UCLA lost only 12 games—*12!*—in those nine years.

One of those defeats came in the game that was absolutely critical in catapulting college basketball to the level of popularity that we know today—the two-point victory in January 1968 by Elvin Hayes and the University of Houston over a Lew Alcindor-led UCLA team that had won 47 games in a row. From a historical perspective, I feel it's the most important sports event I've ever called. As a sophomore the previous season, Alcindor, a three-time National Player of the Year who later changed his name to Kareem Abdul-Jabbar, had led UCLA to a 30-0 record and the national title. In the national semifinal game in March 1967, the Bruins defeated Houston by 15 points.

The 1968 UCLA-Houston game was played in the Houston Astrodome before 52,693 fans, at the time the largest crowd ever to see a basketball game in the United States. It was televised nationally by TVS, a syndicated sports network that was founded in 1965 by Eddie Einhorn, a brilliant entrepreneur who was the first TV executive to see the enormous potential in college basketball. (He later sold TVS to NBC.)

When Einhorn put the Houston-UCLA game together, he didn't know me from a backboard. However, as he told me later, when he was discussing the final terms of the agreement with UCLA athletic director J.D. Morgan, J.D. had one request.

"I also want you to use our announcer."

"Is he any good?" Einhorn asked.

"Of course, he's good," J.D. replied. "He's doing our games."

"That was all I needed to know," Einhorn said later. "I didn't know your work, but if J.D. Morgan said you were good, I trusted that you were."

That was the start of my long relationship with Einhorn. After doing his national telecast of that UCLA-Houston game, I became his lead announcer and did most of his national games and many of his other telecasts when my schedule permitted.

Houston coach Guy Lewis was the driving force behind the matchup in the Astrodome. Wooden, who disliked anything that distracted the team from the conference schedule, didn't want to play the game. But J.D. realized the considerable economic benefits and agreed to sign on. It was always an attractive pairing, but the ingredients made it one of the most eagerly anticipated sports events ever. UCLA, the defending national champion, was ranked No. 1, Houston was ranked No. 2, and both were unbeaten. The game was televised in prime time—the first national prime-time telecast of a college basketball game.

My broadcast partner was Hall of Famer Bob Pettit, the only time we worked together, but what a historical night to share the microphone. Our broadcast location was literally below ground. The court was in the middle of the Astrodome, and they had dug large foxholes in the infield dirt for the announcers.

Despite the buildup, if UCLA had won by 10 or 15 points, it would have been just another big game. Wooden hates it when I say this, but for history, the right team won. The underdog won and won at home, giving the telecast a roaring crowd of nearly 53,000 fans to heighten the drama. And it was close all the way, decided with 28 seconds left on a pair of free throws by Hayes, "the Big E," bringing the final score to 71-69. A six-foot-eight All-America forward with a deft shooting touch, Hayes scored 39 points, hitting 17 of 25 shots from the floor, many from long range. He also blocked four shots, including three by the seven-foot-two Alcindor. Lew, who had missed two games and several days of practice after being poked in the left eye in a game eight days earlier, played all 40 minutes but was sub-par, scoring only 15 points. All-America guard Lucius Allen almost lifted the Bruins to victory with 25.

Most experts point to the Michigan State-Indiana State NCAA title game in 1979—Magic Johnson versus Larry Bird—as *the* game that helped boost college basketball into the stratosphere. I disagree.

I called that one, too, so I don't say this out of bias. UCLA-Houston, 11 years earlier, was the game that really showed the world how big college basketball could be. That was the skyrocket.

My own career was also taking off in those days, and during the next basketball season, I embarked on a schedule that exhausts me just thinking about it. On the weekends that UCLA played at home during the conference season, I announced three basketball games in just over 24 hours, sandwiched around a 4,000-mile round trip.

Einhorn had organized a Saturday afternoon Game of the Week package, signing five Catholic schools from the Midwest—Notre Dame, Marquette, DePaul, Loyola of Chicago, and the University of Detroit (now Detroit Mercy). I called those games when my schedule allowed it. I would do the UCLA game on Friday night at Pauley Pavilion, then rush to Los Angeles International Airport and take an overnight flight to Chicago, Detroit, or Milwaukee for the Saturday game. Arriving in the early morning, I went directly to the arena and used the examination table in the first aid room for a couple of hours' sleep. Then I would shower and shave in the locker room, change clothes, and be ready to call the 1:00 p.m. game. When it was over, I raced back to the airport, flew to L.A., drove to Pauley Pavilion, and arrived in time to announce a UCLA game that night. It was a wild ride, but I fed off it. It was a chance for exposure in the Midwest and East, and it gave my friends and family in Michigan and Indiana a chance to see me announce a game.

KTLA was graciously tolerant of my outside broadcasting activities, but my schedule caught up with me one Saturday night when I didn't make it to Pauley Pavilion. The airport in Los Angeles was fogged in, and as we circled for a while, I knew I was in big trouble. There were no cell phones in 1969, and not only was I about to miss the game, but I had no way of notifying the station. Finally, we landed at a suburban airport in Ontario, California, 55 miles from UCLA. It was after 8:00 p.m., and the game had already started without me!

When I didn't show up, no one from KTLA knew what to do, so, cleverly, they didn't do anything. There was a total panic. Halfway through the first half, they decided to start taping the game with just crowd noise. Finally, I was able to phone from Ontario and told them I could make it to KTLA by 11:00 p.m., in time for the start of the delayed telecast. I rented a car, hurried back to the station, and then called the game in the control booth studio—off the tape. Of course, the tape began halfway through the first half, so we began by informing the audience, "Due to technical difficulties, we're picking up the action midway through the first half with the score… " There were technical difficulties all right.

Having heard the live radio broadcast on the car ride up the freeway, I knew all the critical details, even suggesting in my call in the final minutes of another lopsided win who should take the shot for UCLA: "Bill Sweek is open in the corner; the Bruins should get him the ball. The pass does go to Sweek, and he fires from 20 feet. It's good!" Oh My!

Because UCLA was so dominant, the Bruins were an integral part of Einhorn's national TVS package of four or five games every season. Several of those featured UCLA and Notre Dame, the nation's fiercest intersectional rivalry in the early and mid-1970s. Four of those games were especially memorable.

In 1971, the Irish, coached by Johnny Dee and playing in front of a whistling, stomping, screaming crowd in South Bend, upset the unbeaten and top-ranked Bruins 89-82. All-America guard Austin Carr poured in 46 points and held off UCLA's late surge all by himself, scoring 15 of Notre Dame's final 17 points in the game's last six and a half minutes. The loss snapped UCLA's 49-game, nonconference winning streak.

By 1973, the colorful Richard "Digger" Phelps was coaching Notre Dame, but the Irish were no match for the Bruins that season, losing twice. The second game, an 82-63 UCLA victory in South Bend was the Bruins' 61st straight win, a new collegiate record. The old mark of 60 in a row had been set in the mid-1950s by a University of San Francisco team that was led by superstars Bill Russell and K.C. Jones.

By 1974, UCLA's record winning streak had soared to 88 in a row, a record that may last until the next Ice Age. The Bruins were a spectacular 30-0 in both 1972 and 1973 and had not lost since the Austin Carr-led upset in 1971. UCLA center Bill Walton had his own personal winning streak, 139 in a row, dating back to his junior year in high school. Once again the top-ranked Bruins were in South Bend for the national telecast, and with 3:30 to go, they were on their way to 89 victories in a row, leading the second-ranked Irish 70-59 behind Walton's 24 points.

At that point, Phelps called time out and ordered his team into a full-court, man-to-man press, which led to one of the most shocking turnarounds I have ever seen in sports. Notre Dame forced four turnovers, hit six straight baskets, and scored the game's last 12 points. With 29 seconds left, junior guard Dwight Clay tossed in a high, arching fall-away jumper from the right-hand corner for the go-ahead basket. After he released the ball, Clay, who had earned the nickname "Iceman" for his previous last-second heroics, fell backward into the arms of delirious Irish fans in the first row.

Wooden, who never liked to call timeouts—he saw it as a sign of weakness—finally signaled for one with 21 seconds left. On their last possession, the Bruins had five shots at the basket and missed them all as Notre Dame won 71-70. The main headline in Sunday's *Los Angeles Times* sports section read "Feat of Clay—Irish 71, UCLA 70."

Thirty years later, early in 2004, I interviewed Wooden, then 93 years old, for a feature that was shown during the CBS coverage of the NCAA Tournament. He spoke about that game and alluded to the pressure of the long winning streak.

"Defeat is inevitable," Wooden said. "When we lost our 88-game winning streak, in one sense it's almost a delight. You're almost pleased that you lost. Not really—you didn't want to—but it seems like you've lost a weight off your shoulders."

"It took a lot of pressure off us," said former UCLA head coach and Wooden assistant Gary Cunningham a few months before I talked to Wooden. "I mean, when the streak got up there, the pressure was incredible. I think Coach was relieved."

Not so relieved that he was going to lose again. The unbeaten Irish had leaped past the Bruins into the top spot in the polls, with UCLA tumbling to second. Just one week later, they met again in Pauley Pavilion, and, before a huge national television audience, UCLA won by 19 points 94-75. Walton had 32 points and 11 rebounds, and All-America forward Keith Wilkes scored 20.

UCLA's victory in that game reminded me of 1968. Two months after losing to Houston in the Astrodome, the Bruins met the unbeaten Cougars again in the NCAA semifinal game and blitzed them 101-69.

෯

In my nine years of calling UCLA basketball games, I forged a real bond with the student rooting section at Pauley Pavilion. I was just a few years removed from my career as a college professor and felt comfortable around college students. I still do. I have always loved their enthusiasm, their energy, and the electricity they bring to a classroom or a sports event. My broadcast location at UCLA was in the first row of the second level, just above the student rooting section, and when they flashed the peace sign to me—this was during the Vietnam War—I gave it back to them. It was a natural thing to do. I felt a warm connection with the students, which led in 1970 to one of the more unusual episodes in my career.

UCLA's 1970 team was one of Wooden's favorites, "the team without" as he called it—the team without Lew Alcindor, who came before, or Bill Walton, who came two years later. There were no superstars, but there were five starters who were all *very good* players— Sidney Wicks, Curtis Rowe, and Steve Patterson in the frontcourt, and Henry Bibby and John Vallely in the backcourt. "The team without" went 28-2 and won another national title.

On a rainy Friday night in early January, UCLA opened the 1970 conference season by racing out to a 39-12 lead against undermanned Oregon. But the Ducks kept switching zone defenses, then finally hit on one that worked. They also got hot on offense and reeled off a 21-6 run to trim UCLA's lead to 45-33. Although Wooden always said he disliked stalls, he told his team to hold the ball, which the rules allowed in those days, to pull Oregon out of its zone. There was no shot clock and no penalty for failing to advance the ball if the defense didn't pressure the offense. Oregon, however, stayed packed in its zone.

As always, I was working all alone without a color man, and the only action was a UCLA free throw during the last 4:37 of the first half. As one of the Bruins continued to hold the ball on his hip and everyone else stood and watched him, it became obvious that there was no action to report, so I figured I better fill some time by reviewing the scoring in the game. That consumed nearly a minute. Then I reviewed the remaining schedule, home and away, and, happily, that helped me to make it to halftime with UCLA leading 46-33.

At the start of the second half, UCLA was still holding the ball, still trying to induce Oregon to abandon its zone. As the Bruin crowd booed the lack of action, I suggested the cameras shoot Pauley Pavilion's rafters and the national championship banners. A little bit of UCLA championship history ate up another minute of the stall. However, there were still 17 or 18 minutes left in the game, and the rest of the half yawned in front of me like a vast, empty desert.

With nothing else to say, I decided to be honest with the audience.

"I've exhausted all of my material," I confessed. "I've told you everything that's pertinent to this game and this season. As you can see, there's no action. It's still 46-33, and frankly my mind has wandered off to another place. Maybe it's because of the weather tonight, but this melody is running through my mind. It's 'Raindrops Keep Falling on My Head' [a popular song from the movie, *Butch Cassidy and the Sundance Kid*]."

As 10 inactive athletes stood frozen on the floor, I began humming it. That helped me get through the next few minutes. Sparing the audience anymore of my "musical talent," Oregon came out of its zone midway through the second half and the Bruins started shooting and went on to win by 17 points.

The next night, a talented Oregon State team came into Pauley, and as I settled into my chair, at least a half-dozen students came up and offered me the lyrics to "Raindrops." The game that followed was much different than the previous night's match. It was a close battle all the way. With time running out, Oregon State was on the verge of a huge upset, leading by a point, but reserve forward John Ecker of UCLA hit a three-foot turnaround bank shot with four seconds left to win it for the Bruins 72-71. It was a rare home scare for UCLA. In my game wrapup, I looked at the lyrics to the song and tied them into what we had just seen.

"Many copies of 'Raindrops Keep Falling on My Head' have been given to me tonight," I said, "and that's applicable to how opponents of UCLA must feel. No matter how well they play, those defeats just keep falling on you. No matter how close you come, it's a UCLA win. One after another, after another."

Because the delayed broadcast started at 11:00 p.m., it was about 1:00 a.m. when viewers were listening to my final remarks. Spontaneously, innocently, I added, "and, you music lovers, if and when UCLA wins the conference title, I'll sing those lyrics down at center court. Thank you, and good night."

My offhand pledge almost overwhelmed the rest of the season. Within a couple of games, UCLA's pep band started doing its own rendition of the song. When the Bruins were far ahead in the second half and victory was assured, the band would strike up the "Raindrops" tune, and the student body would turn en masse, point at me, and chant, "You'll sing! You'll sing! You'll sing!" I was trapped by my own big mouth.

Finally, inevitably, the night came. The Bruins defeated California at home to clinch the conference championship, and there was nowhere to hide. After the broadcast ended, I shuffled all my papers, then put them into my briefcase, and took them out again, employing a delaying action in hopes that Pauley Pavilion would soon empty out. But no one left. Slowly, I made my way downstairs to center court for the performance that I'd promised. I was nervous and never came close to locating the same key as the band, so it was awful in that regard, but there were highlights, too. There's a little musical bridge in the song where I inserted "U-C-L-A," and everyone cheered. By coincidence, it was another rainy night in Los Angeles, and when I started to sing, all of the students opened their umbrellas, which, from my point of view, made for a spectacular picture.

I thought, "Wow, is this ever a special moment."

Two weeks later, I received a letter from a UCLA faculty member. I don't have the letter anymore, but, basically, it said, "I'm Doctor -------------, I've been a professor of musicology here on campus for 20 years, and this is my lifetime work. I'm a big basketball fan who has always enjoyed your telecasts, and I was intrigued by your singing performance in Pauley Pavilion a couple of weeks ago. Because of that, I'm requesting your help in my continuing pursuit of knowledge in my academic field. Here's my phone number, and if you're ever in Westwood, I would love to have you stop by and explain to me two notes I've never heard before in my entire life."

Over the years, in airports, or on the street, people have often stopped me and asked when I was going to sing again. Many of them have told me they were in Pauley Pavilion that night, and based on the reaction I've gotten, there must have been 50,000 fans there to see me make a fool of myself.

A year later, several fans, even people at KMPC and KTLA, asked me what I was going to do at the end of the 1971 season, and I thought about it. Should I read a poem? Should I sing another song? Then I decided it would be wrong. It worked the year before because it was spontaneous and honest. If I tried to do something this time, it would be contrived. There would be only one Enberg musical performance. That's a decision worthy of a standing ovation.

❦

As I've spent time with John Wooden since his retirement from coaching many years ago, my appreciation for him has continued to grow. His interests are so much wider than just basketball. Besides his love for poetry—he was a high school English teacher—I think he could quote from every book ever written on Abraham Lincoln. As his players will tell you, he was a brilliant teacher and certainly an inspiration. I found him to be the ultimate example of not only greatness, but also goodness.

Wooden is 94 and continues to lead an active life, making speeches, doing interviews, meeting with other coaches who seek his advice, spending time with many of his former players. Despite his success, which seems more unbelievable as each year passes, he remains modest and self-effacing. I asked him once what he remembered most about his first national championship back in 1964.

"It was in Kansas City, as all the championships were in those days," he answered. "We won the championship on Saturday night, and the next day was Easter Sunday, so my wife, Nell, and I were on our way to church. We had taken no more than two steps out of the hotel when a pigeon dropped a perfect hit right on my head. I said to myself, 'Johnny, maybe you're not as important as you think you are.'"

Of all his records—including 10 national titles, 88- and 47-game winning streaks, four unbeaten seasons, 19 conference titles, and the 149-2 record in Pauley Pavilion—to me the most significant was his team's phenomenal 38-game winning streak in the NCAA Tournament. That run of success lasted from 1964 until the double-overtime, three-point loss to eventual champion North Carolina State in the 1974 national semifinal game. Think of it: 38 in a row, facing only teams good enough to be in the NCAA Tournament.

Wooden's achievements were so staggering that the fans' expectations became totally unrealistic. After the loss to North Carolina State in 1974, which ended a run of seven successive national titles, several fans wrote to the UCLA athletic department, claiming he was over the hill and should be replaced. He won the national championship again the next year and retired.

Surprisingly, the man who won so often never talked about winning and losing. He asked his players to give 100 percent and to play as a team, and believed winning would take care of itself.

"Success is the satisfaction that one gets from knowing he made the effort to do the best of which he is capable," Wooden told me. "No one can do more than that. When I graduated from grade school, my dad gave me a creed, and one of the points in the creed was, 'Make each day your masterpiece.' Just do the best that you can every day. Never cease trying to be the best you can be. That's within your power. We may not be equal as far as ability is concerned, but we're all equal in trying to make the most of what we have.

"I don't believe a player could tell you that he ever heard me use the word 'winning.' Did I want to win? Of course I did. But I wanted it to be the byproduct of doing your best. I didn't want the emphasis placed on winning. I think we've won on occasions when we've been outscored, and I think we've lost on occasions when we outscored the opponent, because we didn't measure up to the level of competency that I knew we had."

To make his point, Wooden often quoted from a short poem by George Moriarty, a Major League Baseball player, manager, and umpire in the early years of the twentieth century. The most important lines were:

"Who can ask more of a man than giving all within his span? Giving all, it seems to me, is not so far from victory."

That very simple philosophy allowed him to go into the locker room after a 30-point win and really let his team have it, because they didn't play their best. In a heartbreaking loss, he could go in and embrace them, because, "I can't ask for more than you gave me. You gave me your best." It's a beautiful philosophy. It's so simple in structure, and it's absolutely applicable in every business and family. He also believed that you worked on what you did best and made that your focus and let the other team take care of their problems. He didn't do much to adjust to the opposition, but his own practices were very demanding.

"He didn't believe in long drills," former player and assistant Gary Cunningham recalled. "Most of his drills were five- and 10-minute segments, but he believed in repetition, day after day after day. Pretty soon you'd be doing it right. He wanted things done precisely the way he believed that they should be done. Footwork, pivoting, balance—all of the things you don't see in basketball as much today—were very important. His whole philosophy was: keep it simple, but be fundamentally sound.

"He was always teaching. Always teaching. He never relaxed. He had an incredible work ethic."

"I always loved practices," Wooden said. "I loved planning them, loved conducting them—more than games. Always did. It's the only thing I've missed."

There were two sides to John Wooden as a coach. There was that gentle, sensitive, cerebral, fatherly figure whom you wanted to impress. As an announcer, I certainly felt that way. Then there was the other John Wooden whom I didn't have to deal with, because I wasn't a player—a man who was tough, in some ways, unrelenting. He was a master at understanding the differences in players. Some can take criticism more easily than others, and those he would not hesitate to berate, sometimes unmercifully. Others he handled much more gently. But with all of them, he was a strict disciplinarian, refusing even to compromise his principles in the more liberal environment of the late 1960s and early 1970s.

"I thought my parents were strict," Walton told me, "but this guy was off the charts. There was never any wavering. There was never any flexibility. The players were into flexibility, but he wasn't. I never felt like a star. People said he let the stars do what they wanted, that he had a double standard. He didn't have a double standard. We all felt our careers could be over at any time.

"While I argued with him about everything else—politics, religion, economics, the legal system, the Vietnam War, lifestyles—we all knew there was no real point in arguing with him about team rules. We challenged him at times about team rules or our style of play, but we never crossed the line. He would listen to you, but if you didn't do what he wanted, he would say, 'I respect your opinions, and we enjoyed having you here, but we're going to miss you.'"

Wooden demanded that his players shave every day and get a haircut once a week. Like a military officer, he would march into the locker room to inspect his troops, making sure that their shirts were tucked in, their shoes were properly tied, their hair was cut, and their faces shaved. But the players never knew when an inspection was coming. The coach might stop a player on campus and tell him he would have to miss practice that day unless he shaved.

On the opening day of practice before his senior year, Walton, already a two-time National Player of the Year, two-time Academic All-America selection, and now one of the team captains, didn't pass Wooden's inspection. The coach rubbed his star's cheek with his hands and said, "That's not good enough, and your hair is not short enough. You can't practice."

Walton argued. The other seniors backed him up.

"Come on, Coach," they pleaded. "Let him practice. He can get it cut tomorrow."

Wooden wouldn't bend.

So Walton jumped on his bike, still wearing his uniform, and frantically pedaled down to a Westwood Village barbershop. There, in frustration, he told the barber, "Cut it all off." While the barber was cutting his hair, Walton shaved his face with a disposable razor and warm water.

"Then I rode my bike back to Pauley Pavilion," Walton recalled, "rode it right into the arena, hopped off, and jumped into a line of players waiting to get into a drill. Coach Wooden was tough but not unfair. Once I met his expectations, I was allowed back into practice."

Now in his early 50s and an NBA basketball commentator who worked many games with me when I was at NBC, Walton has grown very close to his former coach. He calls him as often as he can, sometimes every day.

"It was an ordeal for me to speak until I was 28 when I learned to overcome my serious stuttering problem," Walton said. "Now they're scouring the earth for someone to stop me from talking. Sometimes Coach doesn't take my calls. He tells his friends, 'Walton will leave a 10-minute message and that will be all the information I need.'

"I was Coach Wooden's worst nightmare and slowest learner. Now I thank him profusely for his teachings, his knowledge, his lessons of life, but mostly I thank him for his patience and forgiveness."

TIMEOUT

A Mental Blackout

BESIDES TELEVISING REGULAR-SEASON games, Eddie Einhorn's TVS network showed first-round action in the NCAA Tournament. I called many of those games, including UCLA's regional meeting with Cal State Long Beach in Seattle in 1970. Utah State and Santa Clara were the other two teams in the regional, and Einhorn lined up Connie Alexander, who called football and basketball games for the Southwest Conference network, to announce that game. Connie and I, who had never met before, traded assignments in the telecasts of the two games. I did color on his telecast, and he was the commentator on mine.

The Utah State-Santa Clara game was televised to a much smaller network than the UCLA game, and as fate would have it, that game ran long, ending about two minutes before we were scheduled to come back on the air with the Bruins and 49ers. During the commercial time out, Connie and I unhooked our microphones and raced to the end of the floor to do the on-camera opening for the UCLA game. When the audience joined us, I launched into my typical on-camera opening remarks, "Welcome from the great Northwest as UCLA begins its bid for another national championship tonight against Cal State Long Beach... "

While I continued my pregame patter, I suddenly realized I couldn't remember the name of my co-announcer. As Connie stood patiently next to me, waiting to be introduced, I kept talking, figuring his name was bound to come to me, but it didn't. This had never happened to me before. I couldn't talk forever. Finally, there was no choice but to introduce him. In desperation, I looked over at Connie, thrust the microphone in his direction, and said, "Here with me tonight to bring his color comments to the telecast is... come on in and introduce yourself."

It was like watching the Wicked Witch disintegrate in *The Wizard of Oz*. He almost disappeared from the screen. The look on his face was heartbreaking as he took the microphone and softly said, "I'm Connie Alexander."

Throughout the course of the game, he kept mumbling during commercial timeouts, "I've done that many times. I've done that many times."

It didn't make me feel any better. Here we were in front of a large audience for an NCAA Tournament game, and I couldn't remember the damn name of my partner. However, in a roundabout way, I guess I did him a favor. Word is that he has used that incident as great fodder for his speaking engagements. Needless to say, I'll always remember Connie Alexander.

6

GAME OF THE DAY

"Just report the ball."

—Fred Haney

I n the fall of 2003, I was in Chicago to call a Bears football game the same weekend that the Braves were in town to play the Cubs during the National League playoffs. While I was there, CBS arranged for a box seat behind home plate—my first trip to Wrigley Field in more than 20 years. It's a fabulous old ballpark, immersed in sounds and smells, colorful and intimate, and crowded with fans who care so deliriously. The stands, with their steep, narrow aisles, are a constant beehive of activity.

I sat next to a woman and her husband and was very impressed by her knowledge of the game.

"You've got to hit and run here," she shouted to Cub manager Dusty Baker. "We've got a man on first with one out. This is the time to do it."

Another time she suggested a pitchout. As the game unfolded, we started chatting between innings, and she recognized me, so I formally introduced myself.

"It's nice to meet you," she said, "but right now I'm concerned about the Cubs."

"That's the way it should be," I said. "By the way, it's great to sit next to somebody who really knows baseball. Your dad must have taken you to a lot of Cubs games when you were young."

"He *never* took me to any Cubs games," she said, shaking her head.

"What do you mean?" I asked.

"He was a White Sox fan," she said with disdain. "My *mom* took me to Cubs games."

Like that woman in Chicago, I love baseball. It was the first professional sport I saw as a spectator, the sport that I dreamed about playing on a major league level, and the sport I coached at Valley State. I shared the love my dad and my maternal grandfather, Rudy Weiss, had for the game. I still have the two baseballs Grandpa Rudy willed me, autographed by the 1935 Detroit Tigers and 1935 Chicago White Sox. Later on, I spent 14 seasons with the California

Angels (now the Anaheim Angels), including 11 as their play-by-play announcer on KMPC Radio and KTLA Television.

Because I've called so many different sports, I'm often asked, "What is the most difficult sport to broadcast?"

Even the great Ted Williams was surprised when I answered baseball.

"Damn it," he said. "I thought you were going to say football or one of those other sports."

No question, it's baseball. It's the most difficult, the most demanding, the most challenging, even the most exhausting. Why? Because it's the *longest* season, nearly 200 games, counting spring training. And it's the *slowest* paced game, which pushes the announcer to work hard—particularly on the radio—to fill in those quiet moments when the pitcher is endlessly rubbing a wrinkle in the ball and the batter is loitering outside the batter's box.

For the same two reasons, although this may sound contradictory, it's also the best game for announcers. Because of the length of the season, you have ample time to collect a wealth of personal stories about the players, while the pace of the game gives you the opportunity to weave them into your broadcast in a conversational style. The announcer has the liberty to be very creative. Thus, when I'm asked who the best sportscasters are today, my answer is anyone good enough to call baseball on the radio. They are the verbal artists of my profession.

I enjoy helping young announcers, and often they'll bring me one of their tapes of a high school or college baseball game, proudly urging me to listen to their call of a diving catch or a double play. It's usually very good, and I'll compliment them. However, I know what's coming next.

"What do you do when the pitcher doesn't throw the ball?" they always ask. "What do you do when nothing is happening?"

"Ah, hah. There's the challenge," I'll tell them. "It's what you do with the down time that makes you a believable baseball announcer."

The answer is to fill those gaps with background stories, scene sets, historical notes, and even humor. Baseball then truly becomes the announcer's game. I firmly believe that if a young announcer has the talent to call a baseball game, he can be successful at calling any sport.

Fortunately, baseball gives you more access to the players than any other game. Media are allowed to hang around the batting cage for well over an hour during batting practice, asking questions, listening in on conversations, bantering with the players. You can also wander in and out of the locker rooms and dugouts. Do you get all that access before a basketball or football game? No way. In golf, many players don't mind your presence on the practice range or putting green before a round, but that's the only sport that even comes close.

Of course, as a baseball broadcaster, one of your big challenges is to be able to wander off and tell those stories during pauses in the action and still be alert enough to jump back into the play-by-play call when something important suddenly occurs. There may be only 10 outstanding moments in an entire baseball game—a home run, a double steal, a brilliant catch, a strikeout with the bases loaded—and it's a broadcaster's error if he's so caught up in a story that he's late with the live description.

Because the game moves at such a leisurely pace, the announcer is fully exposed. He not only needs to have plenty of anecdotes and stories at his disposal, it's critical that he thoroughly understands the nuances of the game. In football, you can hide your lack of knowledge behind a good analyst. Basketball and hockey are so fast, that you can hide within the fast-paced action. However, no sport reveals your lack of knowledge like baseball.

~

My first involvement with the Angels came in March 1966, as the host and producer of half-hour pre- and postgame shows for KTLA, which then televised about 40 games each season. Our pregame show usually had three eight-minute interviews, and my debut was in Palm Springs, where the Angels were playing the Chicago Cubs for a spring training weekend. Angels manager Bill Rigney and young outfielder Rick Reichardt, billed by some as the next Mickey Mantle, agreed to be on the show. We needed a representative from the Cubs, and Leo Durocher, their legendary manager, was the obvious choice.

When I told director John Polich and sports director Bob Speck that I planned to ask Durocher, they said he wouldn't do it.

"He'll want to be paid," they both said.

Well, that was all the bait I needed. An hour and a half before the game, I walked onto the field as the Cubs took batting practice. Durocher was leaning on the cage, watching his team, and I slowly edged my way closer and closer, until I was standing at his side.

"Skip," I said, "I'm Dick Enberg, the new announcer with the Angels, and I would like to invite you to be a guest on my first pregame show today."

Durocher was completely unimpressed, not even bothering to look my way.

I pushed on.

"Bill Rigney and Rick Reichardt have already agreed to be guests, and it would make the show perfect if you were on, too. You really should be the other guest."

The Cubs' manager finally turned to look at me.

"It'll cost you a grand," he snapped.

"I won't make $1,000 all spring training," I countered, "but I'll buy you a bottle of whiskey."

Durocher hesitated—and then smiled.

"You got me, kid."

It was a valuable lesson. Sometimes even a large monetary award doesn't have the immediate, powerful impact of a lesser-priced tangible gift.

For the next three seasons, I continued to host pre- and postgame shows, doing the latter from the KTLA studios in Hollywood. After the game, we showed highlights, gave the other scores, and had an inside baseball segment where, as a former coach, I took a couple of plays and analyzed them. We had a seven-foot metal scoreboard on the set that was big enough for all the games, and often I updated it myself, using magnetic numbers.

One night, I was rushing around putting up scores and making sure everything else was ready as time was running out.

"Thirty seconds to air," the floor manager shouted.

I put up the last two or three scores, gathered up my notes, and as the floor manager barked, "Ten seconds to air," tumbled into my chair just in time.

"Hello everyone," I said to the audience. "What a great game tonight, the Angels came from behind to beat the Twins, and we're going to show you the highlights of that big seventh inning. Our inside baseball segment is a look at a unique double play, and we'll also have all the scores from both the American and National Leagues."

While I was talking, the floor manager was waving his arms. Something was obviously wrong, but I forged on while he kept pantomiming. Finally I figured it out. In my haste, I had forgotten to attach my clip-on mike. I was sitting on it. Sitting on my mike. In the middle of a sentence, I said, "Excuse me," reached down, pulled up the mike, put it on, smiled knowingly, and continued talking about the Angels.

Of course, you can imagine some of the mail I got. "You never sounded better," one fan wrote.

It was a technological first. I had created the rectal microphone.

᪣

As the 1968 baseball season ended, I was quite content with my busy broadcasting life, which included the nightly news, boxing from the Olympic Auditorium, UCLA basketball, Angel pre- and postgame shows, and the Rams on radio. With no warning, however, I had a huge decision to make.

Buddy Blattner, lead announcer for the Angels on radio and television since 1962, received an offer to be the No. 1 announcer for the expansion Kansas City Royals, and, having grown up in the Midwest, decided to take it. Several people were involved in the decision to hire me as Blattner's replacement, but the driving force was Gene Autry, who owned KMPC, KTLA, and the Angels. If I had known that Autry was pushing for me—I found out 36 years later while working on this book—I wouldn't have played so hard to get when they asked me to take the job.

As much as I love baseball, when KTLA general manager Doug Finley called me into his office to say they wanted me to become the new Angels announcer, my first reaction was to say no, absolutely no. Finley promised I could keep doing UCLA and the Rams—they would allow me to miss Angels games when the schedule conflicted with those sports—but I would have to give up boxing and the nightly news, which I didn't want to do. Plus, I had two young children, Jennifer, six, and Andrew, three. I knew baseball would take me away from home much more—for 81 games on the road, plus spring training.

Finley persisted.

"Don't you want to be remembered as one of the great announcers some day?"

"Of course, who wouldn't?" I answered.

"Well, name me one great announcer who did not do baseball."

In thinking of outstanding announcers in my time—Red Barber, Mel Allen, Vin Scully, Van Patrick, Curt Gowdy, Ernie Harwell—I realized they had all called baseball. Finley suggested that I try it for a year. He promised me that if it didn't work out after one season, I could come back to KTLA and resume doing boxing and the news. So we agreed on a one-year trial.

Before my first regular-season game in 1969, Fred Haney, who was the Angels' first general manager, came into my broadcast booth at Anaheim Stadium unannounced. As a boy in the San Fernando Valley, I had listened to Haney call Pacific Coast League games. When I was a graduate student at Indiana, he had managed the Milwaukee Braves to National League pennants in 1957 and 1958 and a victory over the Yankees in the 1957 World Series.

"I've been listening to you during spring training," he said, "and I know you're going to do a good job for us. But let me give you one piece of advice. As an announcer, just report the ball. Don't tell me what you hope the ball will do, or what you think the ball will do. Report the ball and you'll be just fine."

Then he walked out.

It was sage advice in many ways. For years, when I ran out of material and action was at a standstill, I'd just find the ball and describe what it was doing: "The pitcher hides the ball behind his back, takes the catcher's sign, backs off the rubber, rubs up the ball, stares in, nods, winds, and throws... and the ball is hammered deep, deep, but foul down the right field line. Look at that scramble for a souvenir. A fan in an Angels cap comes up with it and hands it to his young son. That ball has a proud and happy owner!"

Yes, report the ball.

The first season did not go smoothly, however. My hiring as the Angels' lead announcer was a huge blow to Don Wells, who had been the club's No. 2 announcer since 1961 and assumed he would move up to No. 1. He had paid his dues, but they didn't promote him, and it had to hurt. Instead, they hired a guy who had never done a professional baseball game in his life. I had called a few high school and college games, but that was it. It was pretty hard for Wells to feel warmly toward me, which I anticipated and tried to defuse. From day one, I apologized to him for the cruel circumstances.

"I can understand how resentful you might be of me," I said, "but I'm certainly not one to rub my position in anyone's face. You're the veteran, and I hope we can work together. I expect and want to learn a lot from you."

But he had to be bitter. Most of the time we had a good relationship, but at times it was strained, even on the air. One incident occurred after I used a quote that had struck my fancy. There was talk around the baseball world that year that the ball was livelier, and, when asked a few days earlier if he thought the ball had more life, retired Hall of Fame pitcher Early Wynn said, "I'm not sure, but just the other day, I saw a ball grazing on the outfield grass." I had never seen the line and used it during a game.

On the air, Wells almost snorted. "You haven't heard that one before?" he said. "That's as *old* as grass."

The putdown on the air just destroyed me. I was a new and insecure announcer, it was the middle of the season, and the Angels weren't doing well (they finished 20 games under .500), and it was a long, tiring road trip. That night, I called Stan Spero, the general manager of KMPC (which broadcast all the games), and said, "I'm coming home. I'm quitting. I can't take this anymore."

If he had said, "Come home," I would have hurried back across the country. But he talked me out of it.

"Please don't make an emotional decision," Stan told me. "You've got a great career ahead of you; don't let anybody interfere with it. Don't jeopardize it because of someone else. You have too much to lose."

Stan convinced me to finish the road trip and meet with him when I returned home. By then I had cooled down and decided to stay. Thanks to Stan, I didn't leave the Angels for 10 years.

Despite our occasional differences, I did learn from Wells in the four years that we worked together. In fact, he inspired me with one of his comments. The Angels were in Cleveland late in my first season, and both clubs were floundering. I was thinking, "Who's even listening?" So I asked Wells, who had done baseball for so many years, going back to his days with Bob Elson and the White Sox, how he got up for games like this and how he convinced himself that there was an audience out there hanging onto his words.

"Think of it as the *Game of the Day*," he said. "Imagine that you're broadcasting this game to the entire nation and they don't care what the records are. You have the privilege of being able to call the *Game of the Day*. Do the best you can. Make it interesting. Make them happy they tuned in. *Game of the Day*."

It's a great philosophy, and it helped me get through some long years with the Angels, who had eight losing seasons in my 10 years. (I returned to the Angels' broadcast booth in 1985, the club's 25th anniversary season, to broadcast 40 games, and they finished second in the Western Division under Gene Mauch.)

My first season, 1969, was also marked by the firing of Bill Rigney, the club's highly popular manager since its first season in 1961. When Rigney was cut loose after 39 games, it was a great disappointment for the media in general and me in particular, because there was never a nicer guy or better storyteller. He was a bright, energetic, exciting person to be around and always a good interview. In today's world, if a Bill Rigney had been fired, he would have gone right to the broadcast booth. He had all the goods to be a terrific announcer, but he only worked in the booth briefly much later in his life.

Even in the days when I was only hosting the pre- and postgame shows, Rigney treated me like a full-time member of the broadcast crew. Now I was the lead announcer and had this great relationship with him. I didn't feel like there was anything that I couldn't ask him or that he wouldn't share with me, and suddenly he was gone.

He was replaced by Lefty Phillips, a lifetime Dodgers scout. If Rigney was a 10 in terms of his public relations, Phillips was a two. Here was a guy who had to communicate with 25 players and a media corps, and he had trouble with the English language. When he'd get upset with the team, he'd say, "This is a 'flustrating' ball club." Late in the 1971 season, shortly before he was fired, Lefty saw the handwriting on the wall. Three or four of us were chatting with him around the batting cage, and he looked up, stopped munching his wad of tobacco, and said sadly, "Well, I guess you could call this my 'coupe de ville.'"

The clubhouse attendant who laundered the team's uniforms must have shaken his head every time he looked at Lefty. On

Opening Day, when everything shines, Lefty's home white uniform already had 20 splats of chewing tobacco across the front. It wasn't a team color, but the front of his uniform was always brown.

After Lefty took over in 1969, I went out to County Stadium in Milwaukee on one off day to work out with a few of the players. I was only 34 and in decent shape, so I asked for a uniform and Lefty allowed me to shag flies in the outfield, which was fun. I felt like a real player. Afterward I was in the shower, all soaped up with my eyes closed when I felt something hitting my leg. Then I heard a moronic giggle. I opened my eyes, and outfielder Roger Repoz was urinating on my leg. The other guys in the shower were rolling their eyes. Even they didn't think it was funny. I thought to myself, "Welcome to the big leagues."

A year or two later, I was almost welcomed with a fist. The Angels were playing a weekend series in New York against the Yankees, and they were embarrassingly bad. On Friday night, they made several errors, couldn't get anybody out, and looked like a total bunch of misfits as they lost badly. There's no way to hide that in a broadcast. You've got to call it like you see it, and I did.

On Saturday afternoon, it was no better. Many of the guys went out on the town after the loss on Friday night, and they got pummeled again. I thought they were playing as if they were half asleep, and I said that on the air.

General manager Dick Walsh, who had listened to both games on the radio back in Southern California, called Lefty in anger.

"I don't know what's going on with this team," he complained, "but if they're playing as badly as it sounds, you've got to do something. Are you imposing any curfew at all?"

Lefty told Walsh he would run a room check on Saturday night, and he did. Half the ball club was caught breaking curfew, so Lefty fined them. Baseball salaries were still low 35 years ago, and those fines hurt. By the time we climbed on the bus Sunday morning for the drive to Yankee Stadium, word had spread that the only reason Walsh called the manager was because he'd heard Enberg's broadcast, and it was Enberg who had cost everybody money. I never knew for sure, but I always felt that shortstop Jim Fregosi, as the clubhouse leader, was the one who riled up the team. He was upset because he got fined, too.

As I got on the bus, outfielder Billy Cowan confronted me.

"You cost me $200, you son of a bitch," he shouted. "I ought to take 200 out of your voice."

"All I did was call the game the way I saw it," I answered. "How would you have reported the way you guys played the last two days?"

Cowan didn't want to listen. He acted like he wanted to fight me right there. But fortunately, at this point, Phillips and his coaches boarded the bus, and Cowan backed down. I thought, "Maybe I ought to get more insurance. This could be more hazardous duty than I thought." That's how bad that team was. Not only did they play poorly, they wanted to blame the announcer.

⁖

With nearly 200 games during a baseball season, one of the most formidable tasks for the announcers is lining up obligatory interviews for the daily pre- and postgame shows. With one guest per show and two shows a day, that's nearly 400 guests over the course of the year. Obviously, some are from opposing teams, and it doesn't take long for you to develop a reputation—good or bad—throughout the league. I learned that very early.

The Angels were in Minnesota, and my goal was to get Rod Carew, an outstanding young hitter with the Twins, as our pregame guest. Carew was a tough catch, but I approached him at the batting cage and asked him to be on the show. His first reaction was negative, but after he looked over my shoulder, he said yes. Afterward, I asked one of the writers who was nearby what had happened, and he said Harmon Killebrew of the Twins was behind me. Killebrew heard me approach Carew, and when Carew looked at Harmon, he was asking him silently, "Is this guy okay?" Killebrew nodded yes. It was a keen lesson. Players talk. Don't burn their trust.

I still want the reputation that I'm okay. I don't want it because interview subjects think I'll ask the easiest questions or say the nicest things about them during the broadcast, but because they think I'll be fair and promote what is positive about them. That's my reputation, it's something I've earned, and I plan to continue to embrace it.

When I did get turned down, I didn't take it personally. Star baseball players are probably asked to be guests 50 times during the course of a long season, and they tire of it. In a slump, they're even less inclined to talk. There's an art to knowing people well enough to accept that fact. If they say no this time and you respect it, the next time they might say yes. If you make a big issue out of the turndown, you may never get a yes.

Carl Yastrzemski, the former Boston Red Sox star, was a tough guy to corral as well. He occasionally did postgame shows, but he didn't want to go on before games. I think he felt a pregame interview ruined his focus. Early in my career, the Angels were playing a day game in Boston—I think it was a holiday with a noon start—and he was the logical pregame guest, because he'd had a big game the night before. He had turned me down several times, but, as I said, I didn't take it personally. I went into the clubhouse to try again.

The day before, I had clipped a recipe for cherries jubilee out of the Sunday newspaper. In an effort to try something different, I decided to call it California Angels Cherries Jubilee and convinced Wells to read it with me during the broadcast. I had that idea on my mind when I approached Yastrzemski.

"Yaz, I know you're tired of all the usual questions," I said, "but because we're broadcasting on a holiday and the game is starting so early back in Los Angeles (8:30 a.m. for the pregame show), I thought maybe we'd do something different and talk about food, instead of baseball. Do you like to cook?"

I had no idea if he had ever cooked in his life, but it turned out that he loved to barbecue and had concocted his own special barbecue sauce. He agreed to do the interview and talked about food with all the enthusiasm that he brought to hitting. He even gave the audience the recipe for his sauce. We didn't talk about baseball at all.

During the game, Wells and I read the cherries jubilee recipe between pitches. I'd give an ingredient, "one cup sugar," and he'd repeat, "one cup sugar." Then I'd call the pitch. I'd read another ingredient, "one pound sour cherries," and he'd repeat it and so on. We were copying an old national radio show routine that featured Kate Smith and Ted Collins.

It was late in the season, and I figured almost no one was listening to our broadcast, because the Angels were out of the race and the game came on so early in the morning in Southern California. However, when we returned home, my desk was piled high with mail. Most of the letters were from women who had written to tell me, "I really enjoyed your cherries jubilee recipe and the recipe for Yastrzemski's barbecue sauce. Maybe you'd like my datebread recipe."

Or recipe for lemon meringue pie. Or fruitcake. I could have made a cookbook out of all the recipes. Just shows you never know who's listening!

It proved again just how intimate baseball audiences are, particularly on radio, and how much they get to know you. This was especially true in those days when so few games were on television. A baseball announcer on radio has a connection with an audience that no one else does, touching a fan base that cares deeply about the team. I received more mail in one week with the Angels, even when they were buried in last place, than I get now in a whole year on network television.

∾

After my first four years as Angels broadcaster, KMPC decided to make a change in the announcing team, and it had a profound impact on my life. General manager Stan Spero and sports director Steve Bailey replaced Wells with former Dodgers pitcher Don Drysdale, then working as an announcer for the Texas Rangers. They helped Wells land a position doing sports segments for KFWB Radio (an all-news station), where he worked for many years.

Until the day he died, however, Wells thought I cost him his job, but I had nothing to do with it. As I said earlier, I thought we had a good relationship, despite his frustration with my hiring as the lead announcer. There was a lot to like about Don Wells, and I thought he was an outstanding announcer. But KMPC had a chance to hire a gifted young broadcaster who was a former star player, and Spero and Bailey took it.

Drysdale was a major reason why I lasted so long with the Angels. The dog days in baseball are real, particularly in August with a bad team. But there was never a dog day working with Don. Every day was a great day. He always made the day fun. He wouldn't let you get down. We worked together for six years, and we laughed for six years. I'd like to dedicate the next chapter to our partnership.

TIMEOUT

A Magic Moment

GENE AUTRY HAD A FABULOUSLY successful career as a movie star and entertainer, but that simple little Christmas song, "Rudolph the Red-Nosed Reindeer," made him more money than almost any of his enormous successes. Originally, he didn't even like the song. His first wife, Ina, did though, and she talked him into recording it.

One spring training, he invited all of the players, their wives and children, and the media to a barbecue around the pool at the Gene Autry Hotel in Palm Springs. The western singers, The Sons of the Pioneers, were there to entertain us, but as the evening progressed, the crowd begged Gene to sing a song, too. He was in his 60s then, and no longer had the buttery-smooth, golden voice of his youth. But he finally conceded and sang a song, then another, and finally, at the request of several big-eyed kids, he sang "Rudolph the Red-Nosed Reindeer." It was magic. As he sang, he got better and better. The hoarseness left his voice, and he couldn't have been more brilliant. He became younger before our spellbound eyes and ears.

It was one of those clear, beautiful March evenings in the desert, with the sky dripping with stars, and he knew we were all enraptured by the moment. Here's a man who was a legitimate superstar, and it was our rare privilege to be taken back in time to the halcyon years of "America's Favorite Singing Cowboy."

7

TANANA AND RYAN AND TWO DAYS OF CRYIN'

"If they get hit, it's their fault. Get outta the way. The inside part of the plate is mine, too."

—Don Drysdale

On the mound, Don Drysdale was as imposing as hell. He was six foot six, and his size and wicked delivery—particularly when his long right arm came by way of third base—made him one of the most feared pitchers of all time. His career total of 154 hit batters is a modern National League record.

The big right-hander won 209 games and compiled an outstanding 2.95 earned run average in his Hall of Fame career, before he retired at 33 with a shoulder injury. In 1968 he hurled six shutouts in a row on the way to a then-major league record 58 consecutive scoreless innings.

Off the field, however, he was as sweet as country honey. His laugh was as big as his sidearm breaking ball, and in the six years we shared the Angels' broadcast booth, he not only made a bad day a good day, but also saved my sanity. I took the games way too seriously. I just hated it when the Angels lost. I desperately wanted them to be like the Dodgers and win, because our audience would be bigger, the crowds would be larger, and the entire atmosphere would be more exciting.

I can hear him now, as if he were still sitting next to me.

"Professor, you're taking it too seriously," he said over and over. "Hey, if they don't care about winning, why the hell should you care so much?"

And yet, even in retirement, he was as competitive as anyone. The only time I ever saw him angry was during broadcasts when one of the Angels players, usually one of the pitchers, did something stupid. In particular, he would get incensed when a batter took away the inside corner from an Angels pitcher by crowding the plate, and the pitcher failed to respond by throwing inside, instead offering what would prove to be a fat pitch on the outside part of the plate.

"Damn it, the pitcher's got to make a living, too," he would growl. "A fastball, a foot inside, is not a sin. If they get hit, it's their fault. Get outta the way."

In looking back on his own career, he would never admit that he intentionally hit a batter, no matter what the statistics said.

"They hit themselves," he would cry. "They crowded the plate and stepped into an inside pitch and hit themselves. If you're going to step into the pitch, I refuse to be held accountable."

He used the expression "I've got to feed my family" when he discussed hitters, using the present tense as if he were still employed on the mound.

"You're taking money out of my pocket when you crowd home plate," he would say. "I can't let you do that. The inside part of the plate is mine, too."

He couldn't stand Frank Robinson, because Robbie would typically stand right on that inside corner. They never got along, which is not surprising. He drilled Robinson more than occasionally.

Drysdale also got mad when Angels pitchers lost their control. He'd turn off his microphone and bristle, "What is that bush leaguer doing? Back up the garbage truck and get the sumbitch out of here. He can't even throw strikes." Click. "All right, here's the windup and the pitch. A little outside. Ball three."

Although he was often accused of throwing a spitter, Don never admitted that, either. I came at him from every verbal angle, even trying to sneak my question by him when he'd had a couple of drinks, but his answer never varied.

I'd say, casually, "Don, how did you load up the ball on your spitter?"

He'd give me a generous grin and say, "Professor, you just had to get your fingers up on top of the seams and roll your wrist over, and the ball would come to the plate and dive. Rotating your wrist made it sink."

Then he'd demonstrate by throwing an imaginary pitch. There was no added substance, he said. That was his story and he was sticking to it.

He had a sense of humor that was as wicked as his pitching delivery. One year, they asked the two of us to participate in the ceremonial first pitch of the season at Anaheim Stadium. Drysdale was the pitcher, I was the batter, the Angels' Tom Egan was the catcher, and Gene Autry's guest, Casey Stengel, was the honorary umpire. The day before the ceremony, Don and I agreed that we would give the crowd an added thrill. He would throw the first pitch right at me, and, knowing it was coming, I would do a dramatic flop in the dirt.

I purposely wore white pants and white shoes, so I would be covered with dirt after tumbling out of the batter's box.

As I stood at the plate looking out at Don, I realized how frightening it must have been to face this big, powerful guy. At six foot six, he goes into that elaborate windup, kicks, turns that shoulder, now he's glaring at me, and here comes the ball! As soon as his arm buggy whipped forward, I went down like a sack of potatoes.

And he threw the ball right down the middle. I'd been sabotaged.

One of Don's best friends in baseball was Bob Uecker, the ex-catcher and dry-witted, self-deprecating announcer of the Milwaukee Brewers. When Uecker was breaking in as a rookie with the Milwaukee Braves, Drysdale welcomed him with a fastball in the ribs in an early spring training game.

Painfully making his way to first base, Uecker shouted, "Why are you hitting me? I'm no good. I can't hit you."

"Show me the bruise, and I'll autograph it for you," Drysdale yelled back.

Uecker got even many times over the years, once he discovered that Don was very fastidious, everything about him obsessively neat and clean. For example, his wardrobe was always dry-cleaning perfect, nary a wrinkle, and you could cut your fingers on the sharp crease in his slacks. The condition of his house, his car, and his yard was the same. He could not stand anything messy, dirty, or out of place.

So Uecker would drop by his house and purposely leave his handprint on a mirror, and out of the corner of his eye he'd see Drysdale right behind him with a handkerchief, wiping the mirror clean. Then he'd leave a print or water glass stain on the glass coffee table, and Don would quickly tidy that up. He'd miss the wastebasket with a crumpled piece of paper, and Don would pounce on it like a bunt in front of the mound. Uecker just delighted in driving him crazy, and I don't think Don ever realized it was all a game. You talk about a cleanup hitter. "Big D" was a cleanup pitcher.

He and Uecker were bad influences on me. When Don and I became a broadcast team in 1973, I wasn't much of a drinker. My limited income as a college professor had dictated that a cold bottle of beer was satisfying enough, not only for my thirst, but for my wallet. However, part of the normal postgame routine in baseball, particularly on the road, was winding down with a visit to one of the local watering holes, or in Uecker's words, going "to sprinkle the infield dirt."

What made those nights even more dangerous was Drysdale's generosity. If we went out to dinner, he insisted on paying for it. If we had drinks, he insisted on paying for them. You couldn't pay. You had to fight him to even split the cost. He always had a big wad of money wrapped in a rubber band, and every time he ordered, he ordered for everyone else at the table—even if you still had a drink in front of you. As 2:00 a.m. approached, with foam oozing out of every body orifice, I was often slumped behind five or six bottles of beer, most of them completely full.

Don would look at me and cackle, "Look at the professor. He's hiding behind a brown picket fence."

One night before Memorial Day, Uecker gave us a nighttime tour of Milwaukee, and we stayed out until 3:00 or 4:00 a.m. Bob and Don were not going to let me escape to the hotel. When I finally hit the bed, I knew I would pay for it in a few hours, and I did. When I awoke, I felt miserable. Even worse, we had a day game, and it was my turn to do the pregame interview. I was afraid to even breathe on anyone, so I decided that after what Uecker did to me, his punishment would be serving as my guest.

"We're here in Milwaukee on this Memorial Day," I said at the start of the interview, "and our guest is the former catching star, hah, hah, and current play-by-play announcer of the Milwaukee Brewers, Bob Uecker. Bob, I know you're an entrepreneur and always have a lot of irons in the fire. Would you share some of your current projects with us?"

"As you may know, Dick, I've started a national string of Uecker Passed Ball Schools, teaching kids how to commit passed balls. Thanks to my well-deserved reputation as a catcher, they're very popular."

He's saying all of this with a straight face, and I'm not laughing, I'm just letting him go.

"Because of the incredible response, we're starting to franchise these schools, and if you and Donnie are interested, we'd like to give you Southern California. We've got a winning formula. What we do is find a gravel pit and set up these high-powered guns that shoot baseballs at the Little Leaguers at up to 140 miles an hour. We teach them how to be creative in missing the ball.

"We have a grading system. There are extra points if you not only commit a passed ball, but let the ball hit the umpire. We have model umpires that we put behind the kids when we shoot the gun… "

At this point, although I'm not laughing out loud, tears are rolling down my cheeks. He went on for two or three more minutes, and then we broke for a commercial.

When we came back, I said, "We're back at County Stadium with Bob Uecker, who's discussing his highly successful passed ball schools. You can count me in as a franchise owner, and I'm sure Don will sign up, too. What else are you doing?"

"Well, I've been worrying about hockey," he said. "I'm trying to get more action in hockey. I've designed a crystal clear puck… looks just like ice. You drop the puck, and it doesn't matter who beats up whom, because no one knows where the puck is anyway. It should increase scoring, too, because the goalie won't know where the puck is either."

After he finished his monologue about hockey, I gave it away a little, offering, "You never know what to believe with Bob Uecker, but it's always fun to be with you."

Then I chuckled and said we'd be back with the play-by-play.

A few days later, owner Gene Autry joined the team for a series in Boston. When he saw me, the first thing he asked was, "Well, damn it, Dick, I was listening to your broadcast from Milwaukee, and was that damn Uecker serious?"

I guess we didn't sell the humor well enough—at least with my boss.

❧

If I had ever owned a major league franchise, my first move would have been to hire Drysdale as my manager. He would have been a fabulous skipper. He knew pitching, he knew how to have fun, and he would have been tough when he needed to be tough. In many ways baseball players are like little kids. As Roy Campanella said, "It's the little boy in you that makes you want to play." Players need the kind of discipline that they respect—and fear a little bit. Don would have jerked you by the jersey and shaken you up to demand your attention.

The Angels had eight managers from 1969 through 1978. Aside from Rigney, the most fascinating was Bobby Winkles, who was hired in 1973. Bringing in Winkles was a bold move by the club. He was a bright, enthusiastic college coach who had compiled an impressive 524-173 record and won three national championships at Arizona State with future major leaguers Reggie Jackson, Sal Bando, Rick Monday, and Lenny Randle. However, when he tried to lead the Angels the way he ran a collegiate team, it just didn't work. The hardened veterans wouldn't buy it. You sensed from day one that a certain portion of the ball club was fighting what he was trying to accomplish. The attitude seemed to be, "So fine me or bench me. We're already bad."

As an educator and former college coach myself, I was really pulling for Bobby. But I guess the lesson is a college coach can't stand up in front of some grizzled old veterans who aren't that educated but know baseball, and tell them how to play the game differently. Most of them looked at him and thought, "Hey, you never played big league ball. What do you know?" Winkles's formula was magic with college players, but it failed with the Angels. He was fired midway through his second season.

Winkles wasn't the only person who was frustrated by the Angels. Drysdale was often appalled at the lack of dedication by many of the players. Over and over he would complain, "Hurry in and out of the clubhouse. Hurry in and out of the game." It was an expression that he learned from Pee Wee Reese of the old Brooklyn Dodgers, meaning if you really want to last in baseball, you should get to the park early and be one of the last to leave. Don felt it was important not only to keep working on your skills, but also to spend time bonding with teammates. After a game, whether it was a good win or a tough loss, you should stick around and talk about what had just happened, building team chemistry, maybe figuring out a way for the club and for you to improve. In the old days, when teams traveled by train, players spent much more intimate time together. Now you can sit down on a jet airplane, plug in your earphones, and not even communicate with your teammate-seatmate the entire flight.

Although Drysdale and I had a special relationship away from the field, it was even better in the broadcast booth. Most baseball announcers do their scheduled innings alone, but we developed an open-mike system so that both of us could talk in the same inning. As the lead announcer, I called six innings (first, second, fifth, sixth, eighth, and ninth), and Don called three (third, fourth, and seventh), but we had toggle switches on our mikes that allowed each of us to go on the air whenever we wanted. We knew that going one on one we'd never beat Vin Scully, the broadcasting poet of the Dodgers, but we thought the two of us together would be reasonably competitive for the Southern California audience. No inning was sacred. I could pop into Don's innings, and he could jump into mine, and I thought our play-by-play and chemistry became natural and very rich. We were on the same page all the time.

Whenever our games were televised, Dave Niehaus, a third announcer, joined us and called some radio innings. We had excellent rapport with Dave, too, and he also had the freedom to make his comments in any inning.

Drysdale's analysis of the game was always excellent. If the game was close, he would really lock in on it and take the fan right down on the field. But he had an endless wealth of good stories for the slow moments, too. For a 200-game season, his well was always full. He didn't repeat stories, and each one seemed better than the last. If the game was lopsided, with no doubt about the outcome, we switched styles. We wandered from the action and had some fun with the broadcast; we tried to make it light. That 8-0 game in the third inning is liable to be a 19-1 game. The challenge is to get your audience to stick with you, so we found ways to supplement a bad product.

Many years after both of us had left the Angels, I was driving my car in Los Angeles, listening to Drysdale and Scully call a Dodgers game on the radio. Don was telling a humorous story and started to laugh. I found myself laughing out loud in the car with him, just like I used to do in the Angels' broadcast booth. He had a tremendous ability to reach through the radio, grab you, and make you want to join in on the fun. It was even better in person, and I got to live through it every day with him. I'm not exaggerating. I just never had a bad day when I worked with Don. He wouldn't let you.

His sudden death from a heart attack in Montreal in 1993, while on a Dodgers trip, was a terrible loss for everyone who knew him. He was only 56.

❧

Nothing in all of sports compares to spring training. Everyone is happy and optimistic. There's no pressure to win. Throw in the sunny weather in Florida and Arizona, while people in much of the rest of the country still battle winter, and you're a privileged member of baseball paradise.

In the 1960s and 1970s, the Angels "trained" in Palm Springs, primarily because Gene Autry owned two hotels where the players, officials, and media would stay. It was a four-week baseball Mardi Gras in this chic resort mecca: exhibition baseball in the desert sun until late afternoon and then at 5:30 p.m., an ongoing happy hour. They probably had limited interest in baseball, but the beautiful ladies of Los Angeles quickly migrated to the scene. The Angels may have been the only major league team in history that left spring training in worse physical shape than when they arrived.

Our radio and TV broadcasting accommodations at the Palm Springs ballpark were modest, to say the least. There was no booth; we simply sat on the roof of a little metal press box that perched on top of the stands behind home plate. We reached the roof by a side ladder. In the days before anyone worried about skin cancer, we often took our shirts off as we sat in the sunshine, competing for the spring's best suntan.

Weekend games in Palm Springs were on TV, and one of the orders from Autry was to make sure that the national anthem was played for the television audience, instead of missing it during a commercial break. Arrangements for the anthem were as humble as the accommodations. It was played on a scratchy old record by the public address announcer, who sat in the press box immediately below us. Because he couldn't hear us talking, we would cue him to play the anthem by stomping on the roof. After we banged on the roof, we'd say on the air, "And now, here is our national anthem." In the next couple of seconds, the PA announcer would notify the crowd, put the needle on the record, and the anthem would play.

One afternoon, about half an hour before game time, Drysdale, Uecker, and I were sitting on the roof telling baseball stories, each one crazier than the one before. Director John Polich from KTLA had joined us, and he was enjoying the stories as much as we were. After one story, we all began laughing hysterically. Polich, out of control, started stamping his feet. Of course, the guy below thought we were signaling him to play the anthem, so he did.

On the field, players were still taking infield practice when the national anthem started up, catching them all by surprise. Guys fell all over themselves trying to be patriotic as they skidded to a stop, dropped their gloves, took off their hats, and put them over their hearts. It wasn't exactly what Mr. Autry had in mind.

❧

In 1970 and 1971, the club had a talented but controversial player in outfielder Alex Johnson. He won the American League batting title in 1970, hitting .329, but he often loafed on the field and had a tempestuous relationship with just about everybody. He wouldn't run out ground balls—sometimes he would just stop—and if the ball got by him in the outfield, he would occasionally let somebody else chase it down. Ironically, the single that enabled him to win the batting title in 1970 was an infield hit that he hustled to beat out. We all thought if he ran like that every time he hit a ball, he'd bat .350 every year.

Because he was such a talented player, I was shocked in 1971 when the Angels announced in the middle of a road trip that Johnson had been sent home. In essence, the defending American League batting champion had been fired in the middle of the season. I had mixed feelings about Johnson's dismissal. Although he fought with other members of the media, he was cooperative with me, plus he was always good and generous with kids. Our next game was on television, and I felt, as risky as it was, I should go on the air and relate the other side of Johnson's personality. In my hotel room that morning, I wrote out my thoughts to help me crystallize them. It was a delicate situation.

Basically, I told the audience, "As you all know by now, Alex Johnson has been fired by the Angels. A lot of fans have booed him the last two years, and with good reason. Many writers have criticized him, and he deserved that, too. Because of his lack of hustle in running out ground balls and in playing the outfield, the team had every right to be upset with him. But before we write him off, I wanted to let you know that there was another side to his personality. I never saw him deny an autograph to a young person. He was wonderful with kids. Perhaps that's where his comfort level was. He didn't always show it, but I wanted you to know that there was also a good side to Alex Johnson."

When we returned to Los Angeles, I had a message that Gene Autry wanted to see me. I entered his office with considerable trepidation. I knew what it was about.

Gene looked me in the eye and said, "Dick, I've gotten several phone calls and letters saying that you took an anti-ball club stand in terms of Alex Johnson. I didn't hear your broadcast. What did you say?"

"Mr. Autry," I replied, "here's exactly what I said."

I went on to tell him that I had pointed out that Johnson deserved criticism for the things he had done, that I wasn't defending him, but that in fairness to the man there was a good side, too, and I felt the fans should know that.

When I finished, Autry said, "I've heard a lot of different versions of your remarks, but I wanted to hear it from you. That's exactly what I thought you'd say."

He believed me and that was the end of it.

With all of his brilliance, Autry could be absentminded. In particular, I'll never forget his speaking performance one year during spring training. The Palm Springs Chamber of Commerce annually held a luncheon at the Autry Hotel to kick off the new season, and Gene would be there, along with the manager, maybe a player or two, and the announcers. There was always a healthy turnout. As the emcee, I would give Gene a deserved flowery introduction and he always responded with something like, "Thank you very much. I didn't deserve that fine introduction, but I got the clap a few years ago, and I didn't deserve that either." Later, after some concerned coaching, he cleaned it up to, "I got the lumbago a few years ago, and I didn't deserve that either."

On one occasion, he fortified himself with a few drinks before he came to the microphone, and when he was introduced, he brought a big pile of papers with him. I don't know who wrote the speech, but this looked like a long one. He began his remarks by reading, "I think we'll have a fine ball club this year. With the addition of a good crop of rookies and the trades we made, I'm very optimistic."

He proceeded to run down the team, position by position, and kept turning pages over, and before you knew it, he had talked for 30 minutes. The audience was starting to squirm. As much as we loved Gene, we're all thinking, "Will this ever end?"

Then he turned another page over, and to our horror, he continued, "Thank you very much. I didn't deserve that fine introduction... "

He was starting all over again!

Halfway down the first page, he said, "I think we'll have a fine ball club this year. With the addition of a good crop of rookies... "

And Drysdale leaped to his feet and said, "How about a big hand for Gene Autry? Thank you very much, Gene."

Everyone applauded with great enthusiasm. Don saved us. Gene was going to read it all the way through one more time! And *we* didn't deserve *that*.

∽

There's no event in any sport that a play-by-play man can experience as dramatic as a no-hitter. The drama and tension keep increasing from the seventh inning on, and every pitch and every subtle movement by every player becomes so critically important. It all builds and builds with each pitch to the ultimate climax. The payoff is so enormous and so unlikely that the final out is major league ecstasy. When the Angels had Nolan Ryan, we felt that there was a legitimate chance for a no-hitter every time he pitched.

The records bear me out. In a Hall of Fame career that lasted 27 years and included 324 victories, Ryan hurled seven no-hitters and 12 one-hitters, both major league records. (He shares the record for one-hitters with Bob Feller.) In fact, he came close to pitching a dozen no-hitters, because he lost five of them in the ninth inning. He pitched four of his no-hitters for the Angels, and I called three of them. (I have called six in all, including one by the Angels' Clyde Wright and two by opposing pitchers.)

Ryan's 6-0 no-hitter against Detroit in 1973 was the most dominating game I've ever seen pitched. In the first seven innings, he was absolutely overpowering, striking out 16 batters with 100 mile-an-hour fastballs and hellacious curves. The broadcast booth in Detroit was close enough to the field that you could hear the velocity of his pitches as they smacked in the catcher's glove, as well as his powerful grunts as he delivered high hard ones. When the Angels scored five runs in the top of the eighth inning, the Tigers made several pitching changes. Ryan was on the bench for a long time, and his arm stiffened up. Although he finished without allowing a hit, he only struck out one more batter, finishing with 17—still the most ever in a no-hitter. If it weren't for that uncharacteristic big inning by the Angels, he would have fanned 20. Easily.

With two outs in the ninth inning, first baseman Norm Cash, who had already struck out twice, was the only batter standing between Ryan and his no-hitter. Earlier in the game, umpire Ron Luciano had examined Cash's bat for illegal cork filler. This time Cash, who obviously had a sense of humor, came to the plate with a piano leg. Luciano, perhaps caught up in the drama of the no-hitter, didn't notice.

"Aren't you going to check my bat?" Cash asked.

Luciano did a double take, then called time, and sent Cash back to the dugout to get a bat.

The first baseman laughed.

"What the hell difference does it make?" he said. "I'm not going to hit him anyway."

He didn't. With his regular bat, Cash popped out to shortstop, and Ryan had his second no-hitter of the season.

During that 1973 season, Ryan pitched for a team with a losing record that finished 15 games out of first place. Yet, besides the two no-hitters, he had a 21-16 mark, threw 26 complete games (second in the league), worked 326 innings (third), and compiled a 2.87 earned run average (fourth). He also struck out 383 batters, which is still the major league record. *But he didn't win the Cy Young Award.* He finished second to the Orioles' Jim Palmer. It was criminal.

Palmer is also a member of the Hall of Fame, and he had an outstanding season in 1973 (a 22-9 record, 19 complete games, a league-leading 2.40 ERA, 296 innings pitched, but only 158 strikeouts). However, unlike Ryan, he was pitching for a division champion; Palmer was of Cy Young quality, but not that season. On a good team, Ryan would have won 27 or 28 games. That Cy Young Award should have been Ryan's. It was his best chance. Despite a Hall of Fame career, Ryan never won the prestigious award.

In fact, Ryan was the poster boy for a problem that still exists—the East Coast bias. Drysdale and I talked about it many times during the broadcasts of Ryan's games. With so many night games and a three-hour time difference between West and East, the player in the West is at a considerable disadvantage. Although the feats for players in the East are well chronicled across the country, night games in the West most often don't make Eastern and Midwestern newspapers until a day later, if at all. For a West Coast athlete to be named Player of the Year in any sport, he's got to be considerably better than the guy with comparable statistics, playing in the East. Plainly, he doesn't get the same publicity. Time zones kill.

As a superstar, Nolan Ryan was all you'd want. He was articulate and cooperative. If you wanted him for an interview, he made himself available. I know my oldest son, Andrew, will never forget him. In spring training one year, I introduced Andy, who was about Little League age, to Ryan in the locker room, and when the pitcher noticed Andy's ragged glove, he reached into his locker, pulled out a brand new one, and handed to him.

"You've got a nice glove, but it's got a little wear and tear on it," Ryan said. "Perhaps you'd like a new one. Try this one on. Why don't you take it?"

Talk about a thrill for a kid.

My young children, Andy, Jennifer, and Alex, born in 1972, often went to Angels games with me, sitting in the row right behind us in the broadcast booth. I felt guilty because the baseball season was so long, and I was gone so often that I was denied the normal opportunity to spend time with my young children. This was a way to be together. We could talk driving to and from the game, and they could enjoy the experience of being at the game. In fact, all three, now in their 30s and 40s, say many of their fondest memories of growing up are going to Angels games. The only rule was they couldn't talk during the broadcast. I gave them money for food and showed them where the bathroom was, and they were all set. They even made a few road trips.

In 1975, Andy was in the booth when Ryan threw a 1-0 no-hitter against the Orioles. He kept score, and I got Nolan to sign the scorecard. Andy is nearly 40 now, and that framed box score is still hanging on his wall.

From 1971 to 1977, during seven consecutive losing seasons by the Angels, Ryan and his left-handed teammate, Frank Tanana, were responsible for most of the club's few bright moments. The free-spirited Tanana, who was six years younger than Ryan, won 240 games in a 21-year career with six teams. He was blessed with pin-point control and mountains of moxie. Early in his career, Tanana was a strikeout pitcher, but after he hurt his arm in the late 1970s, he adjusted and was able to keep winning with an 80 mile-an-hour fast-ball and a mixture of off-speed stuff. His fastball became his change of pace. It was tough for batters to read his pitches.

Unlike today, when complete games are almost extinct, both pitchers usually finished what they started—and that was a good thing. Angels relief pitching was so erratic that one year sportswriter Dick Miller of the former *Los Angeles Herald-Examiner* nicknamed the bullpen the "Arson Squad," because they set fires, instead of put-ting them out. The Angels' lack of pitching depth reminded us of that famous jingle from the late 1940s when the Boston Braves' war cry was "Spahn and Sain and pray for rain." In Anaheim, it was "Tanana and Ryan and two days of cryin'."

During that era, my favorite opposing player was Reggie Jackson, who played for Oakland, Baltimore, and the Yankees, before coming to the Angels as a free agent several years after I left the club. Some stars want to be left alone, but Jackson, a future Hall of Famer, was just the opposite. He couldn't wait to talk to us, and that was our good fortune. He always crushed the Angels, so there was plenty to talk about. He was a terrific interview and was entertaining on or away from the microphone. He did impersonations of other players that would have been a hit on *Saturday Night Live*.

Asked once why he didn't like to hit against Ryan, when, after all, he was a fastball hitter and Ryan was a fastball pitcher, Reggie said, "I like ice cream, too, but I don't want it for every meal."

❧

One morning in late 1973—about halfway through my 10 years in the Angels' broadcast booth—I left our house in the San Fernando Valley to run an errand. Our youngest child, Alex, was just a year and a half old, and we needed diapers. When I pulled back in the drive-way, my wife, Jeri, was standing in front of the house. She had been testy and distant lately, and, before I'd left, we'd had an argument. As I got out of the car, she snapped at me again.

"What in the world is wrong with you anyway?" I asked.

She blurted out, "I don't love you anymore."

Boom. Just like that.

It was totally unexpected, but maybe I should have seen it coming. More than a year earlier, she had left in a huff from the Olympics in Munich, flying back to America alone, while I continued to do daily essays. KMPC had sent me to Germany in 1972 to do radio features for Autry's Golden West Network, a trip Jeri thought was going to be a meaningful experience that we would enjoy together. However, I was assigned three features a day, and there was little time to have fun. All I did was work, and she said, the hell with it, I'm going home, and she did.

Years later, Jeri told me that in the two years before she said the words "I don't love you anymore," she felt it. It took her two years to finally verbalize it.

My initial reaction was to try to do everything I could to win her back. Can I bring you flowers? Can I do the dishes? Can I go shopping? What else can I do for you? But the harder I tried, the farther I pushed her away, and we argued more and more. After the confrontation in the driveway, we lived together another six or seven months, until she said finally, "This isn't good for the kids. You've got to get out of here."

To ease me out of the house, she found a place for me to relocate—a little apartment near the San Diego Freeway—and then filed for divorce. To be dismissed from a relationship, not expecting it and not wanting it, was the most painful time of my life. After my parents went through their divorce, it was the last thing I ever thought would happen to me—or wanted to happen to me. Ironically, my own insecurities and fears may have contributed to it. Certainly, in working all the time, I repeated my father's fate.

If it takes the person who breaks up the marriage two years to realize they don't love you anymore, it takes you at least that long to get over it. At the beginning, it was god-awful. A while after I moved out, Jeri moved her boyfriend, an actor she met in a theater group, into the house. Meanwhile, I moved to a larger apartment complex, where I would walk around with my head down, hoping no one would recognize me. Of course, they did.

"Hey, Dick Enberg," other residents would call out, "what are you doing here?"

Indignity.

Coming to grips with your divorce is recognizing and accepting your feelings, your pain, and your anger. I poured out my anguish to Stan Charnofsky, my old baseball coaching associate back at San Fernando Valley State. He was now a psychologist, counseling couples with marital difficulties. Besides his knowledge, I really appreciated his warmth, caring, and understanding.

Imagine my astonishment a year later when the situation reversed itself, and Stan came to me for support after his own wife told him, "I don't love you anymore." I had assumed he was exempt from this mountain of pain, but he suffered under the same despair. I know now that no one is immune. Stan and I spent many conversations sharing our heartache and even collaborated on a book for men going through divorce. Although I later decided to leave the project, Stan did publish an excellent book on the topic, and I wrote the introduction.

In this time of self-pity and self-doubt, my work became my therapy. It was the one thing that loved me back at a time when I needed plenty of love. I was doing 200 baseball games, 20 Rams games, maybe 25 UCLA games a year—the constant work was my escape. Needless to say, announcing with Drysdale, who could get a laugh out of a zombie, was healing for me, too.

But there were many dark days. After calling an Angels game one night, I sat in the radio booth feeling totally beaten. While announcing the games, I was so depressed I wasn't feeling them. They weren't getting to my soul. I was numb. It was just mouth to brain, brain to mouth: "Ball one, ball two, two-and-oh." I felt like I was doing a terrible job and decided to visit Gene Autry as soon as possible. He knew about my divorce.

A few days later, I sat down in his office.

"Mr. Autry," I said, "I came to apologize for my work. I know I'm not operating at my best. I'm going through a real tough time and just want you to know that I'm going to get through this. I can't get any worse. I'm only going to get better, so please be patient with me."

"Well, damn it, Dick," he said, "I was gonna call you in myself, because I know what you're going through right now. I know how upset you are and how painful it is, and I think you're doin' a *hell* of a job."

He just reversed my negative feelings and promoted the positive. That's why I loved Gene Autry. He was like a second father.

During my first Christmas season out of the house, I was deeply depressed and decided to visit Childrens Hospital in Los Angeles. Perhaps by bringing some Christmas cheer to sick and injured children, I could bring some to myself. I gathered some new baseballs, caps, T-shirts, and other souvenirs that I had received from the Rams and Angels over the years and decided they'd be welcome gifts for the children. I called the hospital and asked if I could play Santa Claus, and they warmly invited me to come in. I visited during the day on Christmas Eve, distributing my items to the kids. Most of them were having a tough time, and, seeing their sadness, I soon forgot about myself. Everyone seemed very appreciative, including many of the parents.

A nurse escorted me to the various rooms, including one ward accommodating four children. I gave the gifts to the first three kids, and then we went to the fourth, a girl of about 10, who was lying with her back to us.

The nurse said, "Maria, this is Mr. Enberg, and he's brought some gifts from the Angels and Rams for all the children. He's got a special one for you."

She didn't turn toward us, so I said, "Merry Christmas, Maria," but she continued staring at the wall. I was starting to feel uncomfortable, imposing on this child who obviously didn't want me there. But the nurse kept pushing.

"I think you'd like this T-shirt, Maria. It's a little big, but it's really nice and you can wear it as a nightshirt."

She still didn't respond.

The nurse continued, "Maria, aren't you going to turn and say thank you to Mr. Enberg?"

Reluctantly, agonizingly slowly, she turned and looked at me with these big, brown, beautiful, sad eyes, and said, "Thank you." Then she quickly turned away.

I couldn't wait to get out of the room. It was breaking my heart. My intention was to do something nice, and she didn't want me there. I shouldn't have bothered her. When we got out in the hall, I told the nurse, "I feel terrible."

"What? You feel terrible. Why?"

After I explained my feelings, the nurse said to me, "Do you realize what just happened? She hasn't spoken to anyone in weeks, and she just said thank you to you."

I almost went to my knees. I'll never forget Maria.

Jeri and I were formally divorced in 1975, but it wasn't until I bought a house for myself later that year that I began to feel like I was beginning to mend emotionally. I was buying my own furniture, decorating, cooking for myself, and finally I felt like I was in a real home again. I was beginning to rebuild my confidence. Adults eventually recover.

But the true ugliness of divorce is measured in what we do to our children. We leave indelible burns on them. It angers me when I hear people say, "We got a divorce because of the kids." That's B.S. They got a divorce for themselves.

Children are immensely fragile, psychologically. When they love their mother and father, they can't understand why they don't love each other. "I love my dad and I love my mom," children reason. "Why don't they love each other? It must be my fault. Maybe I'm the problem because they had to discipline me so many times."

I applaud couples whose love has waned, but who hang together as a family until the kids are adults. The children still don't like the breakup, but at least they're mature enough to understand it. I'm not saying it's right for everybody, and there might come a point when parents are fighting so much that it becomes destructive, but it isn't always that bad. It's harder on the kids when you're apart. For kids, divorce is so damn destructive. It's impossible to measure the emotional wounds that it leaves.

When I was asked to leave, my children were only 12, nine, and two. Regrettably, the disruption of the divorce and the subsequent turmoil have had a lifelong negative impact on them.

TIMEOUT

Tears of Joy

IN 2002, WHEN THE ANGELS finally ended 42 years of frustration and heartbreak by winning their first pennant and earning a World Series berth under manager Mike Scioscia, I was on an airplane, flying home from Tampa after calling an NFL game.

The pilot interrupted the flight to announce the day's football scores and then said, "We just received word that the Angels have beaten Minnesota to clinch the American League pennant. The Anaheim Angels are in the World Series."

When he said that, I was jolted by my reaction. Although I had not been associated with the team for many years, I burst into tears. The announcement stirred memories of all the bad years and the long road trips and the good guys and the bad guys and Drysdale and Autry, and it all came boiling to the surface. I couldn't believe how much I still cared.

The woman sitting next to me didn't know what was wrong. When I started crying, she must have thought the plane was going to crash. She took out a rosary and started praying.

I really believe that for those of us who love sports and get passionate about a team, it's once a fan, always a fan. Grandpas care as much as little kids. Two weeks later, when the Angels rallied to tie the World Series with the Giants at three games apiece with an improbable 6-5 win in the sixth game, I was in my hotel room in Kansas City, preparing for another NFL game. The entire wing of the hotel's fifth floor could hear my cheers.

After the Angels defeated the Giants in the seventh game to win the World Series, I spoke at their victory celebration in Anaheim. I told the crowd that those of us who had lived through the dog days, the days of Tanana and Ryan and two days of cryin', were no less excited—and maybe more excited—than the younger people who had cheered their hearts out for them in 2002. How great it was that we all shared the long-awaited payoff now. My only sadness was that Gene Autry, who died in 1998, wasn't there to sing along with us.

8

NO ONE WANTED TO BE THE STAR

"Now that you're back, we want you to know that you're in charge of the microphone again."

—Billy Packer

In 1975, the year of my divorce, I began another relationship that would last for 25 years. NBC inaugurated a college basketball Game of the Week package and hired me to announce the games. Although my entrée to NBC was college basketball—thanks to my connection with John Wooden and UCLA—in the next quarter century, the network sent me everywhere but Antarctica as I also called baseball, NBA basketball, boxing, college and pro football, figure skating, golf, gymnastics, horse racing, tennis, track and field, and the Olympics. It was a busy, fulfilling, and rewarding two and a half decades.

The flexibility of Gene Autry's Golden West Broadcasting enabled me to continue announcing Rams and Angels games in my first two years at NBC, before my second contract in late 1977 increased my network responsibilities and made that dual allegiance impossible, except for one last hurrah with the Angels in 1978.

My very first NBC basketball telecast in November 1975 was a memorable one. Bobby Knight's top-ranked Indiana team, which probably should have won the national title the previous spring, was ready and raring for the season opener with second-ranked UCLA, the defending national champion. The Hoosiers demolished the Bruins and new coach Gene Bartow 84-64 on a neutral court in St. Louis.

UCLA had won the 1975 crown, the last of John Wooden's 10 championships, two days after the Hall of Fame coach announced his retirement. Indiana, which had begun the same season 31-0, lost by two points to Kentucky in the regional final, playing without All-America forward Scott May, who suffered a broken arm in the final game of the regular season. May returned in perfect health the next fall, and, beginning with the convincing victory over UCLA, the Hoosiers went 32-0, winning the 1976 national championship. It's the last perfect record in college basketball.

However, there's another reason why my debut at the Indiana-UCLA game stands out. Years later, I discovered that NBC executives

Chet Simmons and Scotty Connal were watching the broadcast in NBC's control room at 30 Rockefeller Plaza in New York.

Halfway through the game, one of them turned to the other and said with concern, "Do you think he's any good?"

Ken Aagard, a longtime broadcasting friend, working for NBC at the time, was sitting behind them in the control room and overheard the question.

"I had to put my hand over my mouth," Aagard told me later. "I thought, 'Oh, my gosh, what a thing to ask after they'd already hired you!'"

If I had known there was any employer doubt about my ability, I would have broken out in a courtside pool of cold sweat. Aagard never told me the answer to the question, but I guess it was moderately positive, because they allowed me to return the next week.

⁐

When Simmons, the future president of NBC Sports, hired me to do college basketball, he first suggested that I call the games without a color man.

"You worked the UCLA games alone," he said. "You didn't need a color man then. Why do you need one now?"

I took it as a compliment, but I had to be honest with him.

"I'll be glad to do the games alone if you'll guarantee me that they'll all be 81-80," I said, "but I want a partner to help me through the bad games. Don't isolate me. When the margin is 20 or 30 points, two announcers can have a conversation, perhaps have a little fun, and keep the audience interested and engaged."

Then I added, "By the way, if you decide to hire a commentator, I recommend former coach Billy Packer. I've worked with him only once, but he was polished and well prepared. I think he's terrific."

Packer had done commentary on several NCAA Tournament games for NBC the previous two seasons, and Simmons was familiar with him. My recommendation was an added factor in the decision to hire Billy for the new Game of the Week package.

An All-Atlantic Coast Conference guard at Wake Forest in the early 1960s, Packer later served as an assistant coach at his alma mater. He broke into broadcasting in 1972, and we worked together

Oh My! *Memories*

Batter up, age two. Do you think there was any chance I wouldn't love baseball?

San Fernando Valley, 1944. Having gone barefoot all summer, I thought nothing of attending fourth grade without shoes.

Virginia, Minnesota, 1946. The Enberg clan gathers for a family reunion. My parents, Arnie and Belle, are on the far right behind my brother, Dennis (on the end), and me. Third from the left is my "second mother," Aunt Beatrice, with her two children. Next to her are Grandpa and Grandma Enberg, who immigrated from Finland.

Here's the backyard of our farm in Armada, Michigan. Our sauna is on the left (the brown building), and our two-hole outhouse is behind it. In the foreground are beehives, from which we extracted clover and buckwheat honey.

At 13, I spent weekends working at the Enberg fruit stand on our farm in Michigan. My trusty radio—to listen to sports events—was by my left side. We grew 20 varieties of apples, and apples that weren't sold were turned into our famous cider.

This fierce-looking group features the seven seniors on the 1951 Armada High School football team. Included are two spunky 140-pounders—right guard Dave Dunham and quarterback Dick Enberg (No. 30).

The IU Sports Network made its debut in 1957 with future CBS White House correspondent Phil Jones (center) and me behind the microphone. I called Indiana football and basketball for four years.

In December 1957, Jack "Suds" Bailey and I talked our way through the press gate at the NFL Championship Game and later conned our way into the victorious Detroit Lions' locker room. We posed as two reporters from imaginary radio station WCEN in Chillicothe, Ohio.

Check out the new assistant baseball coach at San Fernando Valley State College (now Cal State, Northridge) in 1962. I taught four years and coached three at Valley State.

In my wonderful life, I've rubbed shoulders with many special people. Other than my father, John Wooden is the greatest man I've ever known.

After UCLA clinched the conference basketball title in 1970, I kept my promise and sang "Raindrops Keep Falling on My Head" in front of a packed house at Pauley Pavilion. It was a memorable moment! While I sang, the UCLA students responded by opening their umbrellas.

Leo Durocher, one of my first baseball pregame show guests, joined three Angels stars for this photo. Next to me, from the left, are pitcher Frank Tanana, Durocher, pitcher Nolan Ryan, and outfielder Joe Rudi.

Oh My! That's Hall of Famer Joe DiMaggio in an Oakland A's uniform when he served as the team's batting instructor in 1968-1969.

My oldest daughter, Jennifer, and I joined "America's Favorite Singing Cowboy," Gene Autry, at Anaheim Stadium.

Bob Uecker (far left), Don Drysdale, and I shared a lot of laughs in the 1970s. As announcers, Drysdale and I worked together on Angels broadcasts for six years.

Drysdale and I participated in the ceremonial first pitch of the season at Anaheim Stadium one year when he pulled a fast one. We agreed he would throw the ball at me, and I would flop in the dirt to give the crowd a thrill. Well, I went down, but he threw the ball right down the middle!

Every time Hall of Famer Nolan Ryan took the mound for the Angels, I felt he had a legitimate chance for a no-hitter.

Al McGuire (far left), Billy Packer, and I worked our first national championship basketball game as a threesome in 1978 when Kentucky beat Duke.

Dick "The best Judge" Coach Al

Beautiful family!

Herb Kohl (far left), now a U.S. senator from Wisconsin, annually hosted McGuire (center) and a group of his friends on his Wyoming ranch. It was there one day that we created a fictitious university, Wyoming State. Here, the Wyoming State board of trustees, including me, discusses the homecoming game with the Idaho School of Taxidermy.

My dad, Arnie, cut a dashing figure in his first and only appearance in a tuxedo at the 1980 banquet for presentation of the John Wooden Award.

My wife, Barbara, and I have been happily married for more than 20 years. As you can see, this old farm boy has excellent taste.

Helsinki, 1983. It took some creative camera work to block our lower torsos when we visited a sauna naked for an interview during the World Track and Field Championships.

I interviewed Warren Beatty, as Rams quarterback Joe Pendleton, in the 1978 movie _Heaven Can Wait_, which was nominated for nine Academy Awards. Do you really think I could have been bigger than Marlon Brando?

Baffle was one of several game shows that I hosted more than 30 years ago. This particular week's celebrity guests were Jo Anne Worley and Peter Marshall.

Many of the biggest sports stars in history appeared on *Sports Challenge*, a syndicated game show that I hosted in the 1970s. My guests, from the left, are Jackie Robinson, Joe DiMaggio, Duke Snider, and Carl Erskine.

Analyst Merlin Olsen and I spent many happy Sundays announcing
NFL football games at NBC with producer Larry Cirillo (far left) and director
Ted Nathanson (far right).

Olsen and I were the biggest turkeys in the pen when we filmed this
Thanksgiving promo for NBC about 20 years ago. Merlin and I called
NFL football at NBC for 11 years.

In my three years in the booth with Bill Walsh, I had the privilege of working with a fascinating Hall of Fame coach.

Our Wimbledon broadcast crew gathered for a team photo before the championship. From left to right are John McEnroe, Bud Collins, and Tracy Austin. Covering Wimbledon is two weeks of hard work, but there is always time for a few cheers.

In just my second broadcast as NBC's golf host, I interviewed Presidents George H.W. Bush (far left), Bill Clinton, and Gerald Ford at the Bob Hope Chrysler Classic. Hope is on my left, next to Ford.

For about a decade, I was the host and anchor of the Breeders' Cup on NBC, working with Tom Hammond (far right) who succeeded me as host. This classic event has been held at many of the nation's greatest racetracks, including under the twin spires of Churchill Downs.

The Angels were in Boston, and Ted Williams was in town to support his favorite children's charity, the Jimmy Fund. It gave me this opportunity for a clubhouse interview. Years later, I still wonder at my good fortune. Williams, who was my boyhood idol, later became my friend.

for the first time on a UCLA-Maryland game in 1974 before I came to NBC. As an old teacher rating my broadcast partners, the grade is based on what they can bring to the broadcast that I don't already know. I was stunned with Billy's insights. "He's saying things I've never heard in a basketball broadcast," I thought. "This guy is an 'A' student!"

Packer and I worked together for six years (1976-1981) until he left for CBS before the 1982 season, after NBC lost the contract rights for the NCAA Tournament. He's still CBS's No. 1 commentator. In our last four years together, we were joined by Al McGuire, who coached Marquette to the 1977 national championship and then reinvented himself as a broadcaster. With Packer and McGuire, I was fortunate to become part of one of the most celebrated announcing teams in sports history, although it surprises fans that our threesome was together for only four years (1978-1981).

We had great chemistry because no one wanted to be the star. That isn't Billy's nature. Nor is it mine. No question, Al *was* the star. He was the headliner. This handsome, candid character, fresh from winning the national championship, was the one writers wrote about, but it didn't affect him in his new role.

In Billy's words, "Al was the star without the ego of being a star." In our years together, Al never thought he was very good on the air. He never felt secure. With his fractured English, he was rough and unpolished.

Al spent very little time preparing. He just went on the air and reacted to the game. He had earned a reputation as a brilliant bench coach, and he reacted to the TV action just like a coach. Once the game started, he knew how it operated, when to call a timeout, when to get after the officials, why a game was being won or lost, and, of course, he had a wealth of stories and unique expressions. Big centers were "aircraft carriers." A player with added style was "French pastry." A weak opponent was "a cupcake." A disaster for a team was "Dunkirk." University administrators were "memos and pipes."

"In a bad game, Al was invaluable, because he would entertain the audience," Billy said years later. "Give him the microphone and let him run. I always thought the 1979 NCAA semifinal game, when Michigan State routed Penn [101-67], was one of our best broadcasts, although all Enberg ever said was 'Timeout, Pennsylvania.' The game was one-sided early, and there was no way to analyze it anymore, but Al kept the audience amused all the way.

"As we got to know each other better, he and I realized what the other person's strengths were, and we were able to work off each other. We didn't plan what we did. It just worked. We had excellent teamwork."

Fans often thought Billy and Al didn't like each other, because they often disagreed. One would say black. The other would say white. Billy would suggest zone. Al would argue man-to-man. The truth of the matter is they loved to disagree, but it wouldn't have worked on national television if they didn't truly like each other.

When Al first joined us at the start of the 1978 season, NBC didn't trust him, because he was green and crazily unpredictable. The network also felt a three-man team would never work for basketball, so they banned him from sitting with Billy and me at courtside. For the first few weeks of the Game of the Week package, they put him in a locker room or an unused bathroom somewhere else in the arena. He watched the game on a TV monitor, and if he wanted to make a comment, he pressed a buzzer that simultaneously signaled the director, as well as Billy and me. Then he appeared in a little box up in the corner of the TV screen and offered his analysis, which, by the time all the connections were made, was too late. After that, he disappeared from the screen like a ghost.

There was a bigger problem. When he was away from the court, the TV rookie lost interest in the game. He might wind up talking to the janitor, instead of the TV audience.

It was Billy who finally told NBC, "You've got the best bench coach in basketball sitting in a locker room trying to watch it on TV. That's absolutely insane. He can't even see the whole court. Get him down on the floor with us."

Eventually, they did.

When he first escaped from his locker room, Al wasn't sitting next to me, which I thought was another mistake. So I suggested that our communication would be enhanced if he was positioned between Billy and me, and that's how we did the games for the next four years.

There's an interesting postscript to this saga, which illustrates how much of an operator Al was. At the end of our first season, he sent NBC a bill for double the salary they had agreed to pay him, reasoning that he did twice the work after he was moved to courtside.

After some negotiating, the network reluctantly paid him what he demanded. The genius, McGuire, always on the attack.

"Al never expected to get paid double," Billy told me, "but once NBC said they were sending an executive out to see him, he knew he had the advantage. He wouldn't let the poor guy come to his house, but met him at the airport. Then he walked the guy right down to the coffee shop, where everyone kept interrupting them and saying, 'Coach McGuire, it's great to see you. Good luck next season.' He liked putting people in his own environment, because it made them so uncomfortable that it gave him the upper hand. He was the smartest guy I've ever seen at that. As he always said, 'A genius in a fool's house *is* the fool.'

"After they talked, Al put the NBC guy right back on the plane. The executive went back and told his boss that Coach McGuire was really upset about the money and wouldn't budge. Al was smiling all the way home."

Before Al doubled his salary, we worked our first national championship game as a threesome when Kentucky beat Duke in the Checkerdome in St. Louis in 1978. Because it was our first title game, I was stage-fright nervous, and, as the consolation game between Arkansas and Notre Dame tipped off, I wandered through the bowels of the Checkerdome, looking for an empty room to review my notes again. I found a quiet spot and sat down to study. As I did, I looked over in a darkened corner, and there was Al dozing on a couch. That's Al. Biggest game of the season, and he's taking a snooze.

Al eventually came to life. Nervously making small talk, I asked him if he had ever read the book, *The Little Prince*, which I was reading at the time. It's a beautiful little book about caring and loving and responsibility. Although he was a street-smart genius, Al always claimed he could only read and write at a seventh-grade level, yet he knew all the rich and sensitive details of the book. Here we were about to do a national telecast of the finals, our first one, and, for 15 minutes, we're lost in a conversation about Antoine de Saint-Exupery's *The Little Prince*. It was a wonderful moment, a testimony to the breadth of knowledge Al had. He always knew just a little bit more than you thought.

Of course, there were other times when his lack of knowledge stunned me. In late January 1980 we were scheduled to broadcast an Ohio State-Virginia game in Columbus. The three of us were there the night before to watch the Buckeyes play Wisconsin. Al showed up with a briefcase, rare for him, and out of it he pulled a manila folder. Scribbled on the folder was VAGINA. Billy and I did a double take.

"What's that all about, Al?" we said. "You going to a gynecologist?"

"Whaddya mean?" he sputtered in his New York accent. "VAH-GIN-YA. We got 'em on Saturday."

❦

In 50 years of broadcasting, I've been incredibly fortunate, never missing a game because of illness. I should have, though, early in the 1979 NCAA Tournament when, despite serious laryngitis, I called four games in two days. Early in the tournament in those days, we'd do a doubleheader on Saturday and then fly to another site for another two games on Sunday.

I had been fighting a nagging cold all week, and, as we worked the two games in Providence, Rhode Island, on Saturday, my voice grew weaker and weaker. By the end of the second game, I was reduced to a whisper. Al and I then flew to Murfreesboro, Tennessee, for Sunday's games. (Billy had an assignment at another site that weekend.) I refused to talk to anyone on the plane and didn't utter a peep to anyone in the hotel. All I did was gargle and suck strong lozenges, trying to protect what little was left of my voice.

Awakening the next morning, I looked in the mirror, tried a few words and a scratchy, squawky, fingernails-against-the-blackboard sound came out. I decided I wouldn't try anymore, convincing myself that at least there was something there. We arrived at the arena as usual almost two hours before broadcast time. My voice had loosened up a little, but it was still raspy and rough. During the game, each time we went to a commercial, my throat would tighten, and when I resumed the play-by-play, it was down to a guttural croak, before loosening just enough to continue. Somehow, I made it through the first game as Michigan State breezed past Lamar.

Now we began the second game, Tennessee versus Notre Dame. Sounding like something between a man and a toad, I managed the first half. Now, however, it was really painful. Not only did my throat hurt me, it hurt me to hear myself. I'm sure the audience was saying,

"This guy sounds awful. He's making me clear *my* throat. Get him off the air!"

As we came back from halftime, my voice was dead. I could barely create a sound with an entire half ahead. When we reached the first commercial, I knew I was finished.

Turning to Al, I whispered, "Coach, I can't go any longer. You have to take over. Here's what I'll do. I know you don't know all the players, but I'll assist you by pointing them out on my spotting boards, and I'll underline any statistics that are important. I'll be right here next to you."

With total insensitivity, Al said without a blink, "Dicksie, if you're goin', I'm goin'."

That was all he said. I did the rest of the game.

He was too smart. He was really saying, "You think I'm going to try something I can't do on national television? I'd rather watch *you* die on television. *I'm* not going to die, too." Typical Al. The Fox.

That 1979 season was the year that Michigan State, with Magic Johnson, defeated unbeaten Indiana State and Larry Bird in the championship game. As the season built to its climax and interest in college basketball continued to grow, I remember Al saying, "I can't believe how big the game has become. College basketball is big, big, big." Knowing Al, he was also thinking, "I wish it had been that big when I was coaching. I would have parlayed some major money, money, money out of all this."

Although television ratings for Michigan State-Indiana State are still the highest ever for any college basketball game, it wasn't a great game. Michigan State, the superior team, led throughout and won 75-64.

I was more impressed with 19-year-old Magic Johnson a couple weeks earlier, on the day I lost my voice. When Michigan State's 31-point victory over Lamar had ended, producers asked me to line up Magic and his talented teammate, forward Greg Kelser, for a postgame interview. I brought them to the end of the court, while the network returned to the studio to update other tournament scores. Through my earplug, the producer kept telling me, "Hold them there. Hold them there." Instead of coming back to us after the scoreboard segment, however, NBC switched to another region where a game had reached overtime. Meanwhile, Johnson and Kelser stood patiently with me at courtside, while the network continued to order, "Hold them there."

And we held them—sweaty, but cooling off—for 20 minutes until finally the producer said, "We're not going to need them at all." That's television.

So, taking off my earpiece and turning to Johnson and Kelser, I apologized, "New York says there's no time for the interview. I'm really sorry."

Most athletes would have been totally upset. But the teenager, Magic, turned to me and flashed one of those iridescent smiles of his and said, "Hey, man, that's okay. We'll get you next time, won't we? We'll be back."

He was nice to the point of being naïve. But that's also why he's Magic. Even then, he understood the situation and rolled with the punches, an important quality in life and sports. Knowing that, is there any surprise that he has handled the numbing reality of being HIV-positive as well as he has? If you had to pick someone, God forbid, to be infected because he would inspire and motivate the rest of us to find a cure, who better than Magic? It's like someone said, "That's the guy. Choose him. He'll do something about it. He'll be an inspiration for a cure." And he has been.

In early 1992, 13 years after I first met Magic and less than three months after he had shocked the nation by announcing he had the HIV virus, he consented to be interviewed in depth about his health and future plans. At the time, I was in my second year as NBC's play-by-play announcer for NBA games.

As we taped the interview, to be edited and shown later, Magic responded openly, smiling and incredibly upbeat. If it wasn't for knowing of his infectious joy for life, I would have thought it was an act. However, halfway through the 40-minute session it suddenly struck me that Magic Johnson soon wouldn't be sitting in that chair… that testing HIV-positive was a ticking time bomb, an early guaranteed death sentence. It led me to ask a question I hadn't planned.

As I looked into his face, still filled with that expression of boyish wonder, I said, "Magic, I'm at an age, 57, where I'm counting the good years left. We're all mortal, no matter how often we may deny that mortality. How about you? Have you figured how many good years you have left?"

At the time, he was only 32.

His response, which seemed overly optimistic, was "12 to 15 years." When the interview was over, Magic smiled again and offered a final positive comment. We reached out and touched each other, and I whispered, "I love ya." My producers, cameramen, and the sound technician were all silent. They told me later they were afraid to look up for fear they'd all start crying.

Another 13 years have gone by, and, thank God, Magic Johnson's health is still good. His condition has not deteriorated into AIDS.

᷽

The year after Magic's Michigan State team won the NCAA title, the national championship game was held in Market Square Arena in Indianapolis, where Louisville rallied to beat UCLA for the title. More memorable to me was an incident in the restroom before the game. When you appear on television regularly, people often stare at you, trying to figure out who you are. As I used the facilities, this guy kept staring at me, uncomfortably so. This restroom was reserved for the media, and he should have known who I was. But he didn't take his eyes off me. When I finally finished, he smiled and said, "Billy Packer, you're a lot better looking in person!"

In 1981, the real Billy Packer, plus McGuire and I, were in Philadelphia for the Indiana-North Carolina championship game. To this day, I know that Indiana beat North Carolina, but I can recall zero details. My mind and my heart were never in the game. Like the days with the Angels shortly after my divorce, I called it without ever getting involved.

The game took place a few hours after President Ronald Reagan was shot by a would-be assassin in Washington. We were all shocked that the game was still going to be played. When we heard the news about Reagan, it was totally deflating. It was as if basketball had been vaporized. We went to The Spectrum thinking there was no way the game would be played. You can't play a basketball game when the president might be dying.

The NCAA did not make the decision to go ahead with the title game until about 30 minutes before tipoff. Frankly, it was as if I wasn't even there. I was a college professor in 1963 when President

Kennedy was murdered, and I remembered vividly how emotionally paralyzing it was for our entire country. To have it almost happen again was chilling. And, indeed, we learned later that Reagan, despite his rapid recovery, had come close to death.

By this time, I was also doing NFL football for NBC. Earlier that year, Merlin Olsen and I had called our first Super Bowl, which meant I couldn't join Al and Billy until the middle of the basketball season. While I did the NFL playoffs, NBC would assign other announcers to do the basketball Game of the Week.

When I rejoined Billy and Al for our belated first game together that season, they did something that was highly unusual in our ego-mad business. They had obviously discussed this moment, and, speaking for both of them, Billy said, "While you were away, Al and I got a little careless. Because there were different announcers every week, we ran over a lot of them. We just took charge. We did our thing, and they kind of made room for us. Now that you're back, we want you to know that you're in charge of the microphone again. Run the broadcast the way you always have and the way we've done it before, and we'll fall right back into place. We're not going to do what we've been doing."

"Oh My!" I thought. "That's the ultimate compliment. They're headstrong and making headlines, and they could have just kept on going. But they didn't. They said, 'You're back with us and we trust you. You're in charge of the microphone again.' How nice is that?"

⌇

One of Al's best friends was Herb Kohl, an immensely successful businessman in the Milwaukee area and now a U.S. senator from Wisconsin. When I worked with Al and Billy, Kohl owned a ranch along a mountain-fed river in a gorgeous little valley in Wyoming, and once every autumn, he allowed Al to invite some of his friends there for a "cowboy" vacation. It was like moseying back to another century. Kohl's hired cowboy, Roger Lasson, who managed the ranch, would lead us up into the mountains on horseback, where we'd relax, enjoy a picnic lunch, and admire the incredible scenery. Sometimes, we climbed as high as 10,000 feet. During the trip, we'd see deer, eagles, porcupines, and elk.

On one of those rides, we became involved in an animated discussion of college sports nicknames, and Al took over the conversation.

"I know *every* college nickname," he bragged. "You can't stump me."

"Al," I said, "I'll get you within three."

He scoffed, so I set him up.

"Alabama," I said.

He laughed. "Oh, come on. Crimson Tide."

"Oregon," I said.

He rolled his eyes. "The Ducks."

"All right," I said, "how about Wyoming State?"

There was a long pause.

"Wyoming State? What would they be? The Wolves, maybe?"

"Al, I got you!" I shouted.

Well, of course, there is no Wyoming State. Much later, after I admitted that fact, we decided to create a Wyoming State University. First, we needed a nickname. We decided to call our new team the Fighting Porcupines. Our cheer was "Go Porcs, go!" Kohl's ranch was named Red Rock Ranch, and the Wyoming sky was always a brilliant blue, so red rock red and sky blue became the team colors. On the way to the ranch, there was a little stop-in-the-road, Kelly, Wyoming, of maybe two houses, a post office, and a general store, so we decided the campus site would be Kelly, a place only a few locals even knew existed. Then we sat around and made up opponents for our new college, like the New Mexico School of Turquoise.

During the next basketball season, NBC decided to add a new halftime feature to the Game of the Week telecasts—the network's own Top 20, which we would pick and announce each week. We reported our Top 20 for three or four weeks, and then somebody suggested, "Let's put Wyoming State in there." So we did. I think the Porcupines made their debut at No. 17.

"Hey, look at this," I said on national TV, introducing the Top 20. "Here's a new entry, Wyoming State. We don't know a lot about the Porcupines, but they haven't lost a game in three years."

Well, of course, they hadn't played a game in three years, either. It became our little gag. Al loved it. He felt it was a tribute to all the good times we had enjoyed on Kohl's ranch and even suggested that we sell Wyoming State sweatshirts. Even Billy, always more serious than Al, thought it was funny.

We kept the joke alive for two years. A writer from one of the Chicago papers even called to say he was interested in doing a story on Wyoming State.

"No one can seem to beat those Porcupines," I remember saying. "It may be a small school, but to go so long without losing a game is mighty impressive."

We weren't lying. They hadn't lost a game.

It shows you how innocent sports television was 25 years ago. In today's Internet world, you couldn't get away with that for a second. Recently, I met former Senator Alan Simpson from Wyoming, a modern-day Will Rogers. When I introduced myself, the first thing he said was, "How's that Wyoming State team doing?"

I asked him what he thought of our shenanigans.

"Obviously, I knew what you guys were doing," he said. "I laughed right along with you."

∽

At the end of the 1981 season, NBC lost the rights to the NCAA Tournament to CBS, which still broadcasts the tournament today. CBS hired Billy away from NBC, but Al and I continued to do NBC's regular-season package for three or four more years, because the network hoped to regain the tournament. When the NCAA signed with CBS again, NBC dropped most of its college basketball coverage, televising only occasional games. In 1992, Al also went to CBS.

When Billy migrated to CBS, Al felt like he had lost his security blanket. So, as we prepared for our next season, he said, "Since there are just two of us now, Dicksie, I've got a new idea. If you throw me a question and I don't know the answer, I'll give you a signal. If I touch my nose, it means I don't know the answer, and I won't say anything."

And he was serious.

"Oh sure, Al," I said. "I'm going to be halfway through a question, and you've got your finger on your nose. Then, what am I supposed to do?"

But that was his thinking. As bright as he was, he could never quite understand how television worked. It frightened him. But he felt secure that I understood. No matter what went wrong, he always felt that I would keep talking.

"Dicksie, I can see the train coming and it's about to go off the track," he would say, "but you see it falling off the rails and you put it right back on track. You make it look like there wasn't a mistake at all. The producer looks good, the director looks good, and even I look good."

When he told me that, I thought, maybe that *is* what I do. I see a potential problem coming and work to resolve it so the audience doesn't even know. If things start to fall apart on a broadcast, you don't complain. You make it work.

After Al left NBC, we didn't work together again until early 2000, after I, too, had moved to CBS. We teamed for about half a season, Al's last before he died less than a year later.

To call Al McGuire an unforgettable character doesn't pay proper tribute to him. He was the most fascinating, complex, unique, vibrant person I've ever met, and the next chapter belongs to him.

∼

Although I'm in reasonably good physical condition for my age, I've never wanted to run a marathon. Since coming to CBS in 2000, however, I've participated in a verbal marathon every year in the NCAA Tournament. While at NBC, I never called more than two basketball games in a day. At CBS, all of the network's regular basketball announcers—play-by-play men and commentators—call *four* first-round games on opening day of the tournament, back to back to back to back.

By the time you get to the fourth game, your voice has paid a high price, becoming more and more and more and more hoarse, because there's only so much sound left in your vocal cord tank. It's hard physically. It's even more taxing mentally.

To give you an idea of how demanding this assignment is, let me take you through our schedule for the opening weekend of the 2004 NCAA Tournament. I left my California home on Wednesday for Columbus, Ohio, where I would do four games on Friday and two on Sunday. On Wednesday night, I joined my sidekick, Matt Guokas, and the production crew as we looked at tapes of all eight of our teams. On Monday and Tuesday, I had prepared spotting boards for the eight teams, listing names, numbers, physical characteristics, key statistics, and personal information on all the players. Now, looking at the tapes, I was trying to familiarize myself with the players, most of whom I'd never seen. It was a ton to absorb in a limited time.

The next day, Thursday, we were at the arena at 11:30 a.m. Beginning at noon, each team practiced for an hour. During each workout, we would talk briefly to the coach, then spend time with the sports information director to get additional information and make sure we had the pronunciations of the players' names correct. I don't care how good your color man is, how good your statistician is, how good your producer is, ultimately as the play-by-play man you're responsible for getting things right, and it starts with the pronunciations. You absolutely cannot err on a name.

So we watched practices from noon to 4:00 p.m., took an hour break, then watched the last four teams from 5:00 p.m. to 9:00 p.m. By the time we returned to the hotel, our minds were going in eight directions at once. We were already exhausted, and now had four major games to announce in just 14 hours.

On Friday, Matt and I arrived at the arena about 10:00 a.m., ready for the first game, which tipped off shortly after noon. When you've got eight teams back to back, your head is spinning with names and numbers, names and numbers. Is this one of the two Williams from Cincinnati or the Williams from Illinois? The Smith from Illinois or the Smith from East Tennessee State? One of our games featured Cincinnati versus East Tennessee State. Cincinnati's best outside shooter was guard Field Williams. East Tennessee State had a big guy inside named Jerald Fields. So Fields would score at one end, and Field would counter at the other.

The coach at East Tennessee State was Murry Bartow, but we also had Murray State playing in one of the games. UAB was also playing, and Murry Bartow used to coach at UAB, so those connections were maddening. In addition, UAB had identical twins, guards Donell and Ronell Taylor. Donell was No. 1 and Ronell was No. 2. But Donell, because he was No. 1, wore both of his socks up as a tribute to his brother. Ronell, who wore No. 2, had only one sock pulled up, in respect to his brother. No. 1 had two socks up, and No. 2 had one sock up. Are you still with me? UAB also had two Johnsons, forward Tony Johnson and guard Carldell Johnson. Cincinnati had center Kareem Johnson, and Washington had guard Alex Johnson.

Florida A&M, which played Kentucky, had a forward, Michael Ayodele, pronounced Eye-oh-DELL-ee, and Kentucky had forward Kelenna Azubuike, pronounced Keh-LYNN-uh Az-uh-BOO-kee. East Tennessee State's star was forward Zakee Wadood, pronounced Zah-key Wah-dude. Those are all names you're dealing with in one day, and after each game you have only a half hour to wash old names and numbers out of your brain and absorb the new ones.

By the end of the day, you're a zombie. When we returned to the hotel, it was nearly 1:00 a.m. We'd been at the arena nearly 15 hours. As we were going back to the hotel, one of the producers said, "Quick, who is No. 10 for Cincinnati?" There was no way I could answer. It was gone. It was just out in the stratosphere someplace. I was cooked.

On Saturday, Matt and I were back in the arena to talk to the winning players and coaches. At least now we had a little better feel for the remaining teams. Then we called two more games on Sunday. Although doing two basketball games in one day is a pretty rigorous assignment, after working four, it seems so relatively easy that there's no reason to complain.

So, when fans tune in to watch those first four NCAA games next season, guaranteed, they're going to hear mistakes. We all make them. It's asking for the impossible for someone to do a perfect job, no matter how hard he works. At best in a close game, the flow of the action carries you along. But when the game is one-sided and you have to rely on your memory to come up with material to liven the broadcast, you're in trouble. When they talk about March Madness, I'm absolutely certain an announcer coined the phrase.

The strain of calling four games in one day reminds me of covering Wimbledon. During the years I announced Wimbledon for NBC, I left London totally exhausted every year—the tournament lasts two weeks—and my first thought was, "I'll never do *this* again." A week later, in a state of amnesia, I found myself saying, "I can't wait for next year." It was the same with the first day of the NCAA Tournament. When I flew home, I reasoned, "This is just impossible. If CBS tells me I don't have to do it next year, maybe I should consider that." A week later, I was having a clubhouse meeting with myself. "What am I talking about? I don't ever want to give that up."

TIMEOUT

No Longer at a Loss for Words

WHEN I CALLED THE NCAA TOURNAMENT for CBS in 2001, Hall of Fame UCLA basketball star Bill Walton was my broadcast partner, a fact that would have stunned Walton if he could have foreseen the future 30 years earlier. When I called Walton's games at UCLA in the early 1970s, there was little opportunity to interview the big redhead, because he had a serious stuttering problem.

"Since it was such an ordeal for me to speak because of my stuttering, I wanted no part of the media at the time," Walton told me years later. "Coach Wooden gave each of us the choice, and I elected not to talk to the media. In retrospect, it was a terrible mistake on my part, but I honestly couldn't talk."

After graduation, Walton worked tirelessly to overcome his verbal handicap. Like so many endeavors in his life, he not only won the battle, but he succeeded to such a degree that he makes a good living now as a network TV analyst. He has my complete admiration. When I've shared the microphone with Bill, there have been times within a game when I can tell he's struggling to speak, but it's only momentary. He slows down, quickly adjusts, and then expresses his thought.

On the morning of a telecast he practices his opening remarks for 20 to 30 minutes in front of the hotel mirror. It helps him to relax as he sees and hears himself as the audience will see and hear him later. In fact, it's a good idea for any announcer, whether you're a former stutterer or not. It's a useful technique that anyone in public speaking can employ.

During that 2001 NCAA Tournament, Walton and I called the regional final game between Arizona and

Illinois in San Antonio, with the winner earning a berth in the Final Four. Bill's son, Luke, was a sophomore forward for Arizona that season, and the team's talented sixth man.

After Arizona won the game and the network switched back to New York, the Wildcats, including Luke Walton, celebrated on the court. I looked over and up at my six-foot-11 broadcast partner, and big tears were streaming down his cheeks. "I'm the proudest dad in the whole world," he said.

Walton's son was about to enjoy what Big Bill had experienced as an NCAA Tournament star at UCLA. An hour later, when we boarded a plane to return to the West Coast, Walton still had tears of pride in his eyes.

9

"NO" IS A GOOD ANSWER

"If you don't like my onion sandwiches, too bad.
My personal style is non-negotiable."

—Al McGuire

I always promised myself that if I wrote a book, Al McGuire deserved his own chapter. So here goes.

March 5, 2000. Sheraton Hotel. Madison, Wisconsin.

It was a break in my usual routine before a game. For some reason, at 9:00 a.m. I was magnetically drawn out of my room to the hotel's coffee shop. Down deep I thought my broadcast partner for the day's telecast of the Wisconsin-Indiana basketball game would be there for breakfast. Al McGuire was predictable. There he was. Alone. Through the window behind him the morning sun highlighted the drab winter landscape. The trees were brown and barren, colorless, lifeless. Perhaps that's why the birds of spring are so easily noticed. In fact, Midwesterners look for robins as a sign of early spring. One flew past the window and landed on a tree's empty branch, a signal in these parts that a new season is to be born. Folks in the North Country count on it.

Coach, head low, greeted me with a solemn smile. "I can't do it," he murmured, and he began to cry. Covering his face with a napkin, he apologized for breaking down, adding, "It's become too painful, too difficult to answer the demands of the TV schedule. This is my last game."

I knew he had been taking blood transfusions, his bone marrow producing an insufficient amount of red blood cells. He had refractory anemia, which would ultimately evolve into acute leukemia. At the time, he also thought he was arthritic, explaining, "There's awful pain every day in a different part of my body. What if it hits me in my feet and I can't walk? You'd be left alone to work and I don't wanna stiff ya. But not to worry, Dicksie, the doctors say I've got four more years. So don't feel sorry for me, I'll probably outlive *you*. Anyway, people who worry about the sick may die before the ones they're concerned about."

He had fallen once in his bedroom at home and while his wife and son-in-law tried to assist him to his feet, he cried out, "Leave me down. It's easier, and it feels better."

Al always did like to sleep on the hard floor. His voice softened as he continued with one of his philosophical pearls:

"When you're tired and weak, it feels good to *not* get up. It's better just to lie there. Hey, that may not sound good, but there's times when it's better to give up a little, rather than get up. You're so tired." And he swallowed the end of his sentence.

I helped him up out of his chair. Breakfast was over. We walked slowly to the elevator. His tired eyes were sadder than ever. "I love you, Dicksie."

❧

When I first met Al in the early 1970s, it was difficult to like him, much less love him. As a coach, he was distant, unapproachable, and irascible. When I was in Milwaukee working Marquette games for TVS, he often wouldn't even be at practice the day before the game, and then on game day he wouldn't make his grand arena appearance until we were already on the air. Simply, there was no access to him and he couldn't have cared less. When I tried, I was rejected like a shot that had been fly-swatted away.

Years later, at the end of the 1977 season, he offered me an audience. Marquette was in Ann Arbor to play Michigan in the regular-season finale, televised nationally by NBC. The NCAA was to announce the 32 teams selected for the tournament sometime during that day, and Al's Marquette Warriors were at best a distant long shot to make it. Superstitiously, he'd been wearing the same sport coat for the last several games as his team showed modest late-season life. Before the game he told Billy Packer and me that *if* he heard good news, he'd signal us by taking off his well-worn coat.

Early in the season, Al had announced his retirement, effective after the final game. In what could have been that last game, he came out of the locker room at halftime, sans jacket. Marquette was the last team in, even though Michigan won that afternoon.

It's what makes sports delicious for all of us. A team with no chance does the unexpected. Of all his Marquette teams—and his record was 295-80 with the Warriors—several were considerably better than this one but didn't win the national title. Miraculously, this one did. Al often professed that to win it all, (1) you needed to be lucky, and (2) you had to win a game at the wire. And so it would be. Check the second-round 67-66 thriller over Kansas State.

Then in the national semifinals in Atlanta's Omni, the last-second basket by Jerome Whitehead dismissed North Carolina Charlotte 51-49 in a game I called. In the championship game, when Marquette beat Dean Smith's North Carolina team 67-59, we caught Al in that memorable TV close-up in the final seconds, crying on the bench.

Years later, he told me, "I was cryin' cuz it was really seashells and balloons. National champs. Treetops. I'm not afraid to cry even on national TV. All I could think of was, why me? After all the years of odors in the locker room... the socks and jocks... all the fights in the gyms... just the wildness of it all. And to have it end like this. It's been a great run. Normally, alley fighters like me don't end up in lace."

And Al McGuire was an alley fighter. As a youngster in the McGuire family bar on Long Island's Rockaway Beach, he learned his pugilistic lessons well. His job description, as a teenager, included bouncer. He knew he had to fight and didn't back off from any alcohol-dared challenge. In those high school years McGuire liked to fight, but he fought smart. He once shared an early lesson, "Be wary if you're getting into a fight when the other guy takes off his wrist watch. That guy knows how to fight."

He fought with officials, earning a giant share of technical fouls. He'd work the refs, explaining, "I studied them. Everyone in life has got habits, but sometimes, in tryin' to get an edge I pushed 'em too far."

In the 1974 national championship game against North Carolina State, Al picked up not one, but two "Ts," and it cost Marquette the title. In the locker room after the game, his star Maurice Lucas said to Al, "Thanks Coach, for losing the game."

Al, never totally giving up the fight, replied, "Maurice, you're right, and I guess that makes up for all the games I won for ya."

Make no mistake. During the game Al had a serious hate relationship with officials, but when the game was over, he never held it against the "zebras." He was proud of the fact that he never wrote up a ref and never reported one to the league office, admitting, "Referees don't beat ya. Better teams do. And sometimes bad coaching on my part did."

He was the first coach I ever saw who would let his own players verbally fight him during a game. In 1976, in Baton Rouge, in a tough NCAA playoff game against Western Michigan, Lloyd Walton, his point guard, openly defied Al during a timeout. I couldn't believe it. In my generation no one ever challenged coaching authority. But there in full view of everyone at courtside, Al let Walton shout an emotional rebuttal that consumed almost the entire timeout. He then sent Walton back in the fray with a challenge, "Damn it, then go out there and do it."

Bob Huggins at the University of Cincinnati is the only other coach I've observed in my 50 years who gives players such freedom of expression on a consistent basis. During an early-round game of the 2004 NCAA Tournament, Huggins and his players openly shouted at each other. After the game I told him that his liberal approach was reminiscent of McGuire.

Huggins wrinkled his brow, raised one eye, and replied, "Hey, sometimes my players have good ideas. They don't always have to agree with me. I'm never threatened. Besides, they know who's boss."

Al would have liked Huggins. His practice and game-day "face" mirrors Al's. They both are shouters and poetically profane. In practices Al admitted to coaching by yelling, using swear words to emphasize the importance of the coaching message.

"It was my world of verbal violence," he said. "Shouting, even screaming, that's real coaching. It was by intent. I was tryin' to make men out of kids. Kids who preferred to remain boys, cuz it was easier. My personal style was non-negotiable. That's how I fly. If you don't like my onion sandwiches, too bad. I can't change."

As a coach, he didn't. Later, in his new life as a broadcaster, he did. As he put it, he would re-invent himself. Television helped the transformation. He admitted to becoming mellower, more approachable. He would chuckle when acknowledging that the new Al McGuire became the real one, a nicer guy, all the while confessing, "At the beginning, the new McGuire was an act. I was just bein' 'The Fox.' And then the act became Al McGuire."

Good for us!

It was especially good for me. Al felt he had to protect me, that I was too trusting. He worried I'd be taken advantage of. After all, he was New York City tough, a city-slick street genius. I was farm-raised naïve. He knew all the angles. I trusted all the anglers. So he was quick to step in and protect me from what I didn't know, and in the process taught me a ton of life lessons.

And what a brilliant teacher he was. Perhaps it's because he looked at life from an acutely different angle. All of us watch from our seats in the audience. Al watched as well but was already behind the curtains, seemingly knowing life's full script. We are Dorothys. He was the Wizard of Oz.

Naturally, his favorite stage was New York. Just an hour's walk on the streets with Al was worth a $100 ticket. As we approached a major street intersection, 54th Street and Sixth Avenue, Al pointed to a portable hot dog stand and asked if I was hungry.

"I do like hot dogs," was my reply, "but I taught health science and I think I'll pass on one of those."

He directed me to watch anyway, doing a street play-by-play of the vendor. "Look, he's scratching his ass... playing with the change in his pocket... here's a customer... he's reachin' into the cart with his bare hand for a bun... now grabs a dog... places it in the bun... lathers some mustard... now he's wipin' his chin... a handful of onions... some sauerkraut... and before passing it on to the customer, wraps up the hot dog in a napkin, like the *customer's* hands are dirty."

Whether in New York or Iowa City, he'd insist that wherever we ate, we must be seated by a window. "Whether it's fancy or fast food, why would you want to be in the middle of the restaurant? Get a seat by the glass. It's a chance to watch life go by, an always changing human show. And it doesn't cost another cent. It's insane *not* to sit there."

Al had other principles for good dining. He advised against any restaurant with linen napkins because automatically that told you it was overpriced. Only eat in a place with paper napkins. Maybe it was because he loved to eat with his hands and lick his fingers. His logic: "Why add 15 cents [the cost of laundering the napkin] to my bill when I don't use it?"

The first thing he'd ask when entering the restaurant was who was in the kitchen. If the answer was Mom or Pop, he was convinced the food would be good. Paper napkins, plus Mom or Pop, proved to be a winning equation. On the other hand, if a guy admits to loving a slice of onion on white bread with nothing else on it, how tough is he to please? And spicy hot chili? Another favorite. Al liked food as he described it, "that made his stomach angry."

A favorite Al story was the occasion on which he had ordered lobster for his main course. (Obviously, he wasn't picking up the tab.) When the lobster arrived, one of its claws was missing. Al asked the waiter what happened and was told that sometimes the lobsters fight in the waiting tank and this one lost the battle. Al's response was immediate, "So take this one back. Bring me the winner."

Al was never hesitant in saying "No." It was a good answer whether giving or receiving. We were checking into a Champaign, Illinois, hotel prior to a Big Ten game between the Illini and Purdue, and Al began to argue with a young female clerk at the registration desk. Al preferred rooms on the first or second floor, explaining that in case of trouble you could always jump to safety, but according to the clerk, she didn't think anything was available. She proudly announced that she had a much more elaborate room reserved for him on a higher floor. But Al insisted that's not what he wanted. She said she'd try to talk to her superior, but he was still at lunch, that maybe he could do something or that maybe, just maybe, a room on the third floor would work. Finally, raising his voice for emphasis, Al said, "Young lady, it's all right to tell me, 'No.' The answer I want is 'Yes'; that's the best answer. But 'Maybe' is drivin' me wacky."

Later that night, he reviewed the experience. "Too many people are afraid to give you a 'No' so they give you a 'We'll see' or a 'Maybe.' That's a bad answer. It's a delaying tactic. Eventually, you're probably going to get a 'No' anyway. We do it to our associates, our kids, our players. It's a waste. Tell 'em, 'No.' It's a good answer. It allows you to go on with your business and get a 'Yes' somewhere else. 'Maybe' is the bad answer. It's like ice fishing. It's insane."

Everyone who spent time with Al, including his assistant coaches, received his free advice. Rick Majerus, later to have a sterling career as head coach at Ball State and Utah, brought an attractive date to an NCAA banquet when he was serving as an assistant to McGuire.

During the event, Al leaned over to Majerus and forcefully told him, "Rick, *never* marry a beautiful woman."

"Why?" the confused Majerus replied.

"Because a beautiful woman can leave you," McGuire said.

"Al," Majerus protested, "an ugly woman could leave me, too."

"Yeah," Al said, "but that wouldn't matter."

Al went to many, many banquets. In fact, his second income was from giving speeches. As I've learned, speeches are more demanding of your time than one would think. My fee is healthy, in five figures, but I've never felt overpaid. After you factor in the agent's fee, Uncle Sam, travel time to and from the event, and preparation to gear your talk to the specific theme of the conference, you've earned every penny.

On occasion, for a friend or a good cause, I've offered to give the same speech without any charge. Many times it has stunned me when I haven't even received a thank-you note. I asked Al about it.

"When I get paid," I explained, "I not only receive a handsome check in the mail, but also a highly complimentary thank-you letter from the CEO. When I give the exact same speech for nothing, all I receive is silence."

"Don't you get it, Dicksie," he scolded. "The guy who got you for nothing got the thank-you note. Why would he feel it necessary to send you one? He's the hero."

Why didn't I think of that?

On the subject of favors, Al's advice went to another level. It's another example of his simple sagacity making life easier.

"You gotta know the difference between a favor and a due bill," he said. "It's no big deal that you borrowed a pencil or a quarter and didn't give it back. It was a favor. Favors are things people do automatically with no thought.

"On the other hand, a due bill is something you gotta pay back without any excuse or argument. It's an 'I owe ya one.' If someone has helped you out of serious trouble or gone way out of his way to help you through a tough time, you owe 'em one. There's no forgetting it. That's a due bill. When that person calls and asks you for help, even if it's 10 years later, you gotta deliver. It's like insurance. You gotta pay back. You make your life much simpler and richer if you stop worryin' about favors and do all your concentratin' on the obligations of a due bill."

Of his many former Marquette players Al felt that none meant more to him than Earl Tatum, a multitalented player he called "my black Jerry West." Before an NCAA regional game in 1976, the Warriors were practicing when Tatum tripped and screamed as he fell heavily to the court. With visions of NCAA elimination dancing through his head, Al rushed onto the court to see if his star was seriously injured.

"Earl, Earl," he said, "where'd you hurt yourself?"

Tatum struggled to his feet, limped painfully three steps back, pointed to a spot on the floor, and answered, "Right there, Coach."

As Al explained later, "That's the guy I want shooting free throws at the end of the game with fans behind the basket screaming and waving their arms. He wouldn't overthink. He'd just step up there and knock 'em down."

✍

In his mother's final years, Al would return home to visit with her. He'd often spend an afternoon lying on the couch as she made all the conversation. Without any embarrassment he'd admit to falling asleep while she was talking. He'd awaken and she was still there, sometimes still talking.

"It didn't matter if I dozed off because all she wanted was time with me," he said. "Don't forget, all you can give to the aging is time. They don't want a new sweater, a box of candy, even flowers. They want *time*, time with you."

Now, it was time for Coach. His condition had progressively worsened. He had been placed in a full-care center outside Milwaukee, and I last saw him in early fall. He was McGuire to the very end—on one hand insisting on struggling to get out of bed to give me a hug, claiming he didn't want to show weakness. On the other hand he found amusement in how his many visitors pretended not to see the elephant.

Al smiled as he explained, "We talk and we laugh, but no one wants to see the elephant and talk about it. They pretend it's not there... the elephant, that I'm dying. Hey, it's okay to talk about it. If I was stronger, I'd have a cold beer with 'em with lots of foam. Dicksie, what's really important is to buy your pals a drink while they're still alive. That way you never have to go to their funeral, cuz you bought 'em a drink while they were alive. What the hell good is it to toast a guy after he's on the other side of the grass? That's why I never go to funerals.

"One more thing," he continued, "You gotta make sure when you die, you're dead. That way no one suffers. Not you. Not your family. To string it out is painful and costs too much and ain't no fun for anyone. So make sure when you die, you're dead."

He was still a volcano, spewing hot wisdom.

I asked him what he wanted on his gravestone. His smile went deeper, "Had a good time. See ya." Another hug and that's how we said goodbye.

Alfred Emmanuel McGuire died during Super Bowl week, January 2001. His family asked if I would write a tribute to be used in the program for the funeral mass, a daunting task. Where to start? So much to cover? What to say that was sensitive, yet profound? The answer was to let Al write it. This was the result:

AL McGUIRE

Unforgettable character doesn't pay proper tribute. He's the most fascinating, complex, unique, street-sage genius I've ever met. And he touched us all—each of us now becoming an extension of this magical man. Each with a story of how Coach made us feel important, made us feel good.

So what better way to celebrate his life than to be reminded of his wisdom? Let him speak for himself:

• Just because you have a degree doesn't mean you're educated. Drive a cab for six months and tend bar for six months. Now you got a master's and a doctorate.

• The only time winning is important is in surgery and war.

• A poor man isn't a man without a cent, but a man without a dream.

• When a guy brings his wife flowers for no reason, there's a reason.

• I was a blacktop recruiter. If there was grass in the front yard, I wasn't interested.

• Know your stars. Treat them like stars. They win games. And know your other players. And give them a hug too.

• I never saw color, only character.

• Only the press and the student body can get you fired. If the students and newspapers are for you, it's Dunkirk for the alumni.

• The less rules, the less problems.

• Who cares if your star player is 10 minutes late for the bus? What am I going to do—bench him? Are you crazy? To be a leader, it's okay to be a hypocrite.

• Live in the moment. Do what you have to do as long as you don't hurt people.

• You've got to touch the rank and file. The world is run by C+ students.

• I can't be your friend and your flatterer, too.

• There will always be problems and I feel the greater the problems, the greater the generation is going to be.

• If you really want to know what's going on in a school or a business, ask the custodian.

• When it's dry, think wet.

• When someone calls frantically with a problem, it's never the first thing he says. Wait until the third. That's the one.

• Breakfast meetings are best because they have to end. Lunch meetings go a lot longer, and dinner meetings never end.

• The older you are, the more time flies. I feel like I'm eating breakfast every 20 minutes.

• Ever notice that the largest American flags fly over foreign car dealerships?

That's it. Curtains. Off to the races. Treetops. Seashells and balloons.

TIMEOUT

Taking a Right-Hand Turn

IT WAS EARLY SUMMER and the Angels were opening a weekend series with the Brewers. An unexpected 7:00 a.m. wake-up call in my Milwaukee hotel room was from Al.

"Going to take ya on a right-hand turn this morning. I'll be there to pick ya up at nine."

"Only under two conditions," I replied. "I won't go riding with you on your motorcycle, and I have to be back by five in order to catch the team bus to the ballpark."

Al agreed and was there on time for the pick-up in his beaten-up piece of junk of a car, oft described by his cronies as a moving trash can. In fact his wife, Pat, claimed she needed a tetanus shot just to ride with him.

The mode of transportation on this day was insignificant. It would become one of the great days of my life as well as one of the great life lessons. Al first tidied up the passenger seat by tossing a half-year's accumulation of waste into the back seat.

"Where are we going?" I asked.

"That's the whole point, Dicksie," he said. "We're not goin' anywhere. We're just takin' a right turn."

And we took a right and headed west out of the city.

The right-hand turn philosophy originated at a crossroads near Al's home in suburban Milwaukee. On his way to Marquette each day he would come to a two-way stop. Take a left and he was headed toward the downtown campus. Take a right and he was quickly into the Wisconsin countryside.

Al claimed that at least once a month on the spur of the moment, he'd hang a right. He didn't feel obligated to call in to his office because that would violate the spirit.

They knew where he was. The assistants could handle practice. His definition of these spontaneous days was letting the day come to him, not chasing the day.

In his words, "Take a left and it's Marquette and Milwaukee… concrete, mahogany tables, sport coats with leather patches, plastic. Take a right and go out into the country… sawdust, can of beer, ham sandwich, alfalfa. There was no reason behind it except to get out of my own space; meet the guy with two teeth missing, wearing a ratty cap."

As we drove toward the lake village of Oconomowoc, we saw a sign, PICK YOUR OWN BERRIES, 50 CENTS.

"That'd be fun," I suggested.

He braked and pulled to the side of the road, and we picked a couple dollars worth of strawberries. Reminded me of my Armada youth.

As we drove slowly through a small town, an antique shop window offered an inviting display, prompting my suggestion we check it out. After all, Al loved collecting toy soldiers, stained glass windows, old magazines, and the like, and I have an eye open for copper kettles, wine goblets, and old duck decoys. No purchases were made, but it was an entertaining half hour well spent.

It was well past noon, and my stomach was groaning for food. Al's answer to my query as to where we should eat was simply wherever looked good. We had reached Oconomowoc, and a little eatery on the left side of the street looked right. The food was good. Al was proud of me. I had selected a spot with paper napkins and Mom was working in the kitchen. Who says I'm not a quick study?

En route home we passed a small lakeside park. There was a walking path around the water. We strolled almost silently for about a half hour. The air was cool, the sun warm, a Midwest day at its very best. Words didn't do it justice. Now, it was time to return to civilization.

Returning to the hotel after the baseball game that night, I reflected on the day's gift from McGuire. No game plan. No agenda. No specific appointment times. Just eight free hours, where he helped me experience what it was like to let an entire day come to me. It was rich and everlasting.

To this day, whenever I arrive at two-way stop, I think of Al and relish the McGuire wisdom of allowing yourself the unprompted joys of an occasional right-hand turn. Why don't I do it more often?

10

SISU

*"It's so cold. Why don't you move up here
to the front seat?"*

—Barbara Almori

From 1975 until 1983, I was a single man, but, for the last five years of that era of independence, I had a permanent roommate. My dad and I were reunited.

My father had moved to Southern California several years earlier when I was still married, and he surprised us by falling in love with our widowed babysitter, Gwen. Their romance ended in marriage, and the two of them moved to Ventura, about an hour's drive north of Los Angeles. They lived in her large, comfortable two-bedroom trailer.

One fateful Saturday when I was on the road calling a game, Dad was watching the action in his bedroom on a TV set that I had long before given him as a gift. It blew a tube. Because his wife had a console TV in the living room, he hurried in there to watch the conclusion of the broadcast. As Dad recalled later—and this was all his side of it—Gwen told him, "Arnie, turn off my TV set."

He said, "What do you mean, turn off your set? Dick's announcing this game, and I need to watch the rest of it."

"You've already ruined your set," she argued. "You're not going to ruin mine."

"Are you kidding?" he asked.

"No," she answered, "you're not going to watch my TV."

Dad was always a man of action. He located a ladder, climbed onto the trailer's roof and took down *his* antenna. I can just see the stubborn Finn doing it. A year later, not only were they not interested in the same channel, but the marriage wasn't working, either. They were divorced.

At the time, recently divorced myself, I was living in my new home in the hills above the San Fernando Valley. I invited Dad to move in with me. It was great. We had a perfect division of labor. I cooked and paid the bills. He painted and gardened and did the carpentry and electrical work and anything else remotely mechanical. I was in my 40s and he was in his late 60s, and for the first time, we were on the same page.

Although he had mellowed, I had never been able to tell him I loved him. One day, I finally steeled my courage, grabbed him in a hug and said the words, "Dad, I need to tell you I love you."

He didn't respond. The next time was easier for me, and he seemed more receptive. Then, one morning, as I was leaving for an assignment, I said, "Bye, Dad, I love you," and he answered, "I love you, too, son." Our relationship was now complete, our status equal.

As my divorce receded into the emotional distance, I began to feel better and better about myself. I was ecstatic being single. By 1982, I had come to a decision. "You know what," I'd think to myself, "I have many, many great friends, men and women. I have three kids. I've got my own home. My dad and I are happy together. Things are going well at NBC. Why would I ever want to get married again? Why would I ever disrupt such a great life?" I never needed to be married again.

∽

On January 10, 1982, Merlin Olsen and I were in Cincinnati to call the AFC Championship Game between the Bengals and the Chargers, the so-called "Freezer Bowl," with a wind-chill factor of −59 degrees, still the coldest in NFL history. My birthday was the day before game day, and I planned to meet Jack "Suds" Bailey, my life-long friend from Central Michigan and then a key executive in Procter & Gamble's soap division in Cincinnati. "Suds," who snuck into the Detroit Lions' locker room with me in 1957, had lived through my sportscasting days, and he often joined me on TV basketball weekends, serving as my courtside statistician.

Jack had been eager to throw a birthday party for me at his home. Great idea! I suggested we invite the entire NBC production crew. The party would be a relaxing divergence before the big game. It would be nice way to celebrate the final broadcast of our season. The crew was excited to attend.

Our unit manager for the AFC title game was Barbara Almori. She was blond, pretty, distant, and very efficient. As we planned the buffet at Jack Bailey's house, director Ted Nathanson asked her to arrange for a caterer, a birthday cake, and cars to taxi the staff to and from Jack's suburban neighborhood. In a remarkable coincidence, unbeknownst to me, Barbara's birthday was one day before mine.

Coordinating the party was an extra hassle for her—she spent her birthday arranging a party for me—but the night was special. It felt good to share it with so many people who cared. Nobody stayed late, because we had the playoff game the next day. I asked Barbara to hold one car, so I could thank everyone before being the last to leave. She rode with me in the last car out.

When we went outside, it was bitterly cold, just as it would be on game day. Our driver got behind the wheel, Barbara sat in the passenger seat, and I climbed in back. It was frigid inside the car. You could see the smoke of your breath. She turned and looked at me.

"It's so cold," she said. "Why don't you move up here with us?"

So I did.

"There was nothing romantic about my request," Barbara insisted later. "The only reason I asked you to sit in the front was because I was cold. I was interested in body heat."

Separated two years, Barbara was in the process of finalizing her divorce at the time, and she had never considered dating anyone from NBC. She kept her social life and her business life separate. In my dealings with her, she had never revealed much about herself, being cautious not to be too friendly, as any attractive woman would be in a man's world. She didn't want to give me or anyone else any ideas. On the 30-minute drive back to the hotel, however, we had a very pleasant conversation, discussing a variety of topics. It was our first personal talk, and it turned out to be one of the most important 30-minute trips of my life. When I returned to my room, I thought, "Goodness, there's a lot more to her than I realized—more emotion, more feelings." I had enjoyed the conversation. I liked her.

A little more than two weeks after the game, I called Barbara at her office, explaining that I would be in New York in a few days, and asked her to dinner. She was going skiing that weekend, but said she would give me a call at my hotel when she got back on Sunday night, probably around 9:00 p.m. We could have a light dinner.

When I arrived in New York, it was snowing, and, as I sat in my hotel room that night, I realized I didn't have her home phone number. As it got later and later, I began to wonder if she would make it back in time. I decided if I didn't hear from her by 10:00 p.m., I would go downstairs and eat.

Barbara finally called just a few minutes before 10:00 p.m., and we hastily arranged our first date. We went to a small family-owned

Italian restaurant that had great chicken parmigiana, as well as an indoor boccie ball court. Amid the claps of boccie ball hits, we shared a bottle of Chianti while getting to know each other, not as the sportscaster and unit manager, but as real people. She told me later that she was attracted to me by my sense of humor. I do remember that we laughed a lot during dinner. We saw each other again the next night.

On Tuesday morning, as I was flying back to Los Angeles, I found myself writing poetry. "She's the one," I thought to myself. "I could marry her." Of course, a month before, I was never going to get married again. In the years since, I've told people who have been single for a long time that as soon as you stop chasing love, it finds you. It's like athletes always say, "Let the game come to you."

We dated for a year and meticulously disguised our relationship the whole time. Barbara was still at NBC in New York, and I was living in Los Angeles. We flew back and forth to see each other and occasionally met in other cities where I was doing a game. On New Year's Eve 1982, she accepted my marriage proposal.

When we told our mutual NBC friends that we were engaged, they were all stunned. Producer Michael Weisman's wife, Carol, who had graciously tried to set me up with dates in New York, was intrigued when I broke the news that my fiancée was someone at the network. Her curiosity aroused, she quickly guessed five names in an attempt to identify who my new love could be. Barbara's name didn't get a call. It was evidence of how carefully we had protected our private lives. Even friends who make their living digging for news didn't discover our 12-month romantic adventure. For Barbara and me, it was a sweet victory of sorts.

Now, after more than 20 years of marriage, Barbara and I agree that if we had met two years earlier or two years later, it never would have happened. It was just the right timing in her life and in mine, and I wound up with an extraordinary partner. And a fantastic friend. That's the warmest story of all in this book, and it all began when we were brought together on the very coldest of nights.

We were married in May 1983, by Reverend Donn Moomaw, a two-time All-America linebacker at UCLA in the early 1950s. He's a big, handsome, square-jawed man with a booming voice, and on the day he married us, he looked like he could still bring down ball carriers for the Bruins. He had three other weddings scheduled in his church that day but kindly squeezed us in. Thank God.

Barbara accepted the fact that my three children would be a part of her new life and that my dad would be a member of our household. Sadly, he had been battling prostate cancer. He did feel well enough, however, to join us on a trip to Helsinki, Finland, in August 1983, where I announced the inaugural World Track and Field Championships. It gave him a chance to visit many of his Finnish cousins. Helsinki, which sits on the southern coast of Finland, is the capital and largest city in the country—a beautiful place of scenic bays and broad tree-lined streets. It was a memorable first and only journey to the home of my ancestors.

As I related before, taking a steam bath is a hallowed ritual in Finland, so producer John Gonzalez suggested we do a feature for NBC on how to build an official sauna, speeding up the tape of the construction process so that the one-month effort was reduced to about 30 seconds of TV time. The plan was to conclude the piece with me conducting an interview in the sauna with one of the doctors for Finland's National Athletic Association.

When the cameraman, soundman, and I donned our swim trunks and walked in to do the interview, the doctor held up his hand and announced, "Sauna is sacred. You can't come in with clothes on. I won't do the interview unless you're naked."

I couldn't believe it. It was like being back on the family farm in Michigan. We did the interview sans clothes, the naked cameraman shooting the naked doctor and me, with the naked soundman recording it. Fortunately, a railing discreetly blocked our lower torsos. In the spirit of the occasion, I asked the good Finnish doctor for only the bare facts. Then we shared a cold beer after the sauna. My dad liked that.

The climactic moment of the 1983 World Track and Field Championships came in the women's javelin. Finnish star Tiina Lillak, the world-record holder, was the first athlete I had interviewed on my arrival in Helsinki. She was friendly, attractive, and, like most Finns, spoke excellent English. Finland has a great tradition in the javelin, and the entire nation was eagerly awaiting her performance. When the women's javelin began late in the week, the Finns had not captured a single gold medal, so all eyes were riveted on the infield as the competition began.

Great Britain's Fatima Whitbread seized the lead and held it. When Tiina Lillak prepared for her final throw—the final throw of the entire competition—Whitbread was still in first place. With 50,000 fans cheering their support, Lillak, a Helsinki native, ran forward, gathered herself, turned, and fired the javelin with all of her might. As it sailed high into the late night sky, the crowd noise soared with it, accompanying it through its entire descent. Tiina's final throw had won the gold medal!

The stadium erupted as she sprinted around the track in a state of uninhibited joy—her country's flags fluttering around her. It was a wonderful example of a great Finnish word, *sisu,* which basically means, "unwillingness to be defeated."

A year after we watched Tiina's celebration, our oldest daughter, Nicole, was born. We gave her the middle name Tiina as a tribute to Tiina Lillak. An autographed personal photo of Finland's world champion javelin thrower hangs on the wall in Nicole's bedroom. The picture is inscribed, "To little Tiina from big Tiina."

❧

On that trip to Finland in 1983, I carried a big stack of *The Sporting News*. It was important that I bone up on baseball to prepare for the upcoming playoffs and World Series. I had worked the playoffs for NBC for several years, and in 1982, I called the World Series for the first time, teaming with Joe Garagiola and Tony Kubek when the Cardinals edged the Brewers in seven games. I had been given every reason to believe I would have the role of lead play-by-play man in the playoffs and World Series on my return home. I was excited about the prospect.

Reality hit hard when Michael Weisman, recently promoted to coordinating producer for NBC Sports, paid me an impromptu visit to tell me that NBC executives in New York had asked him to inform me that I would not be doing baseball anymore. The network had hired Vin Scully.

It was the one time in my entire 25 years at NBC that I was very, very upset. I was deeply wounded. I felt betrayed. That was the feeling, betrayal. It was already August, and I had been led down the primrose path, given the impression I was going to do network baseball for many years in the future. Then it was taken away. It hurt as well that Arthur Watson, the respected president of NBC Sports, was not the one who told me.

The only thing that softened the blow was that NBC had replaced me with the man I consider the greatest baseball announcer ever. Scully has a cerebral, melodious rhythm to calling a baseball game. He's the poet laureate of our profession. Besides, I finally rationalized, it wasn't as if baseball was my only sport. I was still NBC's No. 1 announcer for college basketball, NFL football, and various special assignments. Still, it was painful. I had believed the job was mine.

When I returned to the United States from Helsinki, Watson called me into his office and gave me a sincere apology and a sizeable bonus. It was an admission that the whole situation had been handled improperly. Frankly, I have never liked the idea of getting paid for not working, but under the circumstances, I didn't refuse the money.

Recalling the bonus many years later, Weisman told me, "It was guilt, it was goodwill, and it was the right thing to do."

❧

After we returned to America, my dad's condition worsened as the prostate cancer advanced into bone cancer. Barbara and I decided to move from the San Fernando Valley to Rancho Santa Fe, just north of San Diego, so he could be treated at Scripps Memorial Hospital in nearby La Jolla.

Dad was at Scripps for serious treatment when Nicole was born in the same hospital in the spring of 1984. Our daughter was just an hour old when the nurse carried her outside the nursery and placed her in his arms. At first my eyes were drawn to our precious new baby, but when I glanced up at my father's face, he was crying—only the second time I had ever seen him with tears in his eyes. The only other time was when Mom moved out of the farmhouse for good.

Doctors said my dad had the heart of a lion and could have lived to 100, but bone cancer was too tough an opponent. A firm believer in *sisu*, he always thought he was going to beat it, but his condition deteriorated during the summer. He died in September 1984. In the end, he went quickly. I had called an NBC football game in Houston and returning that Sunday night, found him back in the hospital, looking worse than ever. He was black and blue all over. I don't know if it was caused by the chemotherapy, some other medication, or the disease itself, but it looked like half the blood in his body had pooled in blotches just under his skin. His eyes were open, and he could blink them, but he couldn't talk or reach out for me. It was as if he were in a coma with his eyes open.

I remember saying, "You know how much I love you, Dad."

But he couldn't respond, which was anguishing. I spent the last three days of his life just being there for him, sleeping in the room on a cot, staying there until I heard the very last gasp of his life. He was 74 years young.

Not too long ago, I took my son, Ted, to the doctor, and when we entered the office, I recognized the nurse, one who had helped my dad in the hospital 20 years earlier.

"Dick," she said, "we all thought your father was a great man."

A short while after he died, Barbara and I went through his possessions and were surprised to find several shoe boxes, filled with audio tapes. They were all carefully labeled "1969—Rams at Vikings," "1971—UCLA at Notre Dame," "1975—Angels at Boston," and so on. I never knew it, but he had a little tape recorder that he'd place against the speaker of the TV set or the radio to tape my games.

It was his way of showing how much he cared, this tough guy's way of saying, "Hey, son, you're really okay. I'm proud of you."

TIMEOUT

Remembering Arnie

A FEW SHORT MEMORIES of my dad:

• As I related earlier, my father never made more than $8,000 in a year, so he was constantly worried about money. But he always made sure we had Christmas presents. After my mother moved out, he did all the shopping for my brother, sister, and me, with occasional help from Aunt Beatrice.

However, he never bought the Christmas tree or presents until Christmas Eve. When we asked him why, he said, "It's an old Finnish tradition." We found out later it was an old economic tradition. He'd wait for the sales. The tree, in particular, was a lot cheaper on Christmas Eve than two weeks earlier.

• When my father did all the handyman work around my house in the San Fernando Valley, it was just a continuation of life in Armada. He fixed everything on the farm as well. We both realized early that repairing things is not one of my strengths. The few times I tried, I created an even larger problem. So, when something broke, Dad would say, "Get out of here. Go pick apples or hit a baseball, and I'll take care of this."

If it was physical labor, he would lay it on me, but if it was technical, I was chased away—and that was just fine with me.

• My dad was fiercely proud of his Finnish heritage. Every time he saw a story in the newspaper about someone who was Finnish, he would clip it out and put it in a safe place. He did that on the farm, and he was still doing it when he lived with me 30 years later.

One of his favorite athletes of all time was Paavo Nurmi, the Flying Finn, who won nine Olympic gold medals and three silver medals in distance running in the 1920s. I can still hear Dad rolling out the vowels in Nurmi's name with great reverence. To run long distances, to fight off exhaustion, and to not be defeated by the world's best, Nurmi had *sisu.*

11

ON A SET FULL OF STARS

"Play-by-play work is perfect experience for a game show host. You really ought to try it."

—Monty Hall

For a broadcaster, one of the benefits of living in Southern California is the opportunity to appear in movies and television shows. I've never sought work in Hollywood, but I've been recruited to play a sportscaster several times, and it's always been a fascinating experience.

Early in my broadcasting career, I worked in several movies and TV shows as a radio play-by-play announcer, a nebulous voice to be heard in the background. The audience might hear me in the third inning of a baseball game as a burglary took place, then a couple of innings later when the crime had been detected. It was a means for a scriptwriter to show the passage of time.

Directors liked me because they didn't have to script my work. They would ask me to use fictitious names and ad-lib three outs in an inning or five plays in a football game, whatever it was. It was fun to do and a way to earn some easy money. To this day, the mailman still delivers an occasional residual check, sometimes for as little as two or three dollars for a virtually forgotten episode of 35 years ago.

After providing only background work, I came home one day and announced that I had been hired for my first on-camera role.

"I've got good news and bad news," I told my family. "I'm working in another movie, and for the first time, I'm going to be seen on the silver screen. That's the good news. The bad news is it's about a mule that kicks field goals."

My first on-camera role was in the Disney film entitled *Gus,* which was the name of the four-legged placekicker. I appeared in a broadcast booth with Hall of Fame quarterback Johnny Unitas, playing my color man. One of the key scenes featured a shot of us wearing special hats with mule ears.

Of several other films in which I've been seen over the years, the most successful was Warren Beatty's fantasy, *Heaven Can Wait,* nominated in 1978 for nine Academy Awards. Not only was Beatty the star, but he also shared in writing, producing, and directing the film. My scene took place late in the movie, after Beatty, as Rams quarterback Joe Pendleton, led his team to victory in the Super Bowl. I conducted an interview with him in the locker room, while his team-mates celebrated by soaking everyone with champagne.

As is typical for a major film, they shot the scene countless times. On every take, the players—many of them actual members of the Rams—poured the champagne on each other, sprayed it around the room, and pounded each other on the back. It was a delirious cel-ebration. By the middle of the afternoon, they were drinking the champagne, beating on each other with more vigor than ever, and even breaking bottles. The locker room became Lake Champagne.

Everyone was drenched, including me. Unfortunately, I had to drive directly from the movie set to Anaheim Stadium to broadcast an Angels game that night—and I smelled like I'd been on a weeklong bender. The odor of old bubbly is not only strong, but also nauseat-ing. I tried to avoid close contact with everyone in the press box, but Don Drysdale, who had the misfortune of sharing a booth with me, was appalled.

"You smell like a walking frat party," he complained.

Unbeknownst to me, last year, my spotter for NFL games, Kevin Skinner, asked Beatty to autograph a picture of the locker room scene from *Heaven Can Wait*. The actor kindly and kiddingly responded with, "If you'd stuck with it, you'd have been bigger than Brando. This is a photograph of you turning down the Dustin Hoffman role in *Ishtar*."

❧

I may no longer have the matinee idol appeal of Brad Pitt, but I'm still somewhat attractive as a generic play-by-play man. At least, that's how Touchstone Pictures described my role in their movie, *Mr. 3000*, released in September 2004.

I played the role of the Milwaukee Brewers' radio-TV announc-er, who is describing the baseball exploits of star Bernie Mac. Because the film was shot at Milwaukee's Miller Park, my first question to the casting director was, "Why aren't you using Bob Uecker, the team's real-life announcer?"

"He's too well known," was the answer. "You're more generic."

Well, at least, being in Milwaukee gave me an opportunity to visit with Uecker and share that story.

"You've got the facts wrong," he said. "I heard they were actually looking for a geriatric announcer, and that's why you beat me out."

We laughed over that and then laughed many more times as we recounted the good times we shared with Don Drysdale.

While studying my lines, I sought free acting advice from my son, Alexander. Now 32, he has enjoyed success playing character roles in films and on stage.

"Just be yourself, Dad," he said, then added, "On the other hand, that crazy Uecker would be a lot better. Why not try to be like him?"

Doesn't anyone out there love generic?

᠅

Looking back, I was really a man in motion in the 1970s. Besides all of my sportscasting duties, I hosted several game shows, including *Sports Challenge,* which is still seen on ESPN reruns. I also served as co-producer of the PBS documentary, *The Way It Was.*

Monty Hall, the host of *Let's Make a Deal* and a former sportscaster in Canada, suggested I take a shot at game shows.

"Play-by-play work is perfect experience for a game show host, because you have to think on your feet, keep score, and build the drama, just like in sports," Hall said. "You really ought to try it."

Monty was right, and I'm glad I did. Three of the game shows, *The Perfect Match, Baffle,* and *Three for the Money,* lasted a year or less, but they were fun to do, and, as an added bonus on *Baffle,* I got free clothes. The show ran five days a week, and we taped all five half-hour episodes in one day. Before each of the last four shows, I changed my sport coat and tie from a wardrobe on the set and was able to take many of those clothes home. This was quite a fringe benefit for a guy who had to borrow a sport coat for his Armada High School senior picture.

Because I also received a complimentary wardrobe for *Sports Challenge,* I started choosing sports coats with wilder colors and patterns just for variety—such as orange, black, and green plaid and raving raspberry. Years later, after Barbara and I were married, these exotic coats started disappearing. Whenever I asked my wife if she knew where a particular one was, she would plead ignorance. Some time later, she admitted that every time I left home, she gave three of the bright-colored coats away, continuing the give-away plan until the stock was entirely gone. She was embarrassed at the thought I might wear one in public.

You couldn't produce *Sports Challenge* and *The Way It Was* today. The biggest stars in sports history appeared on the shows for $1,000 in cash, plus air travel and accommodations. Today, they wouldn't agree to go to the airport for such a meager fee.

Sports Challenge was syndicated and ran for a decade, and we made more than 100 shows. The format was simple. After showing video clips of great moments in sports history, I would ask two competing, three-man teams of sports stars a series of trivia questions that related to the footage. The highest scoring team was declared the winner and earned $1,000 in sports equipment for their designated charity. The losers earned $500.

Although the show played only once a week, we taped three in one day. So on a production day, we had four three-man sports teams in the studio at once. (The victorious team stayed on as long as they kept winning). There were also three mystery guests (one per show), which brought the total to 15 legendary athletes in the studio at one time. You could walk into the green room and see Joe Louis sitting over here, Joe DiMaggio over there, Mickey Mantle in the corner, and Bronko Nagurski coming in the door. It was fabulous. I never asked for a single autograph; I just relished the chance to rub shoulders with so many Hall of Fame greats.

As an old college professor, I loved writing the trivia questions for the show. I also did most of the play-by-play for the film clips. There were no transcripts. All I had were the old film and the information, and I re-created the descriptions myself. Whenever there was original play-by-play, we would use it, but most of our film was without any narration. If you watch several episodes of *Sports Challenge,* you might hear me announcing a Jack Dempsey fight in one show, the 1946 World Series in the next, and perhaps a 1975 UCLA basketball game in the third. I was truly a man for all seasons. We employed microphone filters to make some of the calls sound plausibly old.

We created about 50 episodes of the PBS documentary, *The Way It Was,* usually bringing back two or three athletes who were instrumental in a historic sports event. Whenever possible, we also tracked down the announcer who called the event, and, when possible, used his original call. If not, I re-created the play-by-play. Curt Gowdy was the host of *The Way It Was*. Gerry Gross was the producer of both *Sports Challenge* and *The Way It Was*.

Proudly, I earned my first Emmy as co-producer of *The Way It Was* for an episode on Roger Maris's 61 home-run season of 1961. As I look back, I still feel fortunate to have been involved with the two shows. Each was a Hall of Fame experience.

TIMEOUT

The Way It Was, 1939

ONE OF OUR MOST DRAMATIC *The Way It Was* shows featured Joe Louis and his 1939 heavyweight championship opponent, "Two Ton" Tony Galento.

At one point, we were discussing Max Schmeling, the German who handed Louis his only loss in his first 62 fights. Two years after being knocked out by Schmeling in the 12th round of their 1936 bout (a year before Louis became heavyweight champion), the Brown Bomber kayoed Schmeling in the first round of their much-hyped rematch.

"Because he was from Nazi Germany, everyone thinks I hated Max Schmeling," Louis said. "That wasn't true at all. I liked Schmeling. He was a good person. There was only one man I ever fought that I hated—and he's sitting right here… Tony Galento.

"Tony, you said some bad things about me before the fight, and I vowed to myself that I wasn't going to knock you out; I was going carry you at least 10 rounds so I could cut you up. I wanted to put at least 100 stitches in your face.

"But you knocked me down in the third round, and I couldn't fool around. I had to get rid of you earlier than I wanted. As I remember, I only got about 40 stitches."

Indeed, after climbing off the canvas in the third round of their title fight, Louis knocked Galento out in the next round.

Louis was honest about his feelings for Schmeling, too. After World War II, they became good friends. The German was a pallbearer at the Brown Bomber's funeral.

12

THE PRESS BOX ELEVATOR WAS FROZEN

"What would you think if I tried an onside kick on the opening kickoff of the Super Bowl?"

—Bill Cowher

Although I've been calling football games for most of the last 50 years, there was no way to be prepared for what happened in a game between the Detroit Lions and New York Jets in late December 1997.

The game—on the last weekend of the regular season—had a playoff atmosphere. The winner would earn a berth in postseason play, while the loser would be eliminated. In addition, Detroit's Barry Sanders was bidding to become the third NFL running back to rush for 2,000 yards in a season. One player in the Silverdome that day said the crowd of nearly 78,000 was so loud that the artificial turf shook beneath his feet.

Early in the fourth quarter, after Sanders ran 15 yards for the touchdown that gave the Lions a 13-10 lead, the crowd noise swelled to a crescendo. After the kickoff, New York quarterback Neil O'Donnell was forced to call a timeout because of the noise and then had to ask for crowd control assistance from the referee before he could run a play.

On the third play after the game resumed, Jets running back Adrian Murrell carried through the left side of the line, gaining only two yards, before he was met by a pair of Detroit defenders, linebackers Antonio London and Reggie Brown. The tackle seemed routine, but Brown didn't get up. In fact, he didn't move. As doctors and trainers rushed to his aid, our sideline reporter, Jim Gray, hurried over to determine the extent of his injury. While the camera focused on the fallen player and the medical staff worked on him frantically, two of his Detroit teammates sprinted to the tunnel to bring a paramedic with his gurney and other emergency medical equipment. It looked extremely serious.

Gray quickly alerted producer Tommy Roy in our NBC truck, and Roy relayed information to our booth that jolted Phil Simms, Paul Maguire, and me.

"The report from the sideline is he may be dead," Roy said. "He isn't breathing."

We all looked at each other, our faces white with fear. Maguire's eyes filled with tears. Suddenly, it's a frightening train wreck, and you've got to call it as it happens on national television. What do you say? You don't know all the details, but you're aware that it's more than awful. I've done football games when players have been knocked out and aren't moving, or when players were suspected of having neck injuries and were carried off after being immobilized—but never when word came from the field that a player had stopped breathing. As we looked down, we could see that a team doctor (later identified as orthopedic surgeon Terry Lock) was giving the fallen linebacker mouth-to-mouth resuscitation. Doctors had also inserted an IV into his arm.

The last thing you want to say is, "We may have a death on the field." You can't speculate. Later, we learned that his mother, who lived in Texas, was watching the game on television. What if we had said that?

"Often, these situations seem worse than they are," I said, a trite phrase, but one I hoped was true.

I talked about the caution that doctors and trainers take today with suspected spinal injuries, and Simms, who had seen many terrible hits in his own career that did not prove disastrous, seconded the motion.

"One of the really good things in the game today is that immediate medical care is much better than it was in the old days," he said. "They have the equipment they need right here, and they're going to take every precaution."

We did not tell the audience that we had a report that Brown had stopped breathing.

We tried to be positive, and we consciously tried not to say too much. The tendency in a situation like that is to want to keep talking, but there's no need. The pictures are more powerful. We needed only to supplement them. Close-up shots of concerned players from both teams—many on their knees in prayer—and 78,000 fans in total silence told the story better than any additional commentary. Director John Gonzalez also did not linger on the injured player too long but tastefully employed only a long-distance camera view.

As the medical staff continued to work on Brown, an ambulance drove onto the field, and Brown, still in full uniform, was strapped to a spineboard, gently placed on the gurney, put in the ambulance, and driven away to a hospital. When he left, we still didn't know whether he was dead or alive. The game had been interrupted for 17 minutes.

Fortunately, this story has a happy ending. As Simms said, medical care for injured players has improved dramatically, and we learned that Brown's life had been saved on the field that day. The top two vertebrae of his spinal column were displaced, and, as Gray had accurately reported, he did stop breathing—for perhaps 90 seconds—and also lost consciousness. According to a story written a few months later by Dennis Dillon in *The Sporting News,* his lips and tongue were turning blue when Dr. Lock started blowing air into his lungs. When the emergency equipment arrived, an artificial respirator, attached by paramedic Bill Grubb, took over. Then, after being placed in the ambulance, Brown was hooked up to an oxygen tank before it departed.

At the hospital, he regained consciousness and, although briefly paralyzed, began breathing on his own. Later that night, he began to regain mobility, and the next day, he underwent spinal surgery. Two days later, he walked 20 yards from his bed and back. Less than a month after surgery, he was jogging and doing other exercises.

When Brown left, the shaken players had no idea if he would recover. Detroit held on to win 13-10, earning a playoff berth as Sanders rushed for 184 yards and finished the season with 2,053, the second highest total in NFL history. Seven weeks after he nearly died, Brown walked to the stage at the ESPY Awards in New York and accepted the NFL Player of the Year award on behalf of Sanders.

༅

I began announcing NFL games for NBC in 1978, ending a wonderful 12-year relationship with the Rams, and except for 1998 and 1999, when NBC did not have pro football, I've called NFL action every year since. Although nothing in my broadcasting career has been as traumatic as the day Reggie Brown stopped breathing, I have endured the usual share of trying times created by equipment failure and bad weather. A prime example occurred two decades ago when we had a nasty technical foul-up on the biggest stage of all— the Super Bowl.

In 25 years with NBC, I was privileged to call eight Super Bowls, including four with longtime partner Merlin Olsen. Neither of us will ever forget the unrehearsed drama that took place in our booth in Super Bowl XVII, as Washington played Miami in the Rose Bowl in January 1983.

Traditionally, the network play-by-play announcer introduces the starting lineups on national television, as well as to the Super Bowl crowd over the public-address system. Immediately following the lineups that day, the network went away for a pregame round of commercials. When we returned and the two teams kicked off, Merlin and I quickly realized we had a huge problem.

When you call a game on radio or television, you hear your own voice and your partner's voice in your headphones. But somehow lines had gotten crossed during the PA announcements, and Merlin and I were now hearing our voices not as we spoke, but after a two-second delay.

If I said, "Here's the kickoff down to the goal line," by the time I'd say "goal line," "Here's the kickoff" would be echoing back through my headphones. It was not only distracting, but also mad-dening. It couldn't have been worse if our enemies had tried to sabo-tage us. The biggest game of the year, biggest television event of the year, a huge national audience, we'd been in hard preparation for two weeks, and now we could barely talk.

We learned quickly that we had to speak in three- or four-word sentences, because any long descriptions caused chaos. Our own words just kept coming back and hitting us. Any sentence longer than "He's out of bounds" was impossible to complete without interfer-ence.

Not only were we hearing an echo, but also there was a loud shriek in the headphones, and we couldn't hear instructions from Larry Cirillo, the producer. As the game analyst, Merlin had no idea what replay was coming until it began. He had to be ready for any-thing. And this is the Super Bowl with 130 million fans watching.

When we reached the first commercial break, Merlin and I both complained desperately to Cirillo.

"Somebody's got to fix this," we screamed. "It's driving us mad. It's impossible to do the game this way."

It wasn't his fault. But we had to yell at someone.

The response, as always, was, "We're working on it. It'll be fine." It never seems that bad to them. By this time, there were electricians crawling all around the booth, like someone searching for a missing contact lens, checking the connections. One of them spilled coffee on my spotting boards. What else could go wrong?

As the game continued, the echo effect continued. Now, we reached the second commercial break, halfway through the first quarter, and they still hadn't fixed the problem. I was furious. This was going to be a career killer. Every critic in the country was going to have a field day with this telecast. I had to make my point, so in my next verbal blast at Cirillo I tossed in plenty of profanity for punctuation. It's the angriest I've been in my entire career.

In those days, when we communicated during commercials to the production truck, the regular audience couldn't hear us, but anyone watching on satellite could. They didn't get the commercials, so they were party to my swearing a blue streak as I tried to get the attention of the truck. A writer in a remote area of Texas heard my fit and wrote about it the next day, not quoting me word for word, thankfully, but saying something like, "Anyone who thinks Dick Enberg is vanilla, don't believe it. I heard proof that he's *a lot* stronger than vanilla."

The problem was finally fixed, but Merlin and I were hardly upbeat about what we felt was a first-quarter disaster. In the parking lot after the game, I refused to even talk to Cirillo and our beloved director, Ted Nathanson.

"I don't want to talk about the telecast," I said. "It's the worst football game I've ever done."

I had planned a Super Bowl party at my house that night. When I arrived after the game, everyone was raving about the telecast. I couldn't believe it. When I told them about the echo torture, they all said the broadcast sounded normal to them.

One of the guys had taped the game, and he said, "Let's play the first quarter and see what you think."

When I listened, I was amazed. It was damn good. In preparing for a Super Bowl, you have so much information that there's a tendency to bombard the audience from the very start, but the echo prevented it. There were plenty of pauses, letting the audience ease its way into the game. It was a good lesson to learn. All announcers talk too much, and sometimes it's good to back off a little. Less can be more.

The next day I hosted a luncheon in Beverly Hills, where Washington's John Riggins, who rushed for 166 yards in the

Redskins' victory, was honored as the game's Most Valuable Player. He arrived late, cradling a bottle of beer. It looked as if he hadn't slept the entire night. His wife and I were seated next to each other at the head table, and it must have been embarrassing for her, so I tried to be philosophical.

"Winning a Super Bowl is such a rare thing," I mused, "and to be the MVP, too, is really rare. It's the kind of career highlight you want to embrace, one you'll be able to enjoy for many tomorrows."

She looked at me and said, "Don't worry about John. He's already enjoying tomorrow. It started last night."

Even before Merlin and I survived Super Bowl XVII, or as we called it "The Echo Game," we suffered through "The Freezer Bowl," the 1981 AFC Championship in Cincinnati (played the day after my first long conversation with my future wife Barbara). It was a game that should not have been played. It was brutally cold. The game-time temperature of nine degrees below zero and wind that gusted to 35 miles an hour created a wind-chill factor of −59, still the coldest in NFL history. Several Bengals and Chargers players suffered frostbite, some of it serious. More than 13,000 ticket holders stayed home.

We walked 100 yards from our car to the stadium, and, in the bitterly cold wind, it felt like somebody was driving nails into our foreheads. The elevator to the press box was frozen. There was no glass in the front of our broadcast booth, so we were totally exposed to the wind and sub-zero conditions. Merlin walked in with a cup of hot coffee, set it down for a minute, and when he picked it up, it was frozen. In fact, if you threw water in the air, it would flash freeze. During the game, we had electric blankets wrapped around our legs, and Merlin was wearing his ski clothes, but we were never comfortable. When Merlin, this big Utah mountain man, with all of his snow gear, started shivering in the middle of the third quarter, I shuddered in unison. When he got silent, I briefly worried he was going into hypothermia.

Not only was the weather dangerous for everyone, it was particularly unfair to the visiting Chargers. If you can't throw and kick properly, it's not football anymore. San Diego was not only a passing team, but a warm-weather team. The Chargers had no chance to win. B-B-B-Bengals 27, Ch-Ch-Ch-Chargers 7.

As a former player who endured his share of harsh conditions, Merlin remains concerned that a game under such extreme conditions will happen again.

"The NFL still has no plan for postponing games," Merlin said as he recalled that frigid day in Cincinnati. "There ought to be something in writing. If it becomes apparent that lives or long-term health are at risk, there should be a way to postpone it. Players or spectators shouldn't have to risk suffering from frostbite for the rest of their lives."

⋘

My first Super Bowl for NBC was Super Bowl XIII in the Orange Bowl, still one of the best ever played as Pittsburgh and Terry Bradshaw outscored Dallas and Roger Staubach 35-31. The game climaxed the 1978 season, the first that Merlin Olsen and I had worked together. The Hall of Famer, Olsen, and I were partners for 11 years at NBC, and we enjoyed great chemistry. He was the ultimate student, always prepared. He not only brought several pages of notes for himself, but had notes for the producer, notes for the director, and notes for our one-on-one byplay as well. He believed that you needed much more information than you would ever use. Besides, it served as added insurance for a lopsided game.

The network's other top broadcasting team that year included Curt Gowdy, nearing the end of a great NBC career, and former quarterback John Brodie. As the game approached, Don Ohlmeyer, the executive producer of NBC Sports, had trouble deciding which of the two teams should call the Super Bowl. I made a suggestion.

"I'm not eager to replace a friend and a legend," I said to Ohlmeyer. "My time will come. Why don't you have Curt call the play-by-play, and Olsen and Brodie share work as analysts, and make me the host? I'll do the opening, the halftime, and the postgame show."

And that's what we did.

My position for the game was on top of a platform, on the very roof of the Orange Bowl press box. Thirteen years earlier, I had found myself on the Los Angeles Coliseum press box roof, when I cut a demo tape for the Rams, and here I was perched on a roof again. It was almost as if I were on my own little planet, looking down into this beautiful jewel box filled with 80,000 people. There was a light rain that stopped before the game, but a strong wind blew throughout the game. The one element that drives me nuts is wind. No one looks good or is comfortable on television with his hair flying to the four points of the compass. In fact, I had mine so lacquered down that one of our technicians said my hair spray should have won an Emmy. Although my hair didn't move, I did loosen my grip on some of my notes and they were last seen floating somewhere over Biscayne Bay.

Two years later, Merlin and I did our first Super Bowl together—my first as the play-by-play announcer—when the Raiders steamrolled the Eagles 27-10 in Super Bowl XV in New Orleans. For a play-by-play announcer, there's nothing to compare with the intensity of being involved in the Super Bowl. It's overwhelming. First of all, there are countless media demands that pull you away from your preparation. The phone rings constantly. All the while, you're trying to get ready for the game broadcast, which is more difficult than any other, because there's so much more information to absorb. It's as if you're studying for a final exam, and when you feel reasonably caught up, the professor says here's another stack of material you better know. While the local papers are cranking out feature after feature on everyone in the game, down to the assistant trainers, so are the national media. You're never done. I consumed everything I could get my hands on and still felt there were stories I had missed.

More people are watching this game than any other event during the entire year on television and that includes every newspaper critic from New York to Anchorage. If you foul up, you'll read about it the next day in the newspaper, and bad reviews never feel very good. So, when finally settling into my seat in the booth, I had prepped hard to get a top grade in this final exam.

While we called Super Bowl XV, Merlin's wife, Susan, was a guest in the private Superdome box of Fred Silverman, NBC's president. When we returned to the network hotel for the postgame party, we were anxious to get feedback on our first Super Bowl together. As we came in the door, Susan rushed over and told us that Silverman had said that he really liked the broadcast. We immediately stood more erect and, with big smiles, asked what our boss really liked about it.

And she answered, "You got off right on time."

The networks always have feature programming billboarded to follow the Super Bowl, and the last thing they want is for the telecast to run long and have people tune out or switch to another channel. Yes, we "got off right on time"—and *that* made it a great telecast.

Nearly 25 years later, it remains a mandate. While I was working on the pregame show for Super Bowl XXXVIII in Houston, a CBS executive was already fretting about the game's length before it even kicked off.

"You don't think this game could possibly go into overtime, do you?" he worried.

He was rooting against overtime, because the network was heavily promoting *Survivor: All-Stars,* which followed. Because overtime means you're having a great game, in essence, as a CBS executive, he was pulling against himself. We missed overtime, but just barely, because New England's Adam Vinatieri was the "ultimate survivor," kicking a 41-yard field goal with four seconds left to defeat Carolina 32-29.

๛

Five years after the Raiders defeated the Eagles—when we "got off right on time"—Merlin and I were back in New Orleans as the Bears and Patriots prepared to play Super Bowl XX in January 1986. A few days before the game, we visited Tulane University to watch the Bears practice. As I stood on the sideline, someone behind me wrapped his arms around my chest and lifted me off the ground. There was a loud crack. When I returned to earth, I turned around to see a smiling Walter Payton, the Bears' All-Pro running back.

"See, Enberg," he said, continuing to grin, "I got your back in place for you."

I reached into the pocket of my sport coat.

"No, Walter," I said, "you've just broken my glasses."

Sure enough, he had snapped the frame. And he thought that was hilarious. He didn't mean to break my glasses, of course; he was just trying to have some fun. He had a smile on his face as wide as a crossbar. That's the way he was with everyone. Nicknamed "Sweetness," Payton was not only a Hall of Fame player, but also a real character whose love of life permeated the locker room and kept his teammates loose. He gave his smile of sweetness to every teammate and his supreme toughness to every opponent who tried to stop him. His loss at such a young age—he died at 45 from a rare liver disease in 1999—was felt deeply by his former teammates and everyone who knew him.

Payton and his teammates overwhelmed the Patriots 46-10 in Super Bowl XX, one of two Super Bowl routs that I called. The other was Super Bowl XXVII when Dallas pounded Buffalo 52-17. I'm extraordinarily proud of both of those broadcasts. Your best work is required in the worst games, and I feel we really answered the challenge. They were as well done as any games in my 50 years, and I give full credit to my partners Merlin Olsen in Super Bowl XX and Bob Trumpy in Super Bowl XXVII.

Too many announcers give up on a one-sided game. They feel it's a personal insult to their talent. Their attitude is, "How could we be saddled with this terrible game?" That's not professional. If it's a bad game, you can't take it personally. We're paid to broadcast the tough games. Anyone can call games that go 43-40 in overtime. The excitement of the game carries the broadcast. You don't even need to think about the words coming out of your mouth.

In a one-sided game, our personal challenge is to keep as many people watching as we can—with humor, with historical notes, and with interesting anecdotes. The ratings of both of those Super Bowls indicated that people didn't tune out in the second half. Super Bowl XX, in fact, is still the fourth-highest-rated sports program of all time. Super Bowl XXVII is sixth on the all-time list of most-watched TV programs of any sort (based on total number of viewers).

In January 1996, 10 years after Super Bowl XX, Simms, Maguire, and I met with Steelers coach Bill Cowher a couple of days before Super Bowl XXX. Besides our team of announcers, the meeting also included producer Tommy Roy and director John Gonzalez. Meetings like this are standard before every televised football game, although as a group, head coaches aren't always the best source of information. Some don't trust anyone in the media, so they feed you a lot of pap. Others are so open that they shock you.

As we sat down, Cowher looked at the five of us, smiled, and said, "What would you think if I tried an onside kick on the opening kickoff of the Super Bowl?"

Simultaneously, five mouths fell open.

"Are you serious?" we all chorused.

"I sure am," Cowher answered, producing a Dallas special teams lineup. "Here's the guy we'll attack. On every kickoff, he leaves early, going back to help form the blocking wedge." Then he showed us where his kicker, Norm Johnson, would put the ball. "We've got to lose the coin toss first," Cowher continued. "But even if we don't, or if we change our minds, I guarantee you I'm going to try it in the game."

What a piece of information! As it turned out, the Steelers did lose the coin toss, but Cowher decided to kick deep on the opening kickoff. Still, on every subsequent Pittsburgh kickoff, there were several cameras focused on the Dallas player, covering him from every possible angle. In the fourth quarter, after Johnson hit a field goal to trim the Cowboys' lead to 20-10 with just over 11 minutes left, we struck gold. As Cowher promised, he went for the onside kick, and Pittsburgh's Deon Figures recovered at his own 48-yard line to set up a 52-yard touchdown drive.

And were we ever ready for the onside kick! Total coverage, front, back, and side views, and Simms and Maguire thoroughly explained why it happened. The touchdown that followed put the Steelers back in business—the score was 20-17 with 6:36 left. The Cowboys, however, eventually prevailed 27-17.

Cowher took a considerable gamble by telling us his plan, but for two days, we kept his secret. Naturally, if one of us had wanted to be a big shot and spill the beans, we would have ruined our relationship with him forever. But our silence only perpetuated his trust in us. It goes both ways.

Although some coaches will share their specific game plans, others are super cautious. Bill Belichick of the New England Patriots is about as careful as anyone can be. He's a good guy and a great coach—he's led his team to two Super Bowl victories in the last three years—but he becomes suspicious if you ask him to give his full name. He figures that no matter what he says, he might be giving away information that could aid the opposition. He'll talk for 10 minutes, but when you look at your notes, where's the meat? His father was an assistant coach at the U.S. Naval Academy for more than 30 years. Apparently the lesson of "Loose Lips Sink Ships" has had permanent impact on his son's style.

Coach Chuck Noll, who won four Super Bowls with the Steelers in the 1970s and is now retired, had a puzzling approach. He wouldn't give us anything close to inside information, yet he always let his assistants talk without restriction, and they couldn't have been more helpful. One time, Merlin and I drove Noll back to his hotel after a Saturday practice, and, even though he spent 15 minutes captive in our car, he was as taciturn as ever. Meanwhile, his assistants, as usual, freely gave us the game plan on both offense and defense.

You can usually tell if an assistant coach has been cooperative in giving critical inside information to the broadcasters, because at some time during the game they'll get a TV shot of him on the sideline or in the press box. Then, one of the announcers will say something like, "Here's one of the top offensive coordinators in the NFL," or "He should be a head coach some day." A little deserved payback from the guys in the booth.

⤳

During the 11 seasons Merlin and I worked together, we did a game on Thanksgiving every year. Merlin, ever creative, suggested one year that we shoot promos for the holiday game on a large turkey farm. NBC liked the idea and sent the two of us to Turlock in Calfornia's San Joaquin Valley. Turkeys are noisy birds, but Merlin knew that with a sharp whistle, they'll go silent for several seconds, before resuming their frenzied gobbling, which gave our producer, David Neal, an idea.

They videotaped the two of us sitting in front of a TV set in the middle of a pen, surrounded by 5,000 turkeys, all gobbling like people at a cocktail party. Over this shot, an announcer's voice said, "When NBC Sports talks… everybody listens." Instantly, the turkeys were quiet. Merlin had whistled, of course, but his whistle was wiped off the tape. After a few seconds, almost as if cued, the turkeys started up again, gobbling more frantically than ever. That's how the promo finished—with a chorus from our cast of thousands.

We had a lot of fun that day, although, as I recall, there was considerable debate as to who were the biggest turkeys.

Besides working with Merlin Olsen, Bob Trumpy, and the two-man team of Phil Simms and Paul Maguire at NBC, I shared a booth for three years with Hall of Fame coach Bill Walsh, winner of three Super Bowls with the 49ers. As a traveling partner, Walsh was absolutely delightful. He's cerebral and an excellent storyteller and loves to have a good laugh. When the producer, director, and the two of us met for our weekly dinner on Friday night, he always brought an issue—international, national, or personal—for us to chew on over dinner.

Shortly after the Berlin Wall had come down, his question for the night was, "What do you think Europe and Germany will be like 10 years from now?" So we discussed that. Another time he asked, "There's a woman in your life, who is not your wife or a relative, but someone you admire tremendously and enjoy being around. You have no romantic or sexual relationship with her. Who is she and why is she important to you?" He always had a thought-provoking question that spurred good conversation.

On Friday nights, Walsh was so charming, so interesting, and so funny that he could have hosted *The Tonight Show*. However, as the next day and a half unfolded, we could see his personality changing. Saturday, we'd go to practice, then have our production meeting, and it was like watching a flower start to close. By game time on Sunday, he was a totally different person than the one who was so entertaining on Friday night. It took a while, but I finally figured out that when the game began, he wasn't just a broadcaster, he became a coach again. He saw the game with a coach's temperament. Something would happen on the field, and it was like tearing a scab off his memory. It reminded him of a play or mistake that had caused him to lose a game. He would become genuinely upset and didn't feel like finding any humor in the moment. His insights as a commentator were terrific, but his analysis lacked the flair and sense of fun that we all knew was hidden somewhere inside.

I used to kid him, "Bill, one of these days when we get in the booth, I'm going to slip you a glass of vodka, instead of water, to see if we can't get you back to Friday night."

He knew that it was happening to him but couldn't change.

I wasn't surprised when Walsh left the booth in 1992 and went back to coaching, taking over at Stanford, where he had coached in the late 1970s. After three more years with the Cardinal, he returned to the 49ers as a consultant and, later, a general manager. He remains one of the great football minds in my 50 years as a broadcaster.

∽

Of all the NFL games I've done for NBC and, now, CBS, the two most memorable featured Denver and John Elway. They were 11 years apart, and the Broncos won both of them. The first was the 1986 AFC Championship Game—which will forever be known as "The Drive"—and the second was Super Bowl XXXII, when the 12-point underdog Broncos upset Green Bay and snapped the AFC's 13-game losing streak in the championship game.

In the 1986 conference title game (played in January 1987), Denver was trailing Cleveland 20-13 with less than six minutes left when Elway brought his team out of the huddle on his own two-yard line. It was first and 98! It was dark, it was cold, the field was worn and partially frozen, and the Broncos were on their heels. Cleveland had just taken the lead on a 48-yard touchdown pass by Bernie Kosar. Denver's Ken Bell bobbled the ensuing kickoff and was tackled at the two-yard line. The howling fans in Cleveland—nearly 80,000 of them—believed they were on their way to the Super Bowl.

Backed up against his own end zone, Elway artfully created one of the most incredible drives in football history. It was a Michelangelo. "The Drive" consisted of 15 tense plays and included nine passes and two runs by Elway. It was filled with small miracles. Facing third and 18 from the Cleveland 48 with only 1:47 left, Elway was in the shotgun when the snap from center actually clipped Denver man-in-motion Steve Watson's rear end and bounced to the ground. Elway, a former baseball player, fielded the ball one-handed, back-pedaled, and rifled a 20-yard completion to Mark Jackson for a first down on the Browns' 28. About a minute later, he zipped a five-yard touchdown pass to the diving Jackson, and the conversion sent the game into overtime. There, Elway drove his team to the game-winning field goal.

When leaving the stadium after the home team loses, particularly a monumental game like that one, it can be frightening and dangerous. There are a lot of angry fans, many fortified with alcohol, who are ready to take out their anger on someone. But on this occasion it was so quiet outside old Municipal Stadium that it had the solemn feel of a mass funeral. It was as if the whole city had collapsed. I'll never forget such a stifling silence.

Eleven years later, the Broncos' 31-24 victory in Super Bowl XXXII in San Diego not only ended the NFC's 13-year winning streak, it stopped Denver's longtime personal anguish. The Broncos had made it to the Super Bowl four times before and lost by ever-increasing margins—17, 19, 32, and 45 points. On the other hand, Green Bay's Super Bowl record was an imposing 3-0.

The Broncos' winning touchdown came with just 1:45 remaining, as MVP Terrell Davis, a San Diego native, scored on a one-yard run, his Super Bowl-record third rushing touchdown of the game. Elway, who was Denver's quarterback in three of its four Super Bowl losses, finally wore his first ear-to-ear victory grin at age 37.

Denver's first Super Bowl victory was historic for another reason. It's the last NFL game NBC has ever done. Only a few days before kickoff, the NFL, in its infinite wisdom, decided to announce that CBS had outbid NBC for the rights to the AFC in the new television package. So we went into the game knowing that it was our swan song. It seemed insensitive to me that the league didn't wait until after the game to make the announcement. The NFL should have realized that because we now knew it would be our last game that it would steal some of the joy. We were all depressed, not only the broadcasters, but also all of the technicians, cameramen, and production personnel.

Shortly after the announcement, Simms, Maguire, and I filed somberly into a room for our pre-Super Bowl interview with Denver coach Mike Shanahan.

"I want to say something before we get into the details of the game," the coach told us. "I've heard that this is going to be your last broadcast, and I'm sure you're all hurting. But I want to tell you how much I've appreciated your work and how much I've enjoyed getting to know you guys. I hope we have a great game for you."

Considering all of the things on his mind, we were totally impressed with his sincerity and sensitivity. I'll always admire his class.

After NBC lost NFL football, Pat Haden and I called six Notre Dame home games in both 1998 and 1999. Although I missed the NFL's 20-game schedule, they were two enjoyable years. My relationship with Notre Dame dated back to doing UCLA basketball more than 30 years earlier, and I loved returning to the Irish campus. All universities talk about being balanced athletically and academically. No one has been perfect, but Notre Dame comes as close to getting it right as any school I've seen.

I knew Haden as the Rams' quarterback in the 1970s and as one of six charter members of the Academic All-America Hall of Fame, along with Merlin Olsen, Donn Moomaw (who married Barbara and me), Bill Bradley, Pete Dawkins, and Tom McMillen. While working with him on those 12 games, I got to know him on a more personal basis. The more time I spent with Haden, the more there was to like.

He called me in my room one Friday afternoon at Notre Dame and said, "You've got to be down in the lobby at 4:30. Don't ask any questions. Just be here."

When I met him in the lobby, he told me to get in a waiting car and then drove us over to the campus. Arriving at a field where the Notre Dame marching band was practicing, he told me, "You are going to lead the band in 'The 1812 Overture.'"

I was floored. On a previous broadcast, I had made an offhand comment that we all have our fantasies, and one of mine is to lead a big orchestra in one of my favorite classical pieces, such as "The 1812 Overture." The Notre Dame band traditionally plays that composition around the start of the fourth quarter.

I scurried up the conductor's ladder, picked up his baton, raised my arms and... nothing. I thought bands started playing when you raised your arms, but it's when you bring them down that they begin to play. After a few misfired trumpets, we got going in full sound. Now I was really into it, waving my arms with great enthusiasm and pointing at the percussion instruments at the appropriate times for the cannons in the piece. The band seemed in high spirits, too. With a final wave of my baton, we finished triumphantly. Oh My! It was a fantasy fulfilled. All thanks to Haden who cared enough to go to considerable trouble to arrange it.

❧

After 25 years at NBC, I joined CBS in January 2000. I was immensely happy at NBC, and I could have stayed. The network had been very good to me and wanted to extend my contract. In fact, I took nearly a million dollars less over four years to go to CBS. But, at age 65, I felt it was time to be a little selfish. I should be doing the sports that I enjoy the most, and at this time of my life, those are football and basketball. NBC no longer had either the NFL or the NCAA Tournament. I went to CBS with the clear understanding that for the first time in more than two decades, I would not be the No. 1

announcer in either football or basketball, and I accepted that. I've had my time.

Calling NFL football for CBS since 2000, I've been teamed with another NFL Hall of Famer, Dan Dierdorf. In many ways, Dan reminds me of Merlin Olsen, not only in size, but also in intellect. They're both very astute and good-humored. As there was with Merlin, there was immediate rapport with Dan. That can't be contrived. The relationship either works or it doesn't.

Our pairing is yet another example of how fortunate I've been throughout my career. Someone outside my control has selected my partners, and without fail, each has been a person who has brightened my professional and personal life. It's fantastic that for 50 years, when I leave home for a game, I'm going to be working with someone I truly enjoy.

One of the added benefits of men the size of Dierdorf and Olsen is that they run terrific interference through public places, especially airports. I just grab my suitcase, duck behind their girth, and like a good running back, take the clear path. A warning, however, if you should ever encounter these former Pro Bowl stars, beware of their handshakes. These two men have the biggest hands I've ever seen. It's intimidating to shake hands with them. When I do, I silently beg that they don't execute a full squeeze. I'd rather slam my hand in the car door.

TIMEOUT

Miss Turkey

As DETAILED EARLIER, when working with Bill Walsh, it was almost impossible to distract him from his coach-like focus once the game began—even in the simplest of ways.

One year, our NBC schedule had us in Texas to televise the Thanksgiving Day game between the Cowboys and Steelers. The Turkish background of Pittsburgh offensive lineman Tunch Ilkin gave us some fodder for potential fun. As a young woman, Ilkin's mother, Ayten, had been selected as Miss Turkey.

Before the game, we planned a little humorous aside. We would take a shot of Ilkin on the sideline and tell the story about his mother. This would give Bill the chance to jump in and say that if the game didn't end soon we would all *Miss Turkey*. We thought it was a good line and a chance to bring a little holiday levity into the game. We even rehearsed it a couple of times as we drove from the hotel to the Silverdome.

The moment arrived. Director John Gonzalez took the close-up of Ilkin. I said, "There's Tunch Ilkin on the sideline. Fans in Pittsburgh may know this, but I'm sure the rest of the country doesn't realize that his mother was a beauty queen back in her native country. She was Miss Turkey." Then I paused.

And Walsh, without hesitation, said, "Yeah, and he's one of the best pass-blocking tackles in the league, too."

O-O-O-O-h My!

13

BREAKFAST AT WIMBLEDON

"Think of me kindly when you get back to the States. I'm a gynecologist."

—anonymous Wimbledon M.D.

NBC's broadcast booth at Wimbledon is as cramped as a tool shed. Located behind a corner scoreboard, just a half dozen rows off the Centre Court playing surface, the booth has a series of glass panels in front. For television on-camera shots it was necessary to open them in order for the announcers to be clearly seen, so the three of us—Chris Evert, John McEnroe, and me—were forced to squeeze our three backsides onto just two chairs. It was the only way to fit three faces into our tiny window frame.

Unfortunately, the glass wasn't soundproof. When we closed it during action, fans in front of us could hear our play-by-play call. This wasn't a problem when I was announcing the match being played on Centre Court. If I shouted, "What a brilliant, running forehand by Sampras!" fans were cheering and didn't hear my call. However, while sitting at Centre Court, we were often required to announce matches on other courts, offering our descriptions from the video monitor in the same booth. So, picture us sitting in this solemn cathedral of tennis, calling a match a quarter-mile away. While we focused on the action on our TV screen, play was continuing immediately in front of us. Now, when I bellowed, "Oh My! Capriati… what a shot!" all the fans in the immediate area would turn around and stare in the booth as if we'd gone mad. You could see in their confused looks what they were thinking, "Capriati? She's not even playing here."

One afternoon, an elderly woman sitting two rows away from us couldn't take it any longer. She stormed up the aisle and began rapping loudly on our window.

"You're being very rude in there," she snapped. "I can hear you announcing, and you're not even talking about the match I'm watching. Now stop it, or I'll report you."

At the first commercial break, we apologized and tried to explain, but there was no way she could understand. A peace offering of an NBC hat didn't appease her, either. I could only imagine her thinking, "I've waited all my life to get precious tickets to Centre

Court, only to have the experience ruined by the Yanks. The noisy colonists."

❧

NBC sent me to Wimbledon for the first time in 1979. I had never announced tennis before. That year, Bud Collins was doing the play-by-play and Donald Dell was his analyst, while my role was to host and conduct interviews. As part of our expanded coverage, the men's singles final was broadcast live for the first time. At the suggestion of NBC executive Bob Basche, we called it "Breakfast at Wimbledon," because the Saturday final would air at 9:00 a.m. New York time.

As the television revenue increased over the years, the All England Lawn Tennis and Croquet Club, which hosts the tournament, switched the men's final to Sunday and the women's final to Saturday. Now we had a double serving of "Breakfast." However, one thing club officials would not do in the early years was help NBC by delaying the starting time for the two championship matches. By tradition the first ball was struck at 2:00 p.m. London time, and that's precisely when the matches would begin.

The problem for us was that our telecast didn't start until 2:00 p.m. How were we going to properly welcome the audience, set the scene, and introduce the United States to our special live coverage when the match had already begun? The men's final in 1979 featured Sweden's Bjorn Borg, a huge favorite, against American Roscoe Tanner. Everybody at NBC, led by executive producer of sports Don Ohlmeyer, was in a quandary.

"The first set could be half over by the time we get on the air," Ohlmeyer lamented.

But we got lucky. Dell was not only our color commentator, but also Tanner's agent. Before the match, he suggested that Tanner use a locker room restroom to kill some time before coming onto the court. So, when the tournament referee went to collect the two players, the American said, "Hold on. I'm so nervous that I'd better go to the bathroom."

And he did. For four or five minutes he crouched in a stall, while everyone at Wimbledon waited. By the time Tanner made his court appearance and he and Borg warmed up for five minutes, we had the necessary time to properly greet our television audience. Collins later tagged Tanner's long pit stop as "Water Closet Gate!"

Roscoe not only gave us a boost in the bathroom, but also gave us a lift on the court. Borg had won three Wimbledon titles in a row, on his way to five straight. But the underdog Tanner battled to a two sets-to-one lead before Borg won two in a row and prevailed 6-4 in the final set.

Thankfully, today we no longer need long bathroom breaks by any of the players. They still announce 2:00 p.m. as the starting time, but play actually begins at 2:05 p.m.

&

When returning home, although totally enchanted with Wimbledon, I also realized the two weeks involved a heck of a lot of work. At the time, my NBC contract was based on a certain number of units in a calendar year. For example, a football or basketball game counted as one unit. To my dismay, Wimbledon also earned only one unit, which, in my mind, was grossly unfair. Fourteen days of Wimbledon wasn't 14 units, but it certainly was worth more than one. I asked my agent, Ed Hookstratten, to renegotiate. I suggested three units would be equitable, figuring with my newfound love for the event, I'd settle for two.

But Ohlmeyer hung tough, refusing to budge. He said, in effect, take one unit or don't go at all. For one of the few times in my career, I took a firm stand.

"That just isn't right," I protested. "I guess I'll stay home."

So, in 1980, on the Fourth of July weekend, I was sitting at home in Southern California, watching a classic on television, as Borg defeated John McEnroe in five grueling sets to win his fifth consecutive Wimbledon title. McEnroe won the incredibly dramatic fourth set tiebreak that lasted 22 minutes, 18-16—"the 18-16 Overture," as it became known. And I kept thinking, *I should be there.*

Well, after that, I was desperate to return. At the same time, NBC was eager to send me back. Despite our dispute, the network had been pleased with my work in 1979.

They compromised by crediting me with two units and without hesitation I accepted.

❧

One of the fascinating aspects of Wimbledon is the manner in which the British public embrace their Grand Slam event. No surprise, they revere and respect what is their equivalent of our Super Bowl.

The world knows that the Brits are amazingly long on patience. Foul weather must teach that. On one particularly nasty day, a long queue of fans had formed in the heavy rain outside our location at Centre Court. Long before airtime, I had made several trips past them en route to our booth. On each occasion, I couldn't help but notice two lovely ladies, at least in their 60s, standing patiently in place for hours under their umbrellas, or brollies. I knew they had seen me rushing by.

Curiosity called, so I stopped to ask, "When I race by you to get to the head of the line, what's to keep you from thinking I'm cutting in front?"

They looked at each other, then at me.

Their eyes tightened and one offered, "Young man, do you realize the damage we could do with our brollies?!?!"

To this day, I'm left with this image of two kindly matrons beating the total crap out of some rude bloke.

❧

In those early years at Wimbledon, Bud Collins was not only a friend, but also an editor and an invaluable resource. When I replaced him as play-by-play announcer in 1981, and he was shifted to the role of analyst, he never showed an ounce of resentment. Instead, he graciously assisted me to understand the sport and its subtleties. If I used an improper expression, he would say, "No, Dick, to be correct, you should say it this way." He could have let me hang myself on several occasions, but he didn't. What a tremendous ally!

Here's a man who has written the encyclopedia of the game. He's been the voice of tennis for five decades. In fact, I can think of only one other man who was *the* dominant announcer of his sport for such a long period, and that's Don Dunphy in boxing. What Bud knows off the top of his head, I would have to research for hours.

To this day, he is willing to share his absolute knowledge with anyone who cares about the game.

Although much of the daily coverage from Wimbledon consisted of two-hour shows, weekends demanded three and even four hours. Our final broadcast on championship Sunday lasted six hours, giving the producers plenty of flexibility. At best, the most we could reasonably expect from the men's final was a three-hour match, so that left three hours to fill. Out of this need, beginning in the early 1980s my "Wimbledon Memories" were born. They were produced by Glenn Adamo for two or three years, and when he left NBC, they were taken over by Ross Schneiderman.

Schneiderman began producing my essays, not only for Wimbledon, but also for golf, college basketball, and the Olympics. Because he also did statistics and research for me on most of the events I announced, everyone at the network kidded us because we seemed inseparable.

"What's going on?" they'd ask. "You guys having an affair?"

"No," we'd answer, "We're just a formidable doubles team."

I've won seven Emmys for writing those essays, and Ross deserves much of the credit, because he has the artistic savvy to select the proper video to fit my words and the ear to pick the right music to accent the moods of the piece. We've worked hand in glove. I could say I need a shot of McEnroe with a facial expression like, "I gotcha, now," and he'd find it. He always sensed the exact shot I was seeking. To my good fortune, Ross has also moved to CBS and continues on occasion to produce my essays.

Most of our wrap-up pieces at NBC ran three to four minutes, but we were allowed to go much longer at Wimbledon, because the final show had so much extra time. Once, we were allowed a marathon 13 minutes, unheard of in today's world of television. There wasn't a strict time limit, but on occasion I would get carried away, and Ross would greet me Sunday morning with the chilling words, "Dick, it's too long. We have to cut out this section."

It was like pulling my heart right out of my chest. When he knew he had to shorten the piece, Ross begged for sympathy by looking even more tired than usual. That wasn't difficult. He hadn't slept the entire night.

Over the years, we've refined the technique, having learned that our essays, no matter the sport, have more impact with fewer words. I found myself writing shorter sentences and using lengthened pauses. Ross would extend the video and the music longer in each segment. It made the finished product much more powerful and poignant.

Little did we realize when we began producing the essays as a time-filler that they would become so important in my career. At the Olympics in Barcelona (1992) and Atlanta (1996), for example, I did them on a daily basis. In Atlanta, they were known as *Dick Enberg's Moments* and had their own sponsor.

The reaction to those essays in Barcelona and Atlanta was interesting and revealing. Both times, upon returning home, there were two stacks of mail waiting for me. In one pile were letters from viewers who wrote beautiful, touching thank-you notes to express how they had watched a particular essay with their son or daughter or wife and found it a moving and inspiring experience.

In the other pile were clippings from newspaper critics who scolded me for being too emotional, too flowery, too sappy. I'm not saying that all of the critics were wrong, but I thought, "Which group are we trying to satisfy with our work—the public or the critics?" Too often, the media feels that to be journalistic one must be tough and unfeeling. I would argue that allowing your audience to feel deeply, as long as it's honest, is just as journalistic.

Years ago, one critic in his review wrote, "Enberg is the kind of guy who probably cries at weddings."

I sent him a letter and said, "How did you know?"

∽

Although tennis is a wonderful game, the players have never been as cooperative as those in other sports. For example, in Boris Becker's 16 years as a pro, I called almost every one of his Wimbledon and French Open matches, yet never talked to him once. Not once. That is mind-boggling. I tried and tried, but he was never available for a 15-minute chat. When he hung up his racquet, I even wrote a memory piece on his retirement but never had a chance to look him in the eye and ask him a question. And it's not as if I have the reputation of being a bad guy.

There are mandatory press conferences after every match, but those are for the writers, not for radio and television. I wanted to sit down with Becker, as I do with other athletes, and get some personal information that I could work into my broadcasts. In effect, I would be asking for notes that would humanize the German star to an American audience. Not talking to Becker in 16 years would be comparable to broadcasting several Green Bay Packers games every year without ever speaking to Brett Favre.

Ironically, as soon as he retired, Becker came into our NBC booth while John McEnroe and I were calling a match. He stayed for an entire set. Maybe I should have pressed harder for an opportunity during his career, but with Becker and several others, there was just so much barbed wire to get through that it was hardly worth it.

All of us who have covered tennis have our stories of frustration. Here's another. In 1995, at Roland Garros, the site of the French Open, I was looking down from the press box at one of the outside courts and saw Conchita Martinez, who had won Wimbledon the year before. I'd never had a chance to talk to Conchita, but here she was, in a quiet moment on an empty court just hitting balls with her coach, Eric van Harpen. There was no one around, so I thought, "Here's a good chance to get five or 10 minutes with her. Anything I learn will help me this week and at Wimbledon later this summer."

I walked down and stood at midcourt, off to the side. One of the balls rolled over to me. I threw it back to Conchita, so she and her coach knew I was there. They finished their workout but didn't come over to say hello. Instead, they walked over to the sideline, took two chairs, turned the backs of the chairs toward me, sat down, and started talking.

I was into a slow burn but tried to be nice.

"Pardon me, I'm Dick Enberg with NBC," I said, "and I'll be calling the matches here at the French Open for the network. I'd like to belatedly congratulate Conchita for her Wimbledon title. I wonder if you could give me five or 10 minutes when you're finished?"

She didn't even look at me.

"You know the rules," she snapped.

I looked at van Harpen.

"Yeah," he said. "If you want an interview, you've got to go through the WTA [Women's Tennis Association]."

And I responded in frustration, "You know something? I really love this game. I'm trying to reach out because I care about the game, care about how I represent it, and you're kicking me out of here? You won't even give me a few minutes?"

There was stony silence. I briefly got the impression that her coach wanted to be helpful, but he saw that his pupil was in no mood to cooperate. He shrugged as if to say, "What can I do? It's out of my control." So I left.

After I told that story to a few people, it spread quickly, and a WTA official came to me and apologized the next day, asking what she could do to help. My complaint seems to have had an impact, because since that time, the WTA has leaned on players and coaches at all tournaments. There has been considerably more cooperation by the athletes. You would think that players would want to work with the networks that are paying millions of dollars to televise these events, dollars that filter down to them in big prize money. One would expect that they'd be bright enough to say, "Part of our financial reward comes through the network rights fees. It's probably a good idea if I spend 10 minutes with their announcer."

Not only are the female players considerably more accessible today, but so are the men. It's one of the brightest developments on the tennis tour. In 2004, at Wimbledon, finalists Roger Federer, Andy Roddick, Maria Sharapova, and Serena Williams all made themselves available for conversations with me. I'm hopeful that the individual tennis empires have finally figured out that I'm not there to impose, but to inform.

～

You didn't have to explain tennis economics or communication skills to Arthur Ashe. He understood both. To be in the same company with the winner of the 1968 U.S. Open and the 1975 Wimbledon championship was to feel enriched by his powerful presence. And he was super serious about tennis protocol.

Many years ago, Hall of Famer Ted Schroeder, the 1949 Wimbledon champion and a San Diego neighbor, was kind enough to present me with a surprise gift, the official dark green- and purple-striped tie of the All England Club. The ties are not for sale to the public, but Ted, as a member of the Club, offered this gesture knowing my sincere affection for Wimbledon.

At the 1990 tournament, I wore the tie in honor of the men's Sunday final.

Early that morning, I ran into Ashe in the TV compound. He furrowed his brow, looked with concern over the rim of his glasses, and chastised, "Enberg, what are you doing with that tie? You're not a member!" And while I was searching for some clever reply, he walked off.

Of course, Arthur Ashe was right. This tennis hacker, Enberg, absolutely does not deserve to wear an official club tie, but I still do. Now I wear it because it reminds me of him. Each time I arrange the knot, I think of that gentleman of the game who taught us all by his elegant, intelligent manner. I respectfully remember Arthur and hope I'm paying him proper tribute.

❧

One year in London, I needed more than a necktie. A tourniquet was more in order. I had finished my Centre Court play-by-play and was returning to the NBC compound to kill time until our final off-air goodbye.

I was jolted to action by a cry from the production staff, "Where's Enberg? He's got to get us out of this taped segment and throw to commercial."

I was off in a 50-yard sprint. At high speed, I reached the three wooden steps entering our makeshift TV studio. Applying the brakes, my shoes slipped and I slammed my shin into the step's edge.

Limping into my on-camera position, I delivered the requisite, "We'll be back to Wimbledon after we pause for these words."

Now that I was done, the cameraman pointed at my bloody pants leg and asked what had happened. After looking at my leg, I hurried to a nearby first aid station to get the wound treated. There was only a half hour remaining before my final closing piece. The woman in attendance checked the injury and announced that it required two or three stitches to close the wound. And it would take a while to anesthetize the area.

"I don't have time for the anesthetic," I replied. "Gotta get back to work."

So she sewed me up, finishing with a plea, "Think of me kindly when you get back to the States."

"Why's that?" I asked.

"Because this is not what I'm normally asked to do," she said. "I'm a gynecologist."

On another trip to Europe, in that same summer of 1987, there was a totally different, but unusual emergency in the Enberg family. Our second daughter, Emily, was just 16 months old, and to entertain her during a car ride to the hotel, my wife Barbara allowed her to play with a coin purse. Its noise served the same purpose as a baby's rattle. Somehow, Emily silently managed to open the zipper, and before Barbara could stop her, the toddler had put a nickel in her mouth. Barbara shouted, "No!" Emily swallowed.

By this time, the car had reached the hotel, and Barbara, in a panic, arranged for an emergency ambulance. On the way to the hospital, Emily became ashen, then ill, and began to vomit. To the immense relief of her mother, she coughed up the nickel. Shortly after, as an added shock, out came a penny.

Only much later could we joke that our baby daughter was a money machine, capable of returning six cents for every five cents. That's a 20-percent return.

∽

As much as announcers may feel that they are distanced from the athletes, they are more closely connected than they think. Prior to the 2003 U.S. Open, I learned of a wonderful personal compliment from Pete Sampras. The USTA officials had planned to have a special ceremony for Pete, not only to celebrate his record 14th Grand Slam win the year before, but also to commemorate his announced retirement.

The ever-modest Sampras's reaction was to say no. I was told that under continued pressure from New York officials, Pete finally succumbed with one caveat, "that Enberg emcee the ceremony." When they told me, I felt like I'd hit a 130 mile-an-hour ace.

On the night of the salute at Arthur Ashe Stadium, while standing in the waiting room with all of the participants, including Pete's wife and young son, I approached Sampras, "Pete, I know your nature is not to openly boast, to showboat, but let me offer one suggestion. After you make your acceptance speech, I think you should acknowledge the crowd by taking a grand tour around the stadium."

His initital response was negative.

I continued, "Think of it this way. If Arthur Ashe were alive tonight and sitting way over on the far side, don't you think it would be the right thing if you walked near him so that he could stand and applaud your great career?"

When I left the room to begin the introductions, I had no idea how Pete would respond.

Touching photographs are evidence of the climax of that evening. Sampras, embracing his baby son, walked and waved his way around the perimeter of the stadium, all to a standing ovation. Many years from now, Pete will be glad he took such an uncomfortable tour. And we will always be grateful he gave us a chance to cheer. Someday, so will his son.

People criticized Sampras throughout his career because he wasn't flamboyant enough. I always thought that to impose a personality on Pete that wasn't his was ridiculous. He was a gentleman who played tennis the way it was designed. His respectful demeanor on court was a tribute to stars of the past, such as Ashe, Stan Smith, Rod Laver, and the rest of the great corps of Laver's Australian countrymen.

∽

Of the many important tennis matches I've called over the years, the most emotionally moving for me took place in 1987, when Australian Pat Cash defeated Czechoslovakia's Ivan Lendl for the Wimbledon championship. During the course of the match, our director, Ted Nathanson, trained an isolated camera on Cash's father sitting in the stands. The old man, a former Australian Rules football player, was a ruddy, rugged-looking character, wearing a cap that was tipped askew. Whenever his son made a brilliant shot, he would clench his fist as if to say, "Atta-boy, mate."

At the conclusion of the match, as Cash won his first and only Wimbledon title, he didn't wait to accept congratulations from the Duke and Duchess of Kent. Instead, he sprinted into the stands, stepped onto the roof of our booth, climbed over the ledge to the second level of the Friends' Box, and bear-hugged his dad. Here were these two tough guys, son and father, meeting in a manly victory embrace. It was every son hugging every dad.

My own father had died just three years earlier, and I choked up. I was on the edge of a serious sob, totally incapable of uttering a single word, as I thought about Arnie and me. Fortunately, it was okay to be silent for a few seconds, because the television pictures were so powerful, but eventually I knew I had to attempt to say something. Finally, I croaked out a few words to get to a commercial before I emotionally "Cashed it in."

The 1996 Wimbledon final between Holland's Richard Krajicek and American MaliVai Washington produced quite a different reporting challenge. Employing the reverent, dramatic tones deserving of such a major occasion, I respectfully welcomed our live audience to the hallowed lawns of the All England Club.

"We're at famed Centre Court for Breakfast at Wimbledon, as two surprising underdogs vie for this coveted Grand Slam championship," I crooned, using my best theatrical whisper.

As I continued in my hushed delivery, the nude form of an attractive 23-year-old barmaid from the village of Wimbledon streaked from one end of Centre Court toward the Royal Box. I saw her but didn't call any attention to such a bold interruption. My years of training have taught me that if something inappropriate occurs in the arena, ignore it, because the cameras probably haven't covered it. So, sanctimoniously, I continued, "... Krajicek and Washington... one will join the elite list of Wimbledon champions."

It was at this point that the ever spontaneous John McEnroe, yet to be introduced, jumped into the broadcast, shouting, "SHE'S NAKED!... NO CLOTHES ON!... GET A SHOT OF HER!... SHE'S STREAKING!"

My attempt at a cover-up was totally shattered. We'd gone from a cathedral mood to cabaret in a matter of seconds.

At this point our NBC cameras tastefully showed Centre Court personnel covering the woman with blankets. Some said after the incident that there was a fight over who would have the honors. Meanwhile, we noticed the Duke of Kent with an appreciative smile. McEnroe was smiling, too.

Oh, the crosses we have to bear, or is it bare?

⮜

Occasionally, people complain about the nationalism exhibited by tennis announcers. "You seem to be pro-American," they cry. Well, we are. And the Germans are pro-German, and the Brits are pro-British, but not to the point that any of us ignore the great play from both sides. Realistically, we all know that our national audience is going to be much bigger if one of our "own" has a chance to win the tournament. When I peruse the draw, I always attempt to handicap whether an American can get to the final. I hope so, because it will make a big difference in our ratings. If we wind up with two Spaniards playing for the French Open title, it might be good tennis, but does anyone care in Chicago? We're not there to make it exciting for Madrid and Barcelona.

That's why it was so captivating in 1989 when Michael Chang became the first American in 34 years to win the French Open. The 15th seed, Chang, only 17 years and three months old, was also the youngest-ever male winner of a Grand Slam event. To get to the quarterfinals, he had to rally from two sets down to upset top-seeded Ivan Lendl and overcome severe cramps in the process. How can anyone forget Chang foiling Lendl with a desperate underhanded serve? He eventually defeated Stefan Edberg in a sensational five-set final.

❧

This may surprise you, but if there's one sport where you *don't* need an intruder like me, it's tennis. Of all sports, tennis least requires an announcer. It's absolutely the simplest TV sport of all to call. It's played in a small, defined area, usually contested between only two competitors, and any good chair umpire offers a reliable call. Those of us in the booth fill in with personal stories and strategy, while fans at home can get the basics by watching the screen and listening to the umpire. In fact, the BBC announcers in England often won't say a single word throughout an entire game.

If anything—and I'm including myself—30 percent of tennis commentary is intrusive, and 70 percent is complementary. All of us could say much less. The challenge is to allow more, by talking less.

Besides working with Bud Collins for more than 20 years, I've shared a booth with many other talented analysts, almost a "Who's Who" of the tennis world. My longest relationships have been with McEnroe, Chris Evert, and Mary Carillo, but I've also worked with Tracy Austin, Jimmy Connors, Mary Joe Fernandez, Billie Jean King, Patrick McEnroe, Pam Shriver, Stan Smith, Tony Trabert, and JoAnne Russell. Most of them are in the International Tennis Hall of

Fame in Newport, Rhode Island. How's that for serving it up in elite company?

To me, it's fascinating how John McEnroe and Chris Evert are so consistent. They have the same personality in the broadcast booth as they did on the court.

As a player, Chris was calculating, unemotional, patient, and precise, and a great sport. Tactically, she liked to hang back on the baseline, rather than charge the net. Her steady on-court demeanor gave you no hint as to whether she was winning or losing the match. Then, she took that on-court personality to the broadcast booth. On the air, she was cerebral, pleasant, prepared, on time, and reluctant to criticize anyone. She emphasized the positives in a player's game.

Johnny Mac, as a competitor, was gifted, unpredictable, volatile, and aggressive. He was always on the attack, charging the net, volleying winners with those magical hands. Serve and charge was his M.O. Opponents had to recognize that he would not only force the action, but also impose his personality on the match. As an announcer, he's the same—candid, shooting from the hip, and never concerned about engaging the brain to soften his reportage. If he feels he's right, he'll passionately pound away. He seemingly wings his material, but he's so intelligent it doesn't matter. As he was on court, Mac is spirited, controversial, and always ready for a good fight.

Since Chris has retired from broadcasting, John and I have worked with Mary Carillo. As New York City teenagers, John and Mary teamed up to win the mixed doubles title at the 1977 French Open. Now they're partners again, but this time they're at war with each other. Their relationship reminds me of Al McGuire and Billy Packer. They love to disagree.

John, basically, is like Al. You never know what he's going to say. His commentary often is brilliantly off the cuff. Mary, on the other hand, is carefully prepared and always ready with the facts to back up her analysis. She's like Billy. It truly makes for good television.

TIMEOUT

Keep Your Shirt On

WHEN SUMMER DAYS SCORCH in London, fans at Wimbledon, unaccustomed to extreme temperatures, find it difficult to cope. Fainting spectators are common.

At the U.S. Open, fans seek relief by taking off their shirts on hot days, but that's forbidden at Wimbledon. The ushers at Centre Court, who are all English military personnel, are very diligent about enforcing the rule.

One sweltering day a few years ago, we opened the window of our booth between matches, hoping for a hint of a fresh breeze. As we looked out, we noticed a fan nearby who had taken off his shirt. Quickly, an army sergeant marched down the aisle and admonished him.

"Young man," he said, "I must inform you that it's against proper behavior to remove your shirt. Please, put on your shirt or I must escort you out of Centre Court."

No argument. The man complied.

As the officer walked back up the aisle, an attractive woman, wearing a tightly fitted tank top, cooed flirtatiously, "Pardon me, Sir, does that rule apply to all of us on Centre Court?"

Without missing a beat, he turned and said, "Madam, there are exceptions to *every* rule."

14

TOO CLOSE
TO CALL

*"Horses are a lot like humans. You can identify
the good ones from the look in their eyes."*

—Seth Hancock

S pending a day at the racetrack is one of the world's great escapes. I live just a few minutes from Del Mar, and, when I feel pressured by life's demands, I can drive over to the track, buy a *Daily Racing Form*, and lose myself for an entire afternoon.

I love the Daily Racing Form. Reading it reminds me of trying to solve a geometry problem. You've been given all the information you need, and the correct answers are right there. You just have to find them. And when you nail a winner, that's an Oh My! It's instant gratification.

Of course, when you pick a horse, it's hard to make your way to the betting window without changing your mind. Everyone at the track has an opinion. If you listen to all of them, you'll bet on every horse in every race. They all have inside information on a "can't-miss winner."

Over the years, I've been enthralled with the variety of characters at the racetrack. They're Runyonesque. You rub shoulders with some of the richest people around—the ones who own the horses—and some of the poorest… the railbirds groping for a couple of bucks to bet on the late double. They all have a story wrapped around a "hot tip."

My broadcast partner, Al McGuire, was one of those racetrack characters. His method of operation was to bet two dollars on every horse in every race. As they streaked across the finish line, he would cry, "Got the winner again!" After the next race, he would celebrate again. "Who won that? No. 8? Got it!" I've even borrowed Al's method when I'm having a rotten day. If I haven't cashed a ticket after six or seven races, I'll buy a two-dollar ticket on every horse just to break out of my slump, knowing I'm going to hit at least one winner. And who knows? It might be a long shot, and I might even break even for the day. (In racetrack terms, *breaking even* means you only lost a little.)

But even if I come home from the track with empty pockets, I've had a full afternoon of entertainment. I've forgotten all my troubles, and it's a lot cheaper than psychiatry.

❦

My first real involvement with the "Sport of Kings" came in my first year at KTLA. The station aired a half-hour show every Friday night that previewed Saturday's feature race at Santa Anita, and I was the host. I was 31 years old, and I didn't know a furlong from a fetlock. I'd gone to the Kentucky Derby once as a graduate student at Indiana, standing with the throngs in the infield, but that was the extent of my experience. I didn't know any of the terminology. To make it even more awkward, people in racing are inherently suspicious of outsiders. There's an immediate distance, a be-wary-of-the-newcomer attitude.

Dan Smith, Santa Anita's assistant publicity director, bailed me out. Before we taped the show early each Friday, Dan lined up guests and prepared questions for me, briefing me on Thursday night. I'd leave KTLA right after the 10:00 p.m. news and drive to Dan's apartment. We'd sit in his kitchen, drinking coffee, eating his wife Erin's brownies, and discussing the questions I was going to ask the jockeys, trainers, and owners whom I would interview the next morning. We usually talked until about 1:00 a.m.; then he went to bed, and I would study some more before dropping off to sleep in their back bedroom. At 5:45 a.m., we'd head for the morning workouts at the track.

I remember the first time I met the great jockey Bill Shoemaker. I could tell from his handshake that he could care less about who I was. Maybe it was my insecurity, but I felt he was thinking, "Why are *you* here?"

After the first three or four shows, I was uncomfortable with my interview sessions. As an interviewer, I knew to listen carefully, so I could follow up on my guests' answers. I also knew that it was important to maintain eye contact with them to encourage their trust, instead of staring at my notes. But I also needed to know enough about the sport to anticipate what the answer would be, and I didn't. Because of that, if my racetrack guests gave me a ridiculous answer, I wouldn't realize it. I would think, "Okay," and go on to the next question. No matter how well I listened, I wouldn't know how to follow up.

"Let's change our game plan," I said to Dan. "Don't just give me the question. Give me the potential answer, too." So, when we prepared on Thursday nights, Dan not only gave me questions, but also coached me on how our guests might answer.

Once I knew what a reasonable answer was, I could play off my guest's response. For example, if he said, "This horse has the biggest heart of any horse I've ever ridden," I could ask, "Why do you say that?" and "What other horses would you put in your top three?" If I didn't do that, his answer would just hang out there, with no transition to the next question, and the audience would be left wanting more. My ability to follow up provided the information and made the interview evolve more as a conversation, instead of a random series of questions.

We did the Santa Anita show for just a year, and I wasn't involved in horse racing again until 1981, while at NBC. That year, the network televised the inaugural Arlington Million at Arlington Park in Chicago—the first million-dollar race for thoroughbreds— and I was the host. We did several Arlington Millions, but the first one was certainly forgettable—one of my most embarrassing moments in broadcasting.

For viewers, the first Arlington Million was spectacular. The mile-and-a-quarter turf race featured a stirring stretch duel between The Bart, a 40-to-one long shot, and John Henry, a rags-to-riches six-year-old gelding, who was the sport's all-time leading money winner when he retired. The Bart was in the lead as they headed for the wire, but John Henry, ridden by Shoemaker, was closing fast, and, as they thundered across the finish line, it was too close to call. Unfortunately for NBC, we called it anyway.

As I recollect, and my memory is hazy, undoubtedly because of selective repression, I either didn't hear the track announcer clearly, or he didn't make a definitive call. But, from my angle, it looked like The Bart had won.

"It was very close at the wire," I said, "but the first Arlington Million has gone to The Bart."

Seconds later, our people in the truck flashed the names of the top three finishers on the screen, led by The Bart. At the top of the order of finish they put "Official Results," which was a terrible mistake. They weren't the official results. They were unofficial.

When the official results were released after analysis of the photo finish, John Henry was declared the winner. For that mistake, we weren't just criticized, we were beaten like an old rug. Can you imagine the mood of those off-track bettors who tore up their tickets?

Our on-screen list that read "Official Results" made it worse, but I was guilty, too. If nothing else, I have a sense for the dramatic, and I got caught up in the excitement of a great horse race and felt I had to make the immediate call. Now I know better. When it's a photo finish, the experienced race callers, such as Dave Johnson, Tom Durkin, or Trevor Denman, will say, "Too close to call," or "There will be a photo to decide this one." Or even, "It looked like The Bart at the wire, but it's too close to call."

John Henry just wouldn't be beaten. That was a good lesson to learn in itself. Three years later, he won the race again at the age of nine.

Despite our Arlington disaster, NBC increased its horse racing coverage by signing a contract to televise the Breeders' Cup World Thoroughbred Championships, which began in 1984. This event, annually held in the fall, brings together the world's best horses for eight (originally seven) classic races, with a different North American track hosting the competition each year. NBC continues to televise this climactic finale to the racing season.

For about a decade, I was the host and anchor of the Breeders' Cup, a daunting task. It was a four-hour show, and, as I have indicated, I wasn't as comfortable doing racing as I was football, basketball, baseball, tennis, or even boxing. Although I didn't actually call the races, I gave an overview of each of the seven races, tied everything together after each race, did interviews, and was the central contact to all of the other announcers. One thing I didn't do was interfere with the flow by offering my opinions. I left those to the experts. In fact, members of the media often asked for my selections. My consistent answer to avoid any commitment was, "Hey, I haven't picked a winner since Secretariat. And I bet him to show."

A few months before the inaugural Breeders' Cup at Hollywood Park, I bumped into my old Santa Anita sidekick, Dan Smith, and asked him if he would consider working in the booth with me again. Fortunately, he accepted.

In my long tenure as Breeders' Cup host, Dan was my security blanket. Not only was he an invaluable source of information, but also I trusted him to correct me should I make a mistake, in effect, to be my on-air editor. As my researcher, before each Breeders' Cup, he jotted down pertinent facts on every horse on five-by-eight-inch cards, one card to a horse. With as many as 14 horses in a race, he had to prepare nearly 100 cards. The night before the races, we'd go over the cards, which gave me a quick feel for the seven fields, and I underlined the facts that were the most interesting to me. As each race came up the next day, Dan handed me the stack of cards for that race and was also quick with the card on the winner at the finish.

One of the interesting assignments at that inaugural Breeders' Cup was conducting interviews with celebrities between races. To boost national interest in this new concept, NBC showcased several of the film and TV stars in attendance. A few were brought to our cramped broadcast location at the Hollywood Park finish line—among them were Fred Astaire, John Forsythe, Tim Conway, and Elizabeth Taylor.

In my wildest dreams, I couldn't imagine the "Armada Tomata" standing in such close quarters with the Oscar-winning beauty, whose face had made stronger men weak in the knees. But out of her element, Miss Taylor seemed uncomfortable and vulnerable, even more nervous than I was. Mind you, I was anything but supremely confident in my own new role as Breeders' Cup host, but my instincts were to give her a big hug and assure her that everything would be just fine. But then I stared into those incredible violet eyes and the best thought I could manage was, "Oh… Oh… Oh… Oh… Oh… My!" So much for *my* acting career.

Unfortunately for my work in horse racing, my life has unfolded backward. I probably should be hosting the sport now, because I'm much more informed than 20 years ago. In recent years, I've been part of syndicates that owned horses, both in England and the United States, and now I know my way not only around the track, but also around the winner's circle. In fact, in England, in 1997, at Royal Ascot, our horse, Heritage, ridden by Frankie Detorri and trained by John Gosden, won The King George V Handicap. That was a top-hat thrill!

∽

In 1990, it was a beautiful, sunny Saturday at Belmont Park, as we prepared for the international array of great horses entered that day. The most eagerly anticipated showdown was the Breeders' Cup

Distaff, matching a pair of 1989 Eclipse Award winners, a six-year-old mare, Bayakoa, the winner of this same race a year earlier, and a three-year-old filly, Go For Wand, the Breeders' Cup Juvenile Fillies champion in 1989. They were about to go head to head for the first time. Go For Wand's brilliant record included 10 victories and two seconds in her 12 starts. Bayakoa had a remarkable 20 wins and eight seconds in her 35 races.

Before they left the gate, it looked like a dream matchup, and as the mile-and-an-eighth race unfolded, it was that and more. For more than a mile, the two horses ran stride for stride, eyeball to eyeball, nose to nose. It was like a match race. Go For Wand was on the rail, and Bayakoa was on the outside as they staged a stirring duel. As the two horses came down the long Belmont Park homestretch, the crowd of more than 51,000 was on its feet cheering their neck-and-neck fight for the wire. Who would win?

Then, suddenly, 100 yards from the finish, immediately in front of the grandstand, Go For Wand crashed to the track with a shattered foreleg, as Bayakoa swept past. Instinctively, the game filly struggled to her feet, limping on three legs toward the finish line as her jockey, Randy Romero attempted to contain her. I can't recall anything in my career that made me more sick to my stomach. It crushed more emotion into a five-second period of time than perhaps any moment in my broadcasting life.

For Go For Wand, there was no hope of recovery. Track veterinarians put up a screen and euthanized her.

As the race was run, we had a camera trained on Go For Wand's owners as they enthusiastically cheered their horse on, thinking they might have a Breeders' Cup winner. Their horrified reaction was heart-rending. Owners of racehorses are like proud parents. They select a sire and a mare for breeding. Then they're blessed with a foal. They give it a name, and they raise it as a weanling and a yearling. They train it and learn its personality. Then they begin its career as a racehorse. Now, this filly, which already had enjoyed great success, was running the race of her life. She was 100 yards from possibly winning this championship race, and, in one false step, with incredible suddenness, she was gone.

We replayed the accident so many times that I finally pleaded on the air, "Please don't show it anymore. Please don't show it again." It was just too painful to watch. Many in the crowd were in tears. In an NBC interview after the race, Ron McAnally, the trainer of Bayakoa, could find little joy in victory, almost apologizing for the win.

"They give their lives for us," he said, summing up all of our feelings.

&

Several years later, my wife, Barbara, and I spent a much more cheerful day at the races. It was midsummer at Del Mar, the charming racetrack "where the turf meets the surf," north of San Diego. Traditionally, so-called celebrities are asked by management to present the trophy and flowers to the winning owner after the day's feature race. They asked me to do the honors that day, and I accepted.

The race featured a fierce three-horse battle down the stretch with all three noses stretching at the wire. While they checked the photo finish, the stewards posted an inquiry, not just on one incident, but two different potential disqualifications. They had a lot to sort out.

I was in the winner's circle primed to hand over the silver trophy and two dozen long-stemmed red roses to the winning owner. Three different sets of owners waited patiently for what seemed an eternity while track officials attempted to determine the order of finish. It took so long that all three trainers decided to take their horses back to the stable area to cool off. Shortly after, the three owners decided to leave, too. So an official from Del Mar graciously relieved me of the trophy and kindly suggested that I give the bouquet of roses to my wife.

Barbara enjoys going to the races and loves making her "monster" two-dollar bets. When track announcer Trevor Denman finally announced the official results, she cheered her winning ticket. As we waited in line for her payoff, fans, seeing the roses cradled in her arms, assumed she was the winning owner and began showering her with congratulations. Rather than try to explain, Barbara found it was much easier to offer her best winning smile and her most sincere thanks. As we moved forward slowly in line, more and more people cheered her success. "Way to go! What a great win! Congratulations!" Like a good actress, she became increasingly comfortable in playing the role of winning owner.

When she reached the payoff window, the clerk offered his hearty congratulations as well. Barbara smiled again, thanked him, and handed in her ticket.

He fed it into the machine and barked loudly enough for everyone in line to hear, "Two dollars to show!"

The gig was up for the pseudo-owner. She'd been discovered. We hustled out of Del Mar faster than the freshest rose could wilt.

TIMEOUT

Meeting Secretariat

ABOUT 25 YEARS AGO, while doing basketball with Al McGuire and Billy Packer, we were assigned a game at the University of Kentucky on Saturday and were scheduled to catch a private jet to South Carolina for another game on Sunday. At the Kentucky game, I met Lexington native Tom Hammond, later to succeed me as host of the Breeders' Cup.

Al, Billy, and I had several hours to kill before our private plane would arrive at the airport, so while talking with Tom, I asked him if it were possible to see the super horse, Secretariat.

"Would there ever be a chance of doing that?"

"Sure," Tom said. "In fact, we could do it today. He's at Claiborne Farm, which is close enough to the airport. I know the people there."

At the time, Claiborne Farm had the greatest roster of breeding sires in the world in retirement, including Secretariat, Buckpasser, Damascus, and Round Table. As we stood outside the stable area, the grooms paraded the great thoroughbreds, one by one. When each one arrived, Seth Hancock, who managed the farm for his family, would tell us the horse's background and pedigree. They saved Secretariat for last.

As the great Triple Crown winner regally posed before us, I said to Hancock, "They all look magnificent to me. How can you tell one from another?"

"I can tell by their conformation," he said, "but there's something else, and this may surprise you. Horses are a lot like humans. You can identify the good ones from the look in their eyes."

When Hancock said eyes, Secretariat, who was turned away from us, snapped his head around, as if on cue, and stared me right in the eye, as if to say, "You better believe it."

"He knows he's good," Hammond said.

Hancock went on to relate that the other horses knew that Secretariat was the champion among champions. When they were romping in the pasture, and the staff brought out feed, he always went first. The other horses waited for him.

If you could say nothing else about me in my 50 years on the air, one thing is true: I'm a fan. I love watching the best, and I love being fortunate enough to rub shoulders with the best. That day, I rubbed shoulders with Secretariat. Of course, I still had plenty of questions. If only Secretariat could talk.

15

THE MOST COOPERATIVE ATHLETES IN SPORTS

"You only borrow it for a little while."

—Dave Marr

G olf didn't like me. I wish the game had liked me. But it didn't like me. It treated me rudely.

At three different times in my life I've seriously tried to play golf, taking lessons, practicing, hitting extra balls—trying everything but psychoanalysis—but I just couldn't conquer it. I had decent baseball talent when I was young—I could hit a line drive off a pitched ball that was curving and dropping and thrown at different speeds. A golf ball just sits there. Why can't I hit it squarely?

When playing golf, you must accept the fact that you will suffer the ultimate indignity. If you make a mistake in any other sport, or any other human endeavor, for that matter, there are many ways to deal with it. You can apologize for it, you can forget about it, or you can even blame it on somebody else. But in golf, if you make a mistake, you're required to go find it and then add it to your score. That's pouring it on!

While my partners would stand impatiently in the middle of the fairway, arms crossed, I would be digging through bushes, ripping up a perfectly good sweater, and trying to find my damn ball. Then, in a hurry to catch up, I'd rush the next shot and wind up in even deeper trouble.

It became so frustrating that at the end of nine holes, I'd often say, "You guys go on and play the back side, and I'll go to the driving range. I'll meet you in the clubhouse. No sense ruining your day."

Then I'd go to the range and hack balls for another hour and a half. It never helped.

It's been said more than once that you don't really know a man's personality until you get him out on a golf course, and I believe that's true. I'm absolutely embarrassed by the inner person who was exposed when I tried to play. I didn't like me. Worse yet, everyone else liked me even less.

I respect my pals who love golf, who can't wait to get out on the course on Saturday morning, regardless of the double bogeys that await. They don't feel beaten up by golf; they look at it as a chance to go out and play a wondrous game in a beautiful environment. But I kept thinking, "Why am I punishing myself?" So I've taken the pledge. I've given up playing the game.

Now I play tennis. I play two, three, or even four times a week, and, in 15 years I haven't lost a single ball. In tennis, I don't have to find my mistake before playing the next shot. Amazing!

⮍

Although the game has rejected me, I do like golf. And I really like professional golfers. My own failures make me more appreciative of the talent of those who can play at a high level. As a group, they're the most cooperative athletes in sports—by far.

In 1995, NBC assigned me to golf for the first time. For five years, I called a dozen or more PGA events a year, working with Hall of Fame PGA star Johnny Miller. Despite all my broadcasting experience, I approached this assignment with considerable trepidation. I had the yips. First of all, I had been warned that golf attracts the most critical audience. There's nothing close. Golfers watch golf religiously, and then they go out and play. They truly understand the finer points of the game. The golf viewer has no patience for any mistakes. That's pressure, a pressure that was constant.

My first event in 1995 was the Buick Invitational at Torrey Pines Golf Course, just outside San Diego. During the practice rounds, I watched the pros fine-tune their game, standing quietly behind them while they worked on the driving range.

Within minutes, I was treated like a visiting dignitary. One after another, the world's top players came to me and said, "I understand you're going to do golf for NBC. It's great to have you with us. If there's anything I can do for you, let me know."

Whether it was Curtis Strange or Phil Mickelson or Davis Love III or Fred Couples or Greg Norman or Payne Stewart or the great older players such as Jack Nicklaus, Arnold Palmer, and Lee Trevino, that warm embrace lasted for all five years of my golf coverage for NBC.

A memorable example occurred during the tournament in New Orleans at English Turn Golf and Country Club early in my first year. Because NBC televised only on Saturday and Sunday, I took a walk onto the course during Thursday's first round and found a small hill that was a good observation point for two different greens. From there I watched Ben Crenshaw—who would go on to win the Masters a week later—hole out on one of the greens. Heading toward the next tee, Crenshaw took a right turn and started walking up the hill toward me.

As he arrived, he extended his hand and said, "Dick, I couldn't help but come over and tell you that I've watched a couple of your telecasts and you're doing a great job."

Here was Ben Crenshaw, one of the leading players on the tour, one of the foremost historians of the game, someone who cares as much about golf as anyone who has ever played it, walking 75 yards out of his way to pay me a compliment. It was a remarkable and sensitive thing to do.

It triggered memories of the incident with 1994 Wimbledon champion Conchita Martinez, who wouldn't even talk to me for five minutes when she sat at courtside after practicing. Crenshaw actually interrupted his round to walk out of his way and give me a compliment. Oh My!

∾

Even for the pros, the game promises a doctorate in humility, and this lesson is driven home every week. No matter how brilliant you may be as a player, if you don't make the cut in a tournament, you don't make a dime. In every other sport, play a couple of days or even a couple of innings and you get a paycheck. In golf, you can practice for three days and play two and if you don't make the cut, you simply toss your clubs back in the trunk of your car and drive to the next event with empty pockets. It doesn't matter how big a name you are. Play on the weekend, or there's no paycheck.

The million-dollar player can swallow the rare bad week—at least financially—but how about the kid scrambling to make it on tour? He's living with his wife in a trailer, and if he misses the cut this week and next week and the one after that, the expenses don't stop. That's the ultimate pressure.

I once asked the late Dave Marr, who won the PGA Championship in 1965 (and went on to become a successful TV golf analyst before passing away from cancer a few years ago), about the capricious nature of the game and how it teaches humility. He responded with a personal story.

"When I became a professional, like all young golfers, I had to find sponsors to help pay my tour expenses," he said. "There are a lot of expenses. I struggled for a while but then started to do a little better, finally winning a tournament. Then I won another one, so it was with great enthusiasm that I returned to Houston to share my exploits with my sponsors.

"'I know it was slow,'" I said to them, "'and you must have wondered if I was ever going to make it. But I won the Seattle Open and I won the Azaela Open and I tied for second at the Masters.' As I rambled on and on about my successes, the men in the room seemed to be nodding their approval. Finally, the oldest gentleman stood and drawled politely, 'David, let me remind you of one thing: You only borrow *it* for a little while.'"

Isn't that a terrific insight? It's true for all of us, whatever our profession. We only borrow success, and often it's fickle and short-lived. It's best not to take it for granted.

Dave was a lovely guy but tough. He didn't hesitate to criticize me after one of my early broadcasts. Trying to speak in golfing lexicon, I used the expression that someone was "bagging" for one of the golfers, instead of caddying for him. Dave called me aside the next day and said, "That's not wrong, but the audience expects more from Dick Enberg than a 19th-hole expression like that." Great advice. He was candid in his critique. He wanted me to be better.

∽

The week after my first golf broadcast at the Buick Invitational, I went to Palm Springs for the Bob Hope Chrysler Classic. Tournament officials had pulled off a major coup in arranging a blockbuster first-day fivesome. It featured host Bob Hope and defending champion Scott Hoch with former Presidents Gerald Ford and George Bush and current President Bill Clinton.

Realizing that President Bush wouldn't play with President Clinton, who had defeated him in the 1992 election, the committee first extended an invitation to Bush to play with Ford, and he accepted. Then they invited Clinton. By the time Bush learned that Clinton was playing, it was too late to renege.

This was the first time a sitting president had played during a PGA event, and perhaps the first time that three presidents ever played together. It was my second PGA telecast, and before it even began, here I was holding a microphone, interviewing not one, but three U.S. Presidents and Bob Hope. Nervous? You bet, but the interview went fine. All I had to do was tee it up. They had all the answers.

As my five years in the 18th hole tower unfolded, I quickly realized that golf, for the announcer, is the most difficult television sport of all. That's because you don't see any of the play until the producer punches it up on the video screen in front of you. The first time the TV audience sees a player is the first time you see him.

In football, baseball, and basketball, you see all of the players, coaches, managers, officials, scoreboards, and fans in one quick glance from the booth. Everything is right in front of you. But you never see a golf shot in person. Like the audience at home, you're watching it on television. Your back is even to the 18th hole, simply a background for the on-camera close ups to prove to the audience that you're really where you say you are.

In my five years working with Johnny Miller at NBC, I marveled at his ability to tell exactly where and how far a shot would go without ever seeing it with the naked eye. Truthfully, he's so good that he could have given the same acute analysis by telephone from the comfort of his own living room. Of course, Johnny always had a wonderful feel for the golf course. When he played on the tour, he won 24 tournaments, and during his best years, his middle and long iron game was so sharp that he would ask his caddie for distances in half-yards. He didn't want to be told that it was 170 yards to the green, he wanted to know if it was 169½.

Johnny would agree that in a live telecast, probably 25 to 35 percent of the shots are on tape. It's the only way you can cover a tournament, because you're following six or seven groups at a time. From the production point of view, it's a real art form and a potential nightmare to coordinate.

For example, while you're calling a live shot by Corey Pavin, they're taping other action on the course. So, when you finish with Pavin, the producer might dictate, "Let's go back to the third hole for Tiger Woods's second shot," adding that it's on tape. On the air, you can indicate that the shot is on tape by simply saying, "Moments ago, Woods with his second shot… " or, if it hasn't been too long since the audience last saw Tiger, the timing may be perfect and you can ignore the suggestion that it was recorded. If it has been several minutes since Woods was on camera, any golf fan would know that the action is on tape and not live, so everyone looks foolish if you don't say, "Moments ago… "

Another complicated task is keeping track of the changes in scoring for the total field. Unlike other sports, the scores you see on the television screen leaderboard are not always current. When I first started, I would look at the scores on my preview monitor and say, "Phil Mickelson, our leader, is seven under par." But I might have just seen Mickelson make bogey and needed to remember that fact, make a quick calculation, and tell the audience that he was actually six under, even though our scoreboard, to be seen by the viewer later, hadn't been updated.

While all of this is happening, the producer, the conduit for what is coming next, is, by necessity, constantly talking in your ear. So part of the challenge is listening to what he's saying while trying to focus on what you're saying, which can be maddening. Too often, you don't even know what you've said. Not a good thing. If you hear a golf announcer deliver a verbal slice, this might explain it. Be kind.

As you can see, there are all kinds of traps, not filled with sand, involved with golf commentary. Maybe this is why there aren't many standout golf anchors. It's also why I have such great admiration for Jim Nantz, the lead golf announcer at CBS. He's a magician at juggling all of these complications while sounding so relaxed. I marvel at how extraordinary his talent is. I only wish I could be that good.

※

Of the annual PGA events that I called each year for NBC, the most significant was the U.S. Open. The 1997 U.S. Open, won by Ernie Els at Congressional Country Club outside Washington, D.C., provided an unforgettable moment. During Saturday's third round, President Clinton, who enjoys playing golf, agreed to join Miller and me in the booth. As he sat between the two of us, he made several insightful comments, while we continued our coverage of the tournament. The president stayed in the booth for 10 minutes or more.

Eventually, our producer, Tommy Roy, decided that the interview was going too long and needed to be wrapped up. Using a TV expression that producers everywhere rely upon when they want to end a segment or delete something from a telecast, he blurted in my ear, "Kill the president. Kill the president." I couldn't believe what I was hearing.

That night, we were able to laugh about it, but I was still shaking my head.

"Whoa, baby," I said to Tommy, "I don't think you want to use that expression with the Secret Service swarming all over the golf course, much less our broadcast location. How about, 'Thank the president, Dick, and if you don't take a timeout, I'll kill *you?*'"

The 1999 U.S. Open, at Pinehurst in North Carolina, was drama of a deeper sort. Mickelson was bidding for his first major title, while back home in Scottsdale, Arizona, his wife, Amy, was awaiting the birth of their first child. She wasn't scheduled to deliver until later in the month, but difficulties with her pregnancy left Mickelson deeply concerned. He announced early in the week that should she go into labor early, he would take a private jet and fly home immediately, no matter where he stood in the field.

"It's not worth the tournament," he said. "As important as the U.S. Open is to me and every other player in the field, this is the birth of my first child."

Mickelson's wife did not go into labor during the tournament, and, on Sunday—Father's Day—he found himself leading 42-year-old Payne Stewart by one stroke with just three holes to play. The two were in the final pair. Stewart, who had won the Open in 1991, also carried the weight of a heartbreaking Open defeat in 1998, when he took a four-stroke lead into the final round but finished second to Lee Janzen at The Olympic Club in San Francisco.

Under heavy gray clouds and a steady drizzle, Mickelson bogeyed the 16th hole, while Stewart canned a 20-foot putt for par. They were tied with two holes to go. Stewart then birdied 17 to take the lead by one stroke. On the 18th, Mickelson delivered a second shot 25 feet from the flagstick, a chance for birdie. Stewart's third shot left him with a 15-foot, tricky uphill par putt. Mickelson still had a solid chance to win. At the worst, we thought there would be a playoff on Monday.

The gloomy weather closed like a curtain on the 18th, contributing to the drama as the two men putted for the U.S. Open championship. It had become so dark that little was visible but the action on the green. Mickelson's 25-footer for birdie missed by inches. Stewart rammed home his 15-footer for par to win the title.

"I just wasn't going to hand the trophy to him," Stewart said of his rally to catch the 29-year-old Mickelson. "Phil is going to have an opportunity to win again. I might be on the short list."

Tragically, Stewart's comment proved too prophetic. It was the last time that I ever saw him. Four months later, he perished in a private plane crash. It was a personal loss for all who knew him. I'll never forget that he was one of the players who had so warmly welcomed me, a novice, to golf. From the media's perspective, he not only was one of the game's biggest stars, he had matured into one of the most cooperative and interesting players on the tour.

⋑

Johnny Miller was the first golf analyst to dare to use the word *choke* in a telecast, while describing players as they misplayed a critical shot. Some of the players didn't like it, but the audience loved his candor, and they're the ones he's obligated to please.

Johnny is in his own world anyway, and that world revolves around golf. Before one of our tournaments, I noticed in my research that the anniversary of the first Superman radio broadcast was 45 years ago to the very day. I thought I might work this little nugget into the broadcast, say, if one of the players made a super effort or super shot to win the event.

But, wisely, before going on the air, I said, "Johnny, if I throw out a line to you that this is an anniversary for the 'Man of Steel,' would you know whom I'm referring to?"

He answered quickly, "Sure. Arnold Palmer."

⋑

Now in his 70s, Palmer, no matter where he goes, is besieged by autograph requests. It still takes him a half hour to walk from the 18th green back to the clubhouse after he plays. But he signs for everyone. He's always accepted those requests as a requisite part of the job and has been a fabulous role model for the players of successive generations.

For a magical half-century, his generous personality and passion have brought generations of fans inside the ropes. When he's on the course, he smiles and gives thumbs up to the gallery, and each of the fans in that direction feels a personal connection with "The King."

Palmer is the host of the PGA Tour's Bay Hill Invitational in Orlando, Florida, each year and because of him, that tournament always draws an excellent field. He also owns the Lexington Cottage on the 18th fairway of the course, and NBC uses its living room as an interview location during the tournament. One year, after Friday's second round, Palmer, then in his late 60s, taped an interview with us in the cottage.

When it was over, he asked one of his assistants to pour his favorite libation.

"Dick," he said, as he placed his order, "would you like to have a drink with me?"

"Absolutely," I said, "and whatever 'The King' is having, I'll have one, too."

So we sat on the same two stools used for the interview and chatted for 30 minutes about the tournament, our families, and our interests, just two blokes having a normal conversation. As we talked, I recalled how Palmer was my dad's favorite, not only because he was so successful and so charismatic, but also because my dad's name was Arnie, too. Although he never met him, my father felt he had a special connection with Palmer. As we said goodbye, I thought that if my dad were still alive, what a thrill it would have been for him to be a part of this 19th-hole conversation and share a sip with one of the greatest golfers ever.

TIMEOUT

Psst… Can I Borrow a Light?

SINCE MOVING TO CBS IN 2000, my golf role has changed. At the Masters, for example, I'm stationed in famed Butler Cabin, conducting interviews and delivering essays. My primary assignment during Sunday's final round is to prepare a three-minute closing essay that highlights key moments during the tournament.

An inherent difficulty is that when I begin working on the essay, there's no way of knowing who the eventual winner will be. In fact, with just a few holes left, there could be several men still in contention. In that case, I'll draft a rough script for three or four different endings, and, at the last minute, edit my copy to specifically feature the winner in his moment of triumph. However, if I'm lucky, one player will enjoy a runaway lead, and I can focus on him with several holes to go. On this Sunday in 2002, it was a gimmee. Defending champion Tiger Woods was on his way to a three-stroke victory over Retief Goosen. Tiger's climactic moment would complete the piece.

With Tiger in command as the final group entered the back nine, I hustled by golf cart back to the CBS compound where producer Ross Schneiderman had carefully edited footage that supported my previously written copy that described the first three rounds. Because I now had the luxury of writing about Woods's presumed victory in advance, Ross could make certain my words fit with the final 30 seconds of music.

As Tiger was finishing the 17th hole, I returned to Butler Cabin, relaxed, because the winner was predictable and everything was under control. I settled into my on-camera position, which is located in the far corner of the room, just opposite the fireplace where the green jacket ceremony takes place. I finished writing the essay and gave it to the teleprompter technician, so that the script would be loaded and ready for me to read. The teleprompter allows you to read the copy as it appears directly over the camera lens.

Everything was now in place to shoot my live on-camera opening. Announcer Jim Nantz at 18 wrapped up his thoughts on the tournament and threw it to me.

Through long experience, however, I have never assumed that everything will go smoothly. Just in case, I had the handwritten copy of the script on my lap, out of camera range. Good thing! As I read my 15-second, on-camera introduction from the teleprompter, there was a rustle in the background. Tiger Woods had arrived in Butler Cabin for the green jacket ceremony much earlier than expected—and everyone panicked.

At the very moment that the video illustrating my essay came up on the screen, the cameraman spun away to set up for his close-up shot of tournament chairman Hootie Johnson, soon to make the presentation to Woods. Unfortunately, the teleprompter and a large monitor left with the camera, and I had to scramble to retrieve the copy from my lap and read it without a noticeable pause. The video was playing, and my words had to fit the pictures.

Disaster didn't end there. When the cameraman left, so did the guy with the lights. I was literally in the dark as I tried to read. The only illumination in the entire area came from a small spare TV monitor to my side. It was like trying to read by the light of a Christmas tree bulb. Here I was, live on national television, at the climax of the most popular golf event of the year, contorting my upper body to get enough light to see my copy, all the while trying to time the words to fit the video shots being shown on the same little TV set. One eye on the picture, one on the copy. It was an agonizing, cross-eyed three minutes, but I made it through without any colossal stumbles.

Later that night, relaxing with a glass of merlot, I realized what a catastrophe it might have been. Had I not written the copy myself, I would have sounded like a drunken sailor because I couldn't see the words clearly. Because I had written it, I was familiar enough with the words and was able to keep going when I came to one I couldn't decipher. And if I hadn't kept my copy with me, I would have been forced into a three-minute ad-lib to the pictures, which would have sounded anything but poetic. That was as close as I've ever come to a personal disaster on network television. Now, wouldn't that have been a stirring finish to the Masters?

16

THE KID

"Come here, Meat. Turn on that tape recorder."

—Ted Williams

oyhood dreams are inspired by heroes—idols often bigger than life. My idol certainly was. And our connection lasted a lifetime. He was baseball's greatest hitter. I taught myself to bat left handed to be like him. He was Ted Williams.

I'm not the only one of my generation to idolize the lanky kid with the handsome swing. Senators John Glenn and John McCain, as well as coach Bobby Knight, are among the large legion of his adult admirers.

In high school I was able to see my hero play in person. My friends and I would hitchhike the 80-mile roundtrip from Armada to Detroit whenever the Red Sox were in town. We rooted for the Tigers, but made sure to get to Briggs Stadium as soon as it opened in order to see Williams take batting practice. It was to witness a virtuoso in action. This was a master craftsman expressing himself better than anyone in the history of baseball—performing, in his words, the most difficult feat in all of sport, "To hit a round ball with a round bat, squarely."

He never took a bad swing. He rarely fouled the ball off or hit a ground ball. It was just line drive after line drive after line drive. He had the same routine before every game. In his first swings in batting practice, he would rip every pitch solidly into right field. In the next round, he tried to drive the ball into the lower deck in right field—between the upper-deck overhang and the fence on top of the base of the right field wall. This space wasn't large, but Williams smashed the ball into that gap with the ease of a pro golfer driving one-irons. He'd finish batting practice with a flourish by trying to hit the ball deep into the upper deck or over the roof.

Ted's talent was made for Detroit. After his retirement I asked him about his dominance there. If he had been traded to the Tigers, as we had hoped, how many home runs would he have hit in a single season? Without hesitation, he answered with total conviction, "About 80!"

In Detroit, the Red Sox stayed at the Book-Cadillac Hotel, about a mile from the stadium, and on occasion the players walked down Michigan Avenue to the ballpark. My friends and I often positioned ourselves across the street so we could catch a glimpse of them as they left the hotel. They were easy to spot, usually well dressed and wearing the giveaway wing-tip shoes. One lucky day, my high school catcher, Dave Dunham, and I were there when Williams and manager Steve O'Neill set out for the stadium.

We followed them all the way down Michigan Avenue. When they stopped, we stopped. When they slowed down, we slowed down. The very thought of asking for an autograph or interrupting them for a handshake would have been much too bold. It was exciting enough to shadow my hero all the way. When Williams and O'Neill finally disappeared in the players' entrance at Briggs Stadium, Dave and I jumped up and down in excitement, slapped each other on the back, and hugged. We couldn't wait to get back to our farm friends to regale them with our successful adventure.

Fast forward to 1969, my first season as the Angels' play-by-play announcer. That year also marked Williams's return to the game as manager of the expansion Washington Senators. Anaheim Stadium was Washington's last stop on its initial swing around the American League, and on the night the series opened, it was my turn to do the radio pregame show. I was determined to interview Williams, whom I had never met.

By the time the Senators had arrived in Anaheim, Ted had fielded questions from reporters all around the league. Not only was he bored at answering the same old inquiries, but also he had a reputation for being antagonistic with the press, openly feuding with baseball writers as a player. He often referred to them with disdain as the "Knights of the Keyboard." Getting him to agree to do our pregame show would not be easy.

I needed a hook. I found it in *The Baseball Encyclopedia*. In 1940, his second year in the majors, Ted pitched the last couple of innings in a 12-1 Boston loss to the Tigers. I knew he had been a star pitcher in high school, but this was the only time he pitched in his big league career. "That's it!" I thought. "That'll get his attention."

Before the game, I bounced down the dugout steps to finally meet my boyhood idol. He was staring out at his players while they took batting practice. At 50, the six-foot-three Williams was still an imposing figure. No other members of the media had dared to approach him. They circled like vultures, but none mustered the courage to enter his electrical field to ask that first question. I boldly jumped right in.

"Hi, Ted, I'm Dick Enberg, the Angels' announcer," I said. "I don't have to tell you how much I admire you. In fact, you were my idol growing up... "

Williams didn't even twitch. He continued to stare straight ahead with the same intense look he once trained on opposing pitchers. I continued my pitch.

"I have the 10-minute pregame show tonight, and I'd be delighted and honored if you'd be my guest." Then I threw him my high, hard one. "And I don't even want to talk to you about hitting. I want to talk to you about the time you pitched against the Tigers in 1940."

He turned toward me, looked me in the eye, reached out his left arm, wrapped it around my neck, and in that booming John Wayne voice, he barked, "COME HERE, MEAT! TURN ON THAT TAPE RECORDER!"

I only had to ask him two questions. He just kept talking, remembering every detail, including the strikeout pitch he threw to Tiger slugger Rudy York. He recounted that York, who hit 33 homers and drove in 134 runs that season, "claimed I threw him a spitball." Never once did we talk about hitting.

For the next decade or so, whenever I encountered Williams—as a manager, at a charitable function, or as a guest on *Sports Challenge*—he always remembered me. A pitching question turned out to be my entrée to closeness with my batting idol. If he saw me in a group of people, he'd call me over, bellowing, "HEY, MEAT, HOW'S IT GOING?" I got interviews that nobody else did. The press always walked on eggs around Williams, and I considered it a special honor to be recognized by him.

We didn't see each other for much of the 1980s. But in the last 10 or 15 years of his life, when he visited his birthplace of San Diego more frequently, I had the opportunity to know him better. I often joined him for lunch or dinner with his close high school pal, Bob Breitbard, still the executive director of the San Diego Hall of Champions, a museum that Breitbard founded.

Ted was fascinating to be around, because he was so passionate about his two main loves, hitting a baseball and fishing. With both subjects, he was very opinionated because he was an expert. When he spoke, you were on the edge of your seat. He loved to teach. If you were a struggling young hitter and asked for suggestions, he was eager to help, even if you were an opposing player. When he was managing the Senators, he spent a good hour before a game one night trying to help Angels catcher Tom Egan with his swing. Egan was limited as a hitter, perhaps beyond help, but it didn't matter to Ted. If you asked him for advice, he was amazingly generous with his time and knowledge.

Twenty-five years later, he was still at it, although his pupil one evening was the immensely talented Tony Gwynn of the San Diego Padres, a lifetime .338 hitter. Gwynn had great respect for Ted—always referring to him as "Mr. Williams." And Williams loved Gwynn, because Tony, too, was a serious student of hitting. A fellow lefty, Gwynn liked to punch the ball to left field, but pitchers had been jamming him a lot, making it increasingly difficult for him to hit the ball the other way.

"If you don't start pulling that inside pitch, they're going to keep throwing it in there," Ted said. "You're strong. You've got to turn on the inside pitch. Once you start yanking a few home runs on the inside stuff, they're going to go back outside, and that's where you want it in the first place. You've got to punish them for throwing inside."

Gwynn took the advice of "Teddy Ballgame." The next year, 1997, he hit a career-high 17 homers, drove in a career-best 119 runs, and still batted a robust .372. All at age 37.

Williams was a mastermind at studying pitchers. He knew how to think the way they did. He honestly felt he was smarter than the men on the mound. In fact, he said openly, "Pitchers are the dumbest sons of bitches in all of sports." He lived a lifetime of disliking pitchers, so much so that he had trouble liking even his own pitchers as a manager.

Ted not only loved to teach, he loved to ask questions. But he wouldn't ask a question because he wanted to know the answer. He knew the answer. He wanted to see if you knew the answer. He was testing, always testing. Before he even asked the question, he would put you on your toes. In that big voice, he'd bellow, "DAMN IT, LET ME ASK YA THIS… "

On one afternoon, I sat with Williams as he discussed baseball with infielder Phil Nevin, reliever Trevor Hoffman, and manager Bruce Bochy of the Padres. He turned to Nevin and challenged, "LET ME ASK YA THIS NOW! WHAT MAKES A BALL CURVE?"

Nevin got four words out. "Well, you know, gravity… "

"GRAVITY!" Williams shouted. "WHAT DO YOU MEAN, GRAVITY?"

And he went on to discuss his theories on the subject. Pointing at Nevin, he also reeled off his A-B-Cs of hitting:

A. "Get a good ball to hit. Don't chase balls out of the strike zone. It's a long season. Be patient. You can afford to wait for a hittable pitch.

B. "When the pitcher is ahead in the count, or in any pressure situation, think about hitting the ball hard through the middle of the infield.

C. "Pull the ball with power only when the count is in your favor [2-0, 3-0, 3-1]. When the pitcher is at a disadvantage and must throw a strike, that's the time to take your best rip."

Three basic rules of hitting that every hitter, from high school to the major leagues, should have in his memory bank, yet how many players with big league potential have failed because they never grasped such elementary wisdom? The idea of getting a good ball to hit is so fundamental that it used to drive him crazy if he'd see a batter with a three-and-one count swing at a pitch in the dirt.

"Why would you do that?" he would snort. "If it's not a good pitch, you've got to be disciplined enough not to swing at it. It's not unmanly to walk."

At the time of his conversation with Nevin, Hoffman, and Bochy, Ted was 81 years old.

"I don't want a job," he said, as he leaned back in his chair. "Damn it, I just want to help the game of baseball 'til the day I die."

And this baseball Einstein—the last of the .400 hitters—did. All at no charge.

Most fans know that Theodore Samuel Williams batted .406 in 1941, but perhaps even more remarkable was his .388 average in 1957, the year he turned 39.

"I didn't get one scratch single that whole year," he told me. "If I had beaten out five infield hits that season, I would have hit .400."

That's correct. Five more hits would have given him his second .400 season. At age 39. Phenomenal!

His lifetime batting average was .344. His lifetime on-base percentage was a staggering .481, the major league record and significantly ahead of Babe Ruth, in second place at .469. In other words, "The Kid" was on base almost one out of every two times he came to the plate. If the measure of a batter's success is how many times he doesn't make an out, Ted's career is nonpareil.

When he died in July 2002, we held a memorial service for him in San Diego. In my remarks, I recounted a story from his youth that he had shared with me. One winter day, during a San Diego rainstorm, Ted and his younger brother, Danny, devised an indoor game of hitting a hard-shelled black walnut with a broomstick. Ted said his brother hit one back at him, striking him directly in the right eye.

"Never did see that well again out of that eye," he said.

"Oh My!" I thought. Here's a man once measured in the military with 20–10 vision, a man who could count the stitches on a fastball, complaining that his sight was impaired by a childhood accident. If not for a misguided walnut, Williams might have hit .500!

~

For much of his life Ted had a reputation—well deserved—of being tough, profane, acerbic, and cantankerous, but, like my father, with age, he mellowed wonderfully. He became softer and friendlier and reached out to people. He was reinforced by the personal contact. And people liked him. When we'd walk into a restaurant or hotel, and strangers would greet him, he'd never brush them off. He would not only shake their hands, he would stop and talk. In fact, he would try to draw them out.

"How ya doing?" he would say. "What's your job here at this hotel? What's going on in your life?"

He went out of his way to relate to people, to make a connection. In that regard, he grew old gracefully.

❦

In the last 10 years of his life, Ted actively campaigned for Shoeless Joe Jackson to be inducted into the Hall of Fame. Jackson had been banned from baseball for life because of the Black Sox Scandal. Ted felt it was a glaring injustice that he had been kept out. Ted reasoned that Shoeless Joe, one of the greatest hitters in history with a lifetime average of .356, wasn't proved guilty of conspiring to throw games in the 1919 World Series, although Joe knew about the conspiracy. In fact, in 1921 a jury acquitted him of charges that he had helped fix the Series. He actually played very well, leading all hitters with a .375 batting average and fielding flawlessly.

Over lunch in San Diego, when Ted brought this up one day, I argued, "Okay, if you're going to put Jackson in the Hall of Fame, you've got to let Pete Rose in, too."

He looked me in the eye and said, "No, I don't."

"It's pretty much the same thing," I said.

"No, it's not." Ted answered. "Joe Jackson was banned for life. He's dead. He deserves to be in the Hall of Fame. Pete Rose was banned for life. He's alive. He hasn't served his sentence. Let him wait."

I think that's the answer to the problem. Pete Rose wants to get in, and some day you may get in, Pete, but you've been banned for life. Simple. Just like he did with his bat, Ted hit the issue right on the sweet spot.

TIMEOUT

Hitting for the Cycle

TO THIS DAY I STILL WONDER at my good fortune. Ted Williams was an influence long before I met him. I dreamed about being him. I taught myself to bat left handed to copy him. I was in the stands to cheer his awesome swing. Then, to get to know him and have him share much of himself and his philosophy with me, completed such a beautiful cycle. My dreams have taken me to a great place. Too bad every kid's idol can't become his friend.

Did he really consider me a friend? Maybe it's presumptuous of me to say that.

It doesn't matter. He included me in many fascinating conversations, and he seemed to genuinely appreciate my work.

"Damn it, Enberg," he proclaimed once, "you're the best there is."

That's good enough.

I like to think that he saw my passion for broadcasting and my passion for sports.

Maybe, it reminded him of his own love for what he did. We were both fiercely driven to succeed. Perhaps that was the mutual magnet.

On March 14, 1988, Barbara and I celebrated the birth of our first son, the new "kid" in our home. We named him Ted.

AFTERWORD

Although it's been nearly 40 years since I taught in college, my passion for education has never subsided. Since 1985 I've been able to combine my love for sports with my love for education as the spokesperson for the Academic All-America Program, a distinct honor. (The program is managed by the College Sports Information Directors of America, known as CoSIDA.)

Young men and women who qualify for this award as outstanding *athletes* and outstanding *students* are the crème de la crème of our society. Consider the time they spend working in their sports all year long—the practicing, the running, the weight lifting, the film study, the mental and physical exhaustion they endure—and yet, they find time to be standouts in the classroom as well, earning a cumulative grade point average of at least 3.20 on a 4.00 scale. Throughout the years, whenever appropriate, I've tried to salute these academic stars competing in sports. It's important to recognize them. They're special people, and the public needs to know who they are.

Whenever I meet them, I always say, "One, you can't have thanked your parents more royally than by earning this award. And, two, understand that this is an exceptional honor, but don't stop here. Continue to aim high. You are destined to be great. Don't be modest."

I'm pleased that the Academic All-America Program is gaining more notoriety these days. Raymond Berry, the Pro Football Hall of Fame wide receiver, earned the honor in the mid-1950s at SMU and admits now that he tried to keep it a secret. As a football player, he was apologetic about being a good student and didn't want his teammates to know. Thank God, we've outgrown that mentality.

In 1988, the program was expanded with the addition of the Academic All-America Hall of Fame, honoring Academic All-America selections who had achieved lifetime success in their professional careers, while being committed to charitable involvement. Four are inducted annually, plus one honorary member—often a person whose college career took place before the Academic All-America Program began in 1952. John Wooden and the late Supreme Court

Justice Byron "Whizzer" White are among those who have been inducted as honorary members.

In 1997, while I was hosting the annual Hall of Fame dinner, it was Wooden and former UCLA star Bill Walton who interrupted the program to announce that I had been selected as an honorary inductee in the Hall of Fame. But, even more importantly, they said CoSIDA was establishing a Dick Enberg Award in my honor. This award would be presented annually to a person like me, someone who didn't qualify as an Academic All-America selection but has been passionate in his or her support of academic-athletic success.

To be included in the Hall of Fame was a great tribute, but to have that award named for me was a phenomenal honor. I was absolutely overwhelmed. I couldn't sleep that night. I kept thinking, 50 years from now, my grandchildren will be presenting the Enberg Award to some great person. Oh My!

In 2004, Ted Leland, athletic director at Stanford University, accepted the Enberg Award. Others have included Congressman and Hall of Fame football coach Tom Osborne; Dr. Donna Shalala, president of the University of Miami (Florida); State Supreme Court Justice and NFL Hall of Famer Alan Page; NBA Hall of Famer Bill Russell; Hall of Fame basketball coach Dean Smith; and former University of Florida sports information director John Humenik, who was instrumental in the continuing growth of the program.

I have a star on Hollywood Boulevard. I'm proud of that, and every once in a while, I go check to see if it's still there. My Emmys, in turn, are a testimony to a lot of hard work, and, I think, good work. But, for a former college professor who has a passion for both education and athletics, having this award in my name, as Al McGuire would say, "is beyond the treetops." In my wildest dreams, I couldn't have created an honor that meant more.

EPILOGUE

Friends of mine occasionally ask me, "Will you ever retire?" And my standard answer remains, "Not in the future."

Seriously, it's hard to imagine retiring, because I love what I do. In 2004, I signed both a new four-year contract with ESPN and a three-year renewal with CBS that are taking me into my second 50 years of broadcasting.

It's a narcotic, my occupation, and right now I enjoy my work as much as ever. The time I might want to consider hanging up the mike is when I don't look forward to my assignments—when the passion is gone. So far that hasn't happened.

Friends have suggested that I cut back, which sounds sensible, but how would I do that? Would I call only tennis? Working for CBS and ESPN, I'll be at the four majors—the Grand Slam—each year, and that's something to eagerly anticipate in the next few years. But it's not enough. I could just call football and basketball. But then I'd have to give up tennis. Or I could do only football and tennis. But then I'd have to eschew basketball. As you can see, it's difficult to let anything go.

At times, I've seriously considered returning to baseball, the best announcer's game, but if I ever signed up for baseball again, it would be necessary to drop everything else. At my age, with a 200-game season, baseball is too demanding to even consider working other sports. I can't go back to the exhausting schedule I had at age 35, when I was busy all year, calling baseball, plus the Rams and UCLA basketball.

Looking into the future, I don't want to arrive at a point where it's necessary to apologize for my mistakes... apologize because I'm not what I once was. As I close in on 70, I understand that I'm not going to get much better at what I do, but I could get worse. So, I would hope, as athletes say, that I'm intelligent enough to see the end before the audience does.

However, I believe I'm still at the top of my game. My health is good. I'm fortunate to be able to play tennis several times a week, when a lot of men my age have switched to golf. I can't do that. You know how that game treats me.

I sincerely believe that I still study as hard as anyone in the business today. Kids hate homework; I enjoy it. I relish searching for the little nuggets and personal notes that no one else has found, material that will make my play-by-play different from all the rest. I don't want to cut back on this preparation. I could fool the network and fool the public for two or three years, but I couldn't fool myself for one game.

In my 50 years, I've never left an event thinking I called a perfect game. If I persevere, there's still that chance to deliver a broadcast no-hitter.

It won't be the constant travel that drives me out of the business, either. Obviously, travel is more demanding and less convenient since September 11, but I still take pleasure in it. I enjoy the quiet time on an airplane. It's important for me. I can accomplish more in a three-hour non-stop flight than I can in three days at home. Because of the lack of interruptions when I'm airborne, there's even time to write a little fractured poetry.

If there's any polar magnetism that would pull me away from play-by-play, it would be to return to teaching. I know I was a good educator. I still have the energy for it, and I would enjoy the academic environment again. As I learned so many years ago, there's nothing more invigorating than the challenge of the raised hand, and you're guaranteed to get it every time you teach. Motivating a roomful of bright students to care about the subject matter and to look forward to learning more is a powerful top-of-the-world feeling.

I couldn't return to teaching health education, because I'd have to be re-educated. However, to go to a school with a strong radio-television-journalism program where I could share my firsthand experiences with young people would be perfect. Now, at least, I'd be teaching something I really know. I'd have the answers.

Teaching again also might force me to author another book, perhaps a textbook used in the class. I love to write, and the experience of writing this book has whetted that appetite. Perhaps, I'll do another book that digs even more deeply into the fascinating sports figures I've encountered in my 50 years of broadcasting.

No matter what other pursuits I may try and what other challenges I may accept, however, I can't foresee any of them being so fulfilling or demanding that they would take me totally away from play-by-play. Even if I returned to the classroom, I can see myself rationalizing, "Gee, I still have my weekends free. I could schedule classes

Monday through Thursday, leave on Friday, do a game on Sunday, and be back on campus on Monday."

There's one other ambitious prospect that I've considered, and it, too, involves education. Perhaps someone on a high local, state, or federal level would be interested in tapping me on the shoulder to work as a government spokesman for education. My assignment could include motivating teachers to improve their skills as educators and encouraging more talented young people to pursue teaching as a career. There's so much that can and should be done to improve education in this country. Maybe I could help. I'd love to give back.

More than half a century later, I still feel the inspiration from my high school English teacher, Norene Johnson. She was strict and demanding. Use words properly. Write clearly. Speak correctly. She was a terrific teacher who brought out the best in me.

It was true when Mrs. Johnson was young, and it's true now. Every teacher is underpaid. We don't give them the proper respect, and I wish I could do something to change that. I've long thought that the economic structure in the field is totally reversed. College professors shouldn't be the highest paid people on the academic ladder. Those who teach kindergarten and the first two grades should make the most money. They're setting the foundation for the entire learning process. They get first crack at kids who otherwise may never make it, except for their teachers' love, understanding, and hard work. Those teachers are saving lives. That would be a goal of mine—to improve the salary of all teachers, but truly reward those who teach the first three years of elementary education.

Of course, if I were going to throw myself into a position like that, I couldn't be doing much broadcasting, unless it was for just a small portion of the year. As you can see, I already have trouble letting go, because I still truly love what I do. My job is a kid's dream come true, and I can't let my dream go.

I've always felt that if you say you're going to work another year before retiring, you've already retired. Part of you has already quit. So, if I ever leave the broadcast booth, the decision might come quickly. Perhaps there will be a signature game that makes me say, "It's the end of the season, the game was terrific, the broadcast was outstanding, people reviewed it well, we had a huge audience. Perhaps this could be a goodbye game."

But if I make that decision and ask CBS to announce that Dick Enberg has done the last game of his career, I know exactly what will happen. I'll go home and sit by the phone, hoping it will ring—hoping someone will call and say, "Don't go away! We still want you!"